Gendered Colonialisms in African History

T0367164

Gendered Colonialisms in African History

Co-edited by
Nancy Rose Hunt, Tessie P. Liu and Jean Quataert

BLACKWELL
Publishers

Copyright © Blackwell Publishers Ltd 1997

ISBN: 0-631-20476-8

First published in 1997

Blackwell Publishers Ltd
108 Cowley Road, Oxford, OX4 1JF, UK

and
350 Main Street
Malden, MA 02148, USA

British Library Cataloguing in Publication Data
Applied for

Library of Congress Cataloging-in-Publication Data
Applied for

Gendered Colonialisms in African History

co-edited by Nancy Rose Hunt, Tessie P. Liu and Jean Quataert

CONTENTS

Editorial

The editorial collective of *Gender & History*, in cooperation with Blackwells, has decided to publish a book series alongside the journal in order to make path-breaking work on the gender dimension of past societies widely available to students, teachers and public audiences. These international, interdisciplinary collections will address the social history of gender relations, changing cultural constructions of feminity and masculinity, and the power of gender to represent and reinforce other forms of difference and hierarchy. We seek especially to trace the links between representations of womanhood and manhood and the social positions of women and men, and to examine the gendered construction of class, race, ethnicity, sexual identity, and other relations of domination and subordination. While the series is open to a variety of theoretical perspectives, we aim to develop feminist scholarship that attends to inequalities of power. Individual volumes will have specific themes, but all will approach topics from a comparative perspective and suggest new conceptual frameworks for gender analysis.

We begin the series with *Gendered Colonialism in African History*, which represents *Gender & History's* first focused look at the history of sub-Saharan Africa. The collection presents essays by younger scholars that address questions which are just emerging in this field. We know this volume will be of great interest to Africanists and to students of colonialism and postcolonial societies in other regions. Europeanists and Americanists have as much to learn as specialists, for placing gender in an African perspective reveals striking new ways of looking at things that are often taken for granted: the body and the construction of the gendered subject; connections between representations and violence; generational relationships among women and among men; the process through which white masculinity was constituted through the exclusion of white womanhood as well as the oppression of black manhood; memory, fantasy, and the gendering of legitimate and illegitimate forms of power; and the contradictions of consumption. These essays question received dichotomies of colonizer/colonized, metropole/locality, hegemony/resistance, and tradition/modernity, and suggest the multifarious ways in which gender became imbricated in relations of power.

The editorial collective is especially grateful to Nancy Rose Hunt, a specialist in African history, who took time from her own archival research and field work in Europe and Africa to conceive this volume, communicate with authors, and write the introduction; and to Tessie P. Liu and Jean Quataert who, as historians of France and Germany respectively, see Europeans' relations with colonial subjects as central to the formation of European identities and worked on this volume in that spirit. The journal's American co-editor, Grey Osterud, tried to ensure that these essays are comprehensible to non-specialists, did the copy-editing and proof-reading, and compiled the index. Finally, the editorial collective is grateful to those in both the book and journals divisions at Blackwells for enabling our dream of a book series to come to fruition, and to Basler Afrika Bibliographien for allowing us to use the stunning photograph on the cover.

ABSTRACTS

Introduction

NANCY ROSE HUNT

This introduction reviews major trends in African women's and gender history since the 1970s, and argues that these essays on 'gendered colonialisms in African history' demonstrate that an important third wave of historical writing in African colonial and post-colonial studies has begun. This third wave is marked by subtle, but cautious 'post-' moves; masculinity studies; and careful attention to memory and secrecy, generational and homosocial struggles, African forms of meaning-making, and a multiplicity of 'metropolitanizations' within colonial and post-colonial Africa.

'Ngaitana (I will circumcise myself)': The Gender and Generational Politics of the 1956 Ban on Clitoridectomy in Meru, Kenya

LYNN M. THOMAS

Drawing on state and mission documents as well as oral interviews conducted in Kenya and England during 1995, Thomas examines the colonial state's unsuccessful effort in 1956–59 to ban clitoridectomy in Meru, Kenya. Thomas challenges the terms of contemporary international debates over 'female genital mutilation' and Kenyan historiography on 'female circumcision' by situating girls and women as the most ardent defenders of clitoridectomy. Thomas's history of the ban also reveals how relations of gender and generation structured and subverted the elaboration of a more interventionist colonial state in postwar rural Kenya.

'Cocky' Hahn and the 'Black Venus': The Making of a Native Commissioner in South West Africa, 1915–46

PATRICIA HAYES

This article investigates the links between gender and administration, ethnography, and violence in the shaping of South African colonial rule in northern Namibia after 1915. The Native Commissioner, 'Cocky' Hahn, elaborated a mode of indirect rule in Ovamboland which depended on local hierarchies and sought to keep rituals intact. Hahn simultaneously practiced violence against the Ovambo and studied them as an ethnographer. The essay explores an incident of violence against an Ovambo woman to show how the invisibility and inaudibility of African women were produced and reproduced in colonialism and in history.

'Not Welfare or Uplift Work': White Women, Masculinity and Policing in South Africa

KEITH SHEAR

Analysing the centrality of gender in the formation of state institutions in early twentieth-century South Africa's emerging segregationist order, the article uses newspapers and government files to reconstruct a campaign by white women to enlist in the police. The ensuing debate, featuring competing visions of the state's role in shaping and maintaining the social order, compelled government officials to articulate their own assumptions about policing in a colonial context. Shear demonstrates that the labeling and consequent suppression of the campaigners' position as 'feminine' gendered officials' contrasting vision of punitive racial policing as 'masculine'.

Love Magic and Political Morality in Central Madagascar, 1875–1990

DAVID GRAEBER

This article focuses on the dangerous forces that people in Imerina, Madagascar, see as lurking in their social worlds and explores how their most intimate fears are related to broader questions of political morality. These fears are often worked out in stories about magic. Asking why ideas about the gender of practitioners of love medicine in Imerina appear to have undergone a dramatic reversal over the past century leads Graeber to a whole series of questions about the links between perceptions of colonialism and, especially, slavery and the association of women with powers of command.

'Fork Up and Smile': Marketing, Colonial Knowledge and the Female Subject in Zimbabwe

TIMOTHY BURKE

Since the 1920s, capitalist professionals in Europe and the United States have frequently feminized the activity of consumption and the figure of the consumer. This article explores this process in colonial Zimbabwe from the 1950s through the 1970s, marking the manner in which colonial institutions and ideologies, particularly those connected to domesticity, were reproduced within marketing. Burke traces both continuities with colonial visions and new contradictions that emerged when marketers conceptualized the ideal African consumer as female.

Introduction

NANCY ROSE HUNT

Masculinity as theme, gender and colony as analytics, men as subjects and authors of gendered histories: these are some of the more striking moves that this set of essays in African history reveals at first glance. The topics explored here from a gendered perspective include generational relationships, representation and violence, colonial state-building, consumption and commodity cultures, memory and forgetting, and languages of domesticity, reproduction, and 'tradition'. Final selections for anthologies of previously unpublished work are necessarily arbitrary, contingent as they are on the predilections and schedules of multiple authors, readers and editors. This collection is no different. Many exciting contributions needed more time than our deadlines would allow, and much that might have been included never reached our mailbox. The chronological and geographical boundaries of this issue are delimited more narrowly than we would have liked, as are authorial identity and location. *Gender & History* welcomes more work from the African continent, essays not originally written in English, and reports of research-in-progress in both fields and archives.

Numerous anthologies devoted to women and gender in African history have been published over the past three decades.[1] This special issue, while making original work available, does not fully do justice to current debates about and shifts in geography and identity that have taken place in the production of historical knowledge about Africa. Our inclusion of essays by a Zimbabwean historian trained in Cambridge (UK) now based at the University of the Western Cape and by a South African historian now based at Northwestern University (USA) is a clue to recent transnational movements within Africanist scholarly production. Yet this selection only hints at realignments that began in the 1980s. More and more African men and women have migrated to African studies centers in the West, especially in North America, for graduate training, post-doctoral fellowships, special institutes, and conferences. The late 1980s and 1990s have also seen the first concerted attempts to promote women scholars as well as gender studies within sub-Saharan Africa through doctoral fellowships, institutes and conferences.[2]

It surely would be incorrect to claim, therefore, that the five essays included here are uniquely representative of the best new work on gendered

colonialisms in African history. Recent issues of major journals, such as the
Journal of African History, the *International Journal of African Historical
Studies*, and the *Journal of Southern African Studies*, reveal how integral to
the field scholarship on women and gender has become. Yet such a conceit
nevertheless shapes my comments here. These five essays represent important new directions in historical studies of colonial Africa, serve to define
a certain moment in historical writing among Africanists, and suggest past
and future lines of inquiry in feminist historical studies of sub-Saharan
Africa.

This collection should be placed within a historical trajectory of studies
on women and gender in Africa. In the early 1970s, North American feminist historians and anthropologists, like feminist scholars in other fields
and regions, embarked on a revolution in the authorship and subject matter
of historical inquiry. Until recently most work in African gender studies has
focused on women rather than men as subjects of history. A first wave of
feminist scholarship focused primarily on the economically productive activities and social agency of African women.[3] A second wave of writing,
latterly influenced by what I call the 'colonialism and culture' school of
colonial studies, turned to questions of gender meanings and relations, to
colonial domesticity, customary law, motherhood, reproduction, sexuality,
and the body.[4] Are we now, with these studies of masculinity, of the formation of subjective, social and institutional identities, and of generational,
homosocial struggles, and with subtle, cautious 'post-' moves, witnessing
the beginning of a third wave in histories of gender in Africa?

It is important to remember the vexed origins of women's history in
North America: women were struggling for their own place within the
academy, all too often against explicit sex discrimination. Women scholars
struggled for recognition, for funding, and for a new vision that would include African women's social action. In those days of self-conscious white
liberal guilt and the search for a useable African past, interest focused on
women in development, especially agrarian change, land tenure, urbanization, and women's roles in formal, informal, and household economies.
Although feminist scholars worked within and against the dominant narratives of economic transformation in Africa, their work was seldom integrated into mainstream scholarship. As Jean Hay has so astutely pointed out,
the marginality of African women's history and Africanist women historians
is evidenced in the kind of publication that ensued: interdisciplinary anthologies and special issues focused on women.[5]

Women's history monographs did, on occasion, receive accolades within African studies. Consider the Herskovits prize, the highest North American
award bestowed on Africanist authors. In 1980, Margaret Strobel's *Muslim
Women in Mombasa, 1890–1975* (Yale University Press, New Haven, 1979)
was the first book by a woman and about African women to receive this
honor. Claire C. Robertson's *Sharing the Same Bowl: A Socioeconomic History of Women and Class in Accra, Ghana* (Indiana University Press,

Bloomington, 1984) won the prize five years later. Women's history again received this recognition in 1991. Luise White's *The Comforts of Home: Prostitution in Colonial Nairobi* (University of Chicago Press, Chicago, 1990) continued the tradition of portraying African women as powerful subjects of their own lives, yet it also suggested how much the field had changed over two decades. Not only did the book highlight sexuality, a theme that had hardly been broached since Strobel's original work on ritual, but women's history was no longer so narrowly tied to marking out the parameters of and justifications for a new field of historical inquiry. Rather, White used the history of prostitution to refigure the history of labor, cities and the colonial state.

The two most recent Herskovits awards have also gone to women: Keletso E. Atkins's *The Moon Is Dead! Give us our Money!: The Cultural Origins of an African Work Ethic, Natal, South Africa, 1843–1900* (Heinemann, Portsmouth, New Hampshire, and James Currey, London, 1993) in 1994, and Henrietta L. Moore and Megan Vaughan's *Cutting Down Trees: Gender, Nutrition and Agricultural Change in the Northern Province of Zambia, 1890–1990* (Heinemann, Portsmouth, New Hampshire, 1994) in 1995. During her acceptance speech, Atkins moved the audience with an auto-biographical sketch of her own migrations, exclusions, and significant turning-points as an African-American woman struggling for acceptance as an African historian. Although Atkins did not define her book explicitly as a study of masculinity, it is an important examination of identity formation and the struggles of washermen in Durban. *Cutting Down Trees* was the first Herskovits prize-winner with the word gender in the title. Co-authored by an anthropologist and a historian, this history of gender relations and the production of knowledge marks out its terrain and analytic through recon-sidering the work of a woman anthropologist, Audrey Richards. *Cutting Down Trees* also marked the emergence of a significant 'post-' move within African history.

The lexicon of cultural history—grammars and tropes, representations and gender meanings, modernity, coloniality and post-coloniality, con-sumption and public culture[6]—has arrived in African historical studies. These paradigm shifts from women's history to gender history and from roles, agency, and oral history to identities, subjectivities, and memory are not, of course, limited to African history. Yet these essays show that such moves are coming into African studies in particular ways, with specific sensibilities and choices in subject matter. These sensitivities involve acute debates about the production of Africanist knowledge and epistemologies in and especially outside the continent.

This collection, therefore, demonstrates that histories of gender in Africa have moved far from the first generation of women's history in their contents and analytic frames, in their use of social theory and evidence, and in authorship. These essays also provide an opportunity to examine the questions that are being marked out as subjects of research and debate in historical studies on colonial Africa. Gender as a set of social and symbolic relations is at the center of analysis here. At the same time, new themes and vocabularies emanating from cultural studies—representation, alterity, cultural production, commodity culture, transnationalism—are at work and play, refiguring the import and methodologies of gender analysis itself. These essays help situate how Africanist scholars are reproducing and disrupting various 'post-' moves, both those which are more generally effecting 'intellectual transformation across the human and social sciences'[7] and those quite particular to new scholarship (some Africanist) in colonial and post-colonial studies.

Colonialism can no longer be viewed as a process of imposition from a singular European metropole, but must be seen as 'tangled layers of political relations' and lines of conflicting projections and domestications that converged in specific local misunderstandings, struggles, and representations (which Graeber alternately terms fantasies). These essays remind us that social action in colonial and post-colonial Africa cannot be reduced to such polarities as metropole/colony or colonizer/colonized or to balanced narrative plots of imposition and response or hegemony and resistance. Such narratives, however refigured and nuanced in recent years, limit our appreciation of the enigmatic mutations and durations, facts and fictions, transgressions and secrecies that sustained research in fields and archives opens up.

The work presented here insists on multiple and distinct colonialisms, metropoles, masculinities, femininities, and domesticities. These pluralities refuse to collapse into easy twos, into binary formulations about African colonial life. Indeed, the most consistent current throughout these five essays is a critique of such reified dualities. David Graeber almost skips over the colonial as a domain of social action altogether (with the exception of the Norwegian missionary, Lars Vig, and his collection of love charms), evoking it rather as a strongly transformative yet parenthetical backdrop for his analysis of memory work, the transformation of social identity, and nightmarish fantasies within Merina social relations. Graeber argues that the important question is not 'how people dealt with their conquerors, but how, as a result, they ended up reconsidering and remaking their relations with each other'.

Lynn Thomas insists that situating such a history within a bifurcated narrative of indigenous responses to European impositions would flatten the complexity of local conflicts, dilemmas, and meaning-making that were at the core of social action. Indeed, such a casting would distort how much of African history was being made, if not wholly outside of colonial power relations, then at least in African terms (and songs) and outside of colonial purview. Keith Shear argues that a binary colonizer/colonized framework would be unable to account for the conflict within white South African society over the gendering of policing. Shear defines identity not in subjective or social but in institutional terms, examining how the masculine identity of the South African police force was defined in reaction to the gender meanings that an alternative policing system advocated and staffed by white women represented. The threat of a new conjunction of women and police power acted circuitously to bolster, or even to forge, the hyper-masculinity that was required to enforce racial domination. In the process, a 'subordinate masculinity' of women was excluded once and for all.[8]

While Thomas rejects the Africanist 'resistance paradigm that reifies dualities', Graeber and Hayes reject respectively the paradigms of hege-mony and colonial representations that have shaped much recent, fashion-able work in colonial studies.[9] Graeber insists that colonized African subjects were not always or only creatures of colonial hegemonic institutions, work spaces, and explicit domesticating projects of identity transformation. Rather, he demonstrates that Merina people were also creatures of their own fears, fantasies, and shifting social relations, of their own memories and inaud-ibilities of previous, precolonial forms of servitude and authority.

Timothy Burke, by contrast, suggests that colonial Africans in the post-war period were creatures of colonial cultural production: they were con-sumers. And, I would add, they consumed more than commodities; they also consumed images, stories, newspapers, cartoons, movies, and music. To explore the full complexity and cultural *métissages* of masculinities and femininities in late colonial Africa, Africanists will need to expand the kinds of sources they examine. These essays demonstrate that the resources for composing colonial identities were vast and various, and that there was much more cultural mixture going on in these compositions and recom-positions than historians and anthropologists have usually allowed for.

Moreover, Africanists will need to dismantle the notion that there was any single metropole for any given African locality, colony, identity, or gender crisis. Political metropole? Perhaps. Yet social, cultural, or economic metro-pole, one external capital for impositions and borrowings? No. Just as Hayes's and Shear's contributions insist that we avoid imagining any linear transfers from Europe of languages of masculinity and domesticity, so Burke's work on advertising suggests the new possibilities for cultural meaning pro-vided by other media such as popular literature, radio and cinema. How would these multiple forms of cultural production have intersected with the lives and meaning-making of such social types as Kenyan female and white South African male initiates, stoep-cleaning Ovambo women, European tour-ists curious about 'native tribes', colonial ethnographer-officials, Merina love-medicine users and accusers, middle-class white South African police women and poor white prostitutes, and advertisers and consumers? How did such new cultural forms become part of various men's and women's composition of masculine and feminine (among other) identities? In Cyprien Ekwenzi's novel, *Jagua Nana*, young Freddie may have looked from Lagos to London for his dreams of manhood, but his middle-aged girlfriend, named after a fancy motor-car, looked to Accra as her cultural capital for the latest clothing fashions as late as the early 1960s.[10] When, if ever, did

Hollywood become yet another cultural metropole within specific African localities? And what kinds of gendered iconography did men and women quote or censor from these kinds of resources?

A key question that Burke's work helps us pose is: how did the lives, aspirations, and gendered styles of Africans, white and black, intersect with various forms of cultural production within what was an increasingly global *ecumene*, not necessarily those cultural forms emanating from London, Paris, or Lisbon alone, but from Lagos, Accra, Onitsha, Johannesburg and Bombay as well?[11] My sense is that eventually, hopefully sooner rather than later, Africanists will begin to compare and contrast their micro-histories of colonial Europeans and 'colonial middle figures'[12] in a growing variety of complex milieux so as to begin to note some of the grids and grammars— geographic, linguistic, denominational, representational—to which these people were mutually subject, some of the ideas, images, commodities, and styles around which 'modern' (and 'pre-modern') European and African colonial men and women forged their 'differential identities'. Indeed, one of Patricia Hayes's central points is that 'Cocky' Hahn was consuming Hottentot Venus postcards, organizing flogging spectacles in his domain for Ovambo chiefs, displaying dances of female initiates for official South African visitors to his territory, and attending them himself in local Kwanyama leather clothes.

What kinds of principles and practices of 'mutuality and exclusivity' were at work in the formation of colonial identities and situations? Consider again Shear's essay, which turns precisely around the historical emergence of a principle of exclusivity, the rigidifying of the masculine here reinforcing racial domination. Moreover, where did women's and men's 'differential power relations among each other'[13] converge with the composition and identification of any individual or social category? Consider rugged, rugby-playing 'Cocky' Hahn in relation to his frail accuser, the mandolin-playing Percival Chaplin, in Hayes's study. Homosocial tensions were also at work among Meru women and girls in post-war Kenya. Thomas's essay transforms how we think about female rites of passage in Africa, including those that have embraced forms of body marking such as clitoridectomy. Such a gendered practice can no longer be uniquely scripted as a struggle between colonizer and colonized, or between men and women. Rather, Thomas highlights the generational conflicts among women over this homosocial domain of life.

Africanists have long negotiated issues of racial mutualities and exclusivities in colonial history. We need now to consider intra-male and intra-female forms of social organization, leisure, institution building, and domination and submission. Thomas, Shear, and Hayes explicitly point to homosocial identity formation, whether in social, institutional, or subjective identities. Shear reminds us that the language of domesticity and of female difference which underlay the white, middle-class movement for female preventive policing was based on a metropolitan discourse that ultimately reinforced the conviction that the South African police force should be a homosocial domain of men. Advertising and the development of consumer cultures in post-war Africa were mediated by similar languages. The very focus on creating African 'middle figures' in single-family, urban homes had important consequences for homosocial forms of organization and leisure in colonial and post-colonial Africa.

Demeaning an effeminate subordinate or controlling rebellious, youthful girls in these homosocial situations were signs of manhood and woman-hood, just as the insistence on a homosocial police force was a way to reinforce state power and racialized violence. What kinds of historical antecedents do these forms of intra-male and intra-female domination and submission have in particular historical settings? It is not possible to read Dunbar Moodie and Patrick Harries on mine marriages in South Africa and not wonder about the performative quality and emotional depth such relationships might have had. I do not intend to suggest that homosexuality was part of these homosocial relations in Kenya and South Africa.[14] I do think, however, that the analytic vocabulary of homosocial and hetero-social which has proven so useful in American and European gender hist-ories would be immensely helpful in sharpening gender analysis here. Thus I signal its curious absence from African histories.[15] These essays show that men and women were defining and expressing masculinities and feminin-ities according to generational, institutional, and work rhythms and prac-tices. They also show that whether men and women were interacting with each other or primarily in relation to others of their same gender *mattered*. A vocabulary of homosocial and heterosocial would help in locating these differences, alongside age and race, as axes of power, and would enable an even more complex tracing of gender within men's and women's lives in colonial and post-colonial Africa.

New questioning of what we mean by metropole and colony has been a critical line of thought since Bernard Cohn, Ann Stoler, Fred Cooper, Nicholas Dirks, and Jean Comaroff and John Comaroff began writing new histories, organizing conferences, and assembling collections, generating what might be termed the 'tensions of empire' or 'colonialism and culture' school of historical ethnography. This school still poses immense challenges to European and American historiographies. Indeed, one can lament how little sustained social history research has yet been done on the internal colonies of Europe and the historical formation of European colonial iden-tities on metropolitan terrain.[16] Future work will likely include much more comparative analysis, multi-sited histories, and an examination of both the internal colonies and colonizations of Europe and the external 'metropoles' and 'metropolitanizations' within Africa suggested by Burke, Hayes, and Shear.

The challenges along these lines are myriad. The question of how to effect a recentering of the production of knowledge about Africa within Africa itself has received considerable attention in recent years.[17] Yet the challenges for African colonial studies do not lie only there. The questioning

of what we mean by 'metropole', a question that is raised at least impli-
citly in all these essays, poses immense difficulties to Africanist historians
long accustomed to approaching colonial studies through a single European power. Scholarly work has too long been marked out along the
lines of scholars' linguistic competencies and national identities. This kind
of specialization has papered over transnational processes and hybrid
colonial situations, where multiple metropolitan identities and projections
overlapped and conflicted. Just as anthropology may in future years be
reshaped by an increased awareness of the need for 'multi-sited ethnography',[18] these essays pose questions about the historical processes of
gendered and colonial identity formation that will likely only be answered
through comparative and multi-sited research methodologies. Language
skills, national identities, funding sources, research itineraries, and perhaps
even intellectual inquisitiveness have, thus far, worked against such approaches. French and francophone Africanists have tended to write French
colonial histories, British and anglophone Africanists to write British colonial histories. Sustained communication and cross-fertilization across this
key linguistic divide is rare indeed. Belgian (post)-colonial and lusophone
Africa have been characterized by greater diversity in the linguistic competencies and nationalities of practitioners. Yet the linearity of most historical formulations of what constituted metropole still stands in much of
these more marginalized literatures.[19]

Finally, these essays testify to a firm refusal to fetishize the domains of
archive, representation, text. There are certainly signs of a shift toward
'post-ness' in African studies here, yet on no easy, unproblematized terms.
Rather, these essays turn away from the recent fashion of studies in colonial
representations, too often facile, literary rereadings of such public forms of
colonial discourse as memoirs, travelogues, fiction, and photographs. They
insist that the politics of representation cannot be confined to European
geographies and imaginaries, but must extend to African ways of conceptu-
alizing time, space, and social relations. Equally important, these essays
examine the concrete historical practices which flowed from such European representations, integrating the histories of Africans in all their diversity with those of Europeans, and in the process transforming both.

Hayes's essay represents a strong and significant criticism of what has
become a fashionable enterprise, studies of European iconographic and
discursive projections of Africa which often border on the prurient and, in
the very act of republishing this negativity, risk restimulating the perverse
Euro-American fascination with the colonial encounter. Hayes insists that
studies of representation not be detached from histories of the implications
of this sexualized form of degradation for social action, especially
violence. The point is not to reject a 'post-' lexicon of representations and
the production of knowledge, but to make sure that studies of the colonial
Africanist imaginary are anchored to specific, local historical contexts,
power relations, and human interactions.

Recent work on imperial manliness, especially studies of the social codes and fantasies of white, European 'soldier-heroes', hunter-pioneers, British public school-trained athletes and former Boy Scouts, has drawn attention to the ways that Africa became a colonized, racialized, and gendered terrain where these men played out and realized their masculinity. The best of these studies have reminded us not only that 'gender was an important axis along which colonial power was constructed' but also that European projections of Africans and other colonized peoples as a demonized, sexualized, feminine 'other' worked to feminize and tame, and thus to diminish and control, colonized men and women.[20] Yet such studies have too often focused on European and especially English identities, and thus have distinct limitations in what they offer for a social or cultural history of Africa and Africans. Indeed, they have operated analytically through a rather straightforward polarity between the manliness of imperial heroes and adventurers and their subordinate variants, effeminate male or tamed female colonized subjects or sexualized territorial spaces. A key innovation in Hayes's treatment is that she locates imperial masculinity within a South and South West African field, embracing the complexities of multiple metropoles and colonies and localizing their specific histories, identities, and effects. Hayes's perspective, too, encompasses the usually absent or merely metaphorical Africans, and thus reveals the violence that such codes authorized. African bodies were marked by imperial masculinity in ways that the historical record reveals but seldom confronts.

Hayes's problematic also centers on what cannot be recovered. How to conjure up, read, and interpret absence, silence, invisibility, secrecy, and song is a subtle current running through several of these essays. Mutedness as a gender theme dates to the 1970s,[21] but approaches to it have varied markedly. Hayes does not try to compensate for the archival absence of African female voices. Rather, it is the very contrast between the conflicting European male voices that can be heard in her sources and the inaudibility of the sexually assaulted African woman in question that is the defining tension of her analytic. She wants to know not just how such representations were reproduced but also how invisibility and secrecy were reproduced both in the historical record and in historians' narratives. Graeber, too, explores the unspoken and invisible, whose very secrecy gives it power. The ambiguity of what constituted metropole or colony, danger or domesticity, real or imagined, wild or tamed, male or female, representation or violence shines through both Hayes's and Graeber's essays.

Graeber, like Hayes, grapples with 'post-' veerings that seem to lead to a fascination with European fantasies and intentions to the near exclusion of everything else. Graeber's argument that '"political reality" can never be really distinguished from its representations', based as it is on changes in Merina social and gender relations, resembles Hayes's perspective. These two essays help to anchor some of the major fault lines involved in the shift towards 'post-ness': the need not to rule out an examination of representations, but to find specific linkages among such projections (whether in Merina love medicine or Hottentot Venus postcards decorated with swastikas) and social and political realities (such as colonial relations of command or a sexual assault on a female domestic worker). Their work proposes more than just an exploration of the ways that European projections and pathologies were played out on the dark slate of Africa as a primal, sexualized body. Nor are they satisfied with explicating the ways that formations of colonial masculinity played into the construction of European identities alone. Either representations or political economy alone would be inadequate, they suggest; each must be considered as both projection and effect.

Whereas Hayes and Shear stimulate us to rethink the category metropole from various metropolitan and colonial sites within South Africa and on its imperial frontier, Burke suggests that we rethink metropoles in relation to new literatures on and realities of transnationalism, globalization, and the refiguration of local public cultures in the post-World War II period. Metropole looms more as academic and development adversary in the problematics posed by Graeber and Thomas. Continuing projections of Africa as savage are brilliantly challenged in Thomas's essay, where the *riposte* at work (to borrow a term from the Comaroffs) consists less in African social and symbolic action than in the act of history-writing itself. Thomas's choice of clitoridectomy as topic could not be more compelling, given the continuing saliency of obscene, reductionist representations produced by post-colonial, Euro-American 'feminist' missionary workers operating under the name of women in development.[22] Nor are these gestures of saving African women from themselves, from their men, and from their 'barbaric', pre-modern cultures limited to the distortions of 'post-colonial' development schemes imagined in Washington and Geneva and imposed on the 'post-colonized'. Indeed, they are used to represent Africans in general, and African women in particular, as savage, backward, and perversely traditional. One need only turn on the television (or teach African history in an American university) to notice the continuing cultural production of projections of Africa as a promiscuous continent plagued by AIDS, patriarchal possession, and brutality. What is at stake in writing new, canny narratives of historical process at work could not be more acute. The riposte lies in undercutting the continued reproduction of colonial projections and epistemologies in and through what Burke calls 'post-colonial analogues'. Indeed, all the essays in this collection tread carefully in the face of matters of representation, tracing the inevitable yet not always visible connections between knowledge production and power relations in both past and present.

Notes

1. Denise Paulme (ed.) *Women of Tropical Africa* (University of California Press, Berkeley, 1963), originally published in France in 1960, was the first collection devoted to women and gender. Many special issues and anthologies have followed: Audrey Wipper (ed.) 'Rural Women: Development or Underdevelopment?', *Rural Africana*, 29 (1975–76); Nancy J. Hafkin and Edna G. Bay (eds) *Women in Africa: Studies in Social and Economic Change* (Stanford University Press, Stanford, 1976); Edna G. Bay (ed.) *Women and Work in Africa* (Westview Press, Boulder, Colorado, 1982); Margaret Jean Hay and Marcia Wright (eds) *African Women and the Law: Historical Perspectives* (African Studies Center, Boston University, Boston, 1982); Deborah Gaitskell, comp., 'Special Issue on Women in Southern Africa', *Journal of Southern African Studies*, 10 (1983); Shula Marks and Richard Rathbone (eds) 'The History of the Family in Africa', special issue of *Journal of African History*, 24 (1983); Claire C. Robertson and Martin A. Klein (eds) *Women and Slavery in Africa* (University of Wisconsin Press, Madison, 1983); Claire C. Robertson and Iris Berger (eds) *Women and Class in Africa* (Africana, New York, 1986); Audrey Wipper and Harriet Lyons (eds) 'Current Research on African Women', special issue of *Canadian Journal of African Studies*, 22 (1988); Patricia W. Romero (ed.) *Life Histories of African Women* (Ashfield, Atlantic Highlands, New Jersey, 1988); Bolanle Awe et al. (eds) 'Women, Family, State, and Economy in Africa', special issue of *Signs*, 16 (1991); Jane L. Parpart and Kathleen A. Staudt (eds) *Women and the State in Africa* (L. Rienner, Boulder, 1989); Cheryl A. Walker (ed.) *Women and Gender in Southern Africa to 1945* (Indiana University Press, Bloomington, 1991); Karen Tranberg Hansen (ed.) *African Encounters with Domesticity* (Rutgers University Press, New Brunswick, 1992). In addition to the Paulme volume, works in French include: a 1977 special issue of *Cahiers d'études Africaines* on African women, vol. 27, no. 65 (including a famous essay in English by Mona Etienne); Groupe 'Afrique Noire', *Histoires des femmes en Afrique*, a special issue of *Cahiers*, 11 (Harmattan, Paris, 1987); 'Femmes coloniales au Congo belge', special issue of *Enquêtes et documents d'histoire africaine*, 7 (1987); and Catherine Coquery-Vidrovitch, *Les Africaines: histoire des femmes d'Afrique Noire du XIXe au XXe siècle* (Desjonquères, Paris, 1994).

2. These schematic remarks apply only to sub-Saharan Africa, reflecting the long academic tradition of treating North Africa as separate and distinct. These comments also do not do justice to the distinctive histories or transnational migrations of scholars based in Africa or identifying as African within post-colonial academic production. Systematic documentation of this matter is needed; the following observations are, at best, only suggestive. CODESRIA (Conseil pour le Développement de la Recherche en Sciences Sociales en Afrique, based in Dakar) and the Ford Foundation (with offices in several African capitals) have been at the forefront of initiatives to sponsor special gender institutes in Africa. The Women's Caucus of the African Studies Association, notably Claire Robertson, organized an important workshop on women's studies initiatives in Africa during the 1991 annual meeting of the ASA in St. Louis; some of the most complete information on African women scholars and gender initiatives was compiled at that time. Women's studies programs have been founded in academic institutions in Nigeria, Senegal, South Africa, Tanzania, and Uganda. The 'Women Writing Africa' project, organized by The Feminist Press (311 East 94th Street, New York, NY 10128) and supported by the Ford Foundation, is compiling information on African women scholars, gender studies initiatives, and relevant literary and historical archival sources. Appointments of African women to academic posts in African history

remain quite recent. Prominent among African women historians are Tabitha Kanogo (Kenya), Nakanyike Musisi (Uganda), and Bolanle Awe (Nigeria). David William Cohen, Jane Parpart, and Luise White have been at the forefront of efforts to include African women in institutes and doctoral programs in North America. African women scholars based in the United States and Belgium seem to cluster more in literary studies than in history; consider how difficult it is to find historian counterparts to Tuzyline Allan (from Sierra Leone), Abena Busia (Ghana), Irène d'Almeida (Bénin), and Clémentine Madiya Nzuji (Zaïre). Many African-American and Afro-Caribbean women have also been involved in the study of African history and culture since the 1980s.

   3. This schema is based on my argument in Nancy Rose Hunt, 'Placing African Women's History and Locating Gender', *Social History*, 14 (1989), pp. 359–79. The two principal works to treat ritual rather than economics in this first wave were Margaret Strobel, *Muslim Women in Mombasa, 1890–1975* (Yale University Press, New Haven, 1979), and Iris Berger, *Religion and Resistance: East African Kingdoms in the Pre-colonial Period* (Musée Royal de l'Afrique Centrale, Tervuren, Belgium, 1981). Other works that take stock of African women's history include: Margaret Strobel, 'African Women: A Review', *Signs*, 8 (1982); Claire Robertson, 'Developing Economic Aware-ness: Changing Perspectives in Studies of African Women, 1976–1985', *Signs*, 13 (1987), pp. 97–135; and Margaret Jean Hay, 'Queens, Prostitutes and Peasants: Historical Per-spectives on African Women, 1971–1986', *Canadian Journal of African Studies*, 22 (1988), pp. 431–47. For a selective bibliography of important English-language publica-tions, see Nancy Hunt, 'Women', in 'Section 19: Sub-Saharan Africa', ed. Margaret Jean Hay and Joseph C. Miller, in *The American Historical Association Guide to Historical Literature*, ed. Mary Beth Norton (Oxford University Press, Oxford, 1995); readers should also consult the general index, as many of the most important works in women's history are included in the various geographical sub-sections rather than under this thematic heading. For French-language work, see Achola O. Pala and Madina Ly, *La femme africaine dans la société précoloniale* (Harmattan, Paris, 1987); Groupe 'Afrique Noire', *Histoire des femmes en Afrique*, *Cahiers*, 11; and Catherine Coquery-Vidrovitch, *Les Africaines: histoire des femmes d'Afrique Noire du XIXe au XXe siècle*.

   4. This school emerged from a Wenner-Gren conference, 'Tensions of Empire', organized by Frederick Cooper and Ann Stoler in 1988, and two related anthologies: Nicholas Dirks (ed.) *Colonialism and Culture* (University of Michigan, Ann Arbor, 1992), and Frederick Cooper and Ann Stoler (eds) *Tensions of Empire: Colonial Cultures in a Bourgeois World* (University of California Press, Berkeley, forthcoming). Notable scholarship within this expansive second wave includes: Kristin Mann, *Marrying Well: Marriage, Status, and Social Change among the Educated Elite in Colonial Lagos* (Cambridge University Press, Cambridge, 1985); Luise White, *The Comforts of Home: Prostitution in Colonial Nairobi* (University of Chicago Press, Chicago, 1990); Hansen (ed.) *African Encounters with Domesticity*; Birgitta Larsson, *Conversion to Greater Freedom? Women, Church, and Social Change in North-Western Tanzania under Colonial Rule* (Acta Universitatis Upsaliensis, Uppsala, Sweden, 1991); work on mater-nity, reproduction, and medicine, including Jean Allman, 'Making Mothers: Mission-aries, Medical Officers, and Women's Work in Colonial Asante, 1924–1945', *History Workshop Journal*, 38 (1994), pp. 23–47; Nancy Rose Hunt, '"Le bébé en brousse": European Women, African Birth Spacing and Colonial Intervention in Breast Feeding in the Belgian Congo', *International Journal of African Historical Studies*, 21 (1988), pp. 401–32; and Carol Summers, 'Intimate Colonialism: The Imperial Production of Reproduction in Uganda, 1907–1925', Signs, 16 (1991), pp. 787–807; Leroy Vail and

Landeg White, 'The Possession of the Dispossessed: Songs as History among Tubmbuka Women', in *Power and the Praise Poem: Southern African Voices in History*, ed. Leroy Vail and Landeg White (University Press of Virginia, Charlottesville, 1991), pp. 231–77. Many biographies and life histories of African women have been published since the mid-1980s. Exceptional among them are: Shula Marks, *Not Either an Experimental Doll: The Separate Worlds of Three South African Women* (Indiana University Press, Bloomington, 1987); Belinda Bozzoli with Mmantho Nkotsoe, *Women of Phonkeng: Consciousness, Life Strategy, and Migrancy in South Africa, 1900–1983* (Heinemann, Portsmouth, New Hampshire, 1991); Jean Boyd, *The Caliph's Sister: Nana Asma'u, 1793–1865, Teacher, Poet, and Islamic Leader* (Cass, Totowa, New Jersey, 1989); and Marcia Wright, *Strategies of Slaves and Women: Life-Stories from East/Central Africa* (Barber, New York, 1993).

5. Hay, 'Queens, Prostitutes and Peasants', p. 432.

6. This new 'post-' lexicon is part of what distinguishes these essays as part of a third wave in gendered studies of African (post-) colonialisms. Notable histories within this new wave are: Megan Vaughan, *Curing Their Ills: Colonial Power and African Illness* (Stanford University Press, Stanford, 1991); David William Cohen and E. S. Atieno Odhiambo, *Burying SM: The Politics of Knowledge and the Sociology of Power* (Heinemann, Portsmouth, New Hampshire, 1992); Paul Landau, *The Realm of the Word: Language, Gender, and Christianity in a Southern African Kingdom* (Heinemann, Portsmouth, 1995); and Timothy Burke, *Lifebuoy Men, Lux Women: Commodification, Consumption, and Cleanliness in Modern Zimbabwe* (Duke University Press, Durham, 1996). The term 'public culture' derives from the journal, *Public Culture*, founded by Arjun Appadurai and Carol Breckenridge. Whether there is also a third wave in pre-colonial African gender histories, as the uneasy precolonial/colonial divide undergoes fresh consideration, is neglected here; see David Schoenbrun, 'Gendered Histories Between the Great Lakes: Varieties and Limits', forthcoming in *International Journal of African Historical Studies*.

7. Frank Mort, 'Crisis Points: Masculinities in History and Social Theory', *Gender & History*, 6 (1994), p. 127.

8. I draw this terminology of subordinate masculinities from Stephan Miescher, a historian of Akan Presbyterian masculinities in Ghana, who in turn drew inspiration from Robert Connell.

9. Hegemony has entered African historical studies from Gramsci via work in Subaltern Studies. For notable examples of effective but different uses of such vocabulary, see Steven Feierman, *Peasant Intellectuals: Anthropology and History in Tanzania* (University of Wisconsin Press, Madison, 1990), and Jean Comaroff and John Comaroff, *Of Revelation and Revolution: Christianity, Colonialism, and Consciousness in South Africa* (University of Chicago Press, Chicago, 1991). See also the critiques in *Contesting Colonial Hegemony: State and Society in Africa and India*, ed. Shula Marks and Dagmar Engels (I. B. Tauris, London and New York, 1994). Patricia Hayes cites the Comaroffs in her critique of the recent fashion for representations, but it would seem more appropriate to lay the blame for prurient academic and popular forms of colonial nostalgia elsewhere. Sander Gilman's work on the Hottentot Venus, for example, contains a disturbingly prurient tinge; Sander L. Gilman, *Difference and Pathology: Stereotypes of Sexuality, Race, and Madness* (Cornell University Press, Ithaca, 1985). The fashion of reproducing iconographic evidence has also produced much fruitful work, although much more of it published in Italy, France, Belgium, and Holland than in Britain and the USA (perhaps a sign of what British and North American sensibilities will allow).

The Dutch exhibition catalogue by Jan Nederveen Pieterse, *Wit over Zwart: Beelden van Afrika en Zwarten in de Westerse Populaire Cultuur* (Koninklijk Instituut voor de Tropen, Amsterdam, n. d. [1990]), has been published in English by Yale University Press, which also published Annie E. Coombe's *Reinventing Africa: Museums, Material Culture and Popular Imagination* (1994). Among numerous works on colonial images of Africans and Africa, many of which emerged from special conferences and museum exhibitions, see from France: Nicolas Bancel, Pascal Blanchard and Armelle Chatelier (eds) *Images et Colonies: Iconographie et propagande coloniale sur l'Afrique française de 1880 à 1962* (BDIC and ACHAC, Paris, 1993); Pascal Blanchard and Armelle Chatelier (eds) *Images et Colonies: Nature, discours et influence de l'iconographie coloniale liée à la propagande coloniale et à la représentation des Africains et de l'Afrique en France, de 1920 aux indépendances* (ACHAC and SYROS, Paris, 1993); *Coloniales 1920–1940* (Musée Mûnicipal de Boulogne-Billancourt, 1990); Jean-Marc Boutonnet-Tranier, *L'Afrique fantastique: par les explorateurs et les déssinateurs du XIXème siècle* (Aethiopia Editions, Ivry-sur-Seine, 1993); Pascal Blanchard et al. (eds) *L'Autres et Nous: 'Scènes et Types'* (ACHAC and SYROS, Paris, 1995). From Italy: *Colonialismo e fotographia: il caso italiano* (Sicania, Messina, 1989); 'Fotographia e colonialismo/1–2', special issues of *Revista di storia e critica della fotographia*, 2 (1981) and 4 (1983); Nicola Labanca (ed.) *L'Africa in vetrina: storie di musei e di esponsizioni coloniali in Italia* (Pagus Edizioni, Paese, 1992); Luigi Goglia, *Storia fotographia dell'Impero fascista 1935–54* (Editori Laterza, Roma, 1985). Also published in Italy are the proceedings of an international conference: Alessandro Triulzi (ed.) *Fotographia e storia dell'Africa: Atti del Convegno Internazionale, Napoli-Roma, 9–11 Settembre 1992* (IUO, Napoli, 1995). From Belgium: Luc Vints, *Kongo Made in Belgium: Beeld van een kolonie in film en propaganda* (KRITAK, Leuven, 1984); *Zaïre 1885–1975: cent ans de regards belges* (CEC, Bruxelles, 1985). From Germany: Thomas Theye, *Der Geraubte Schatten: die Photographie als ethnographisches Dokument* (Münchner Stadtmuseums, Munich, 1989).

10. Cyprien Ekwenzi, *Jagua Nana* (Heinemann, London, 1961).

11. For recent work on globalization and culture along these lines, see Carol A. Breck-enridge (ed.) *Consuming Modernity: Public Culture in a South Asian World* (University of Minnesota Press, Minneapolis, 1995). Also noteworthy is Phyllis Martin, *Leisure and Society in Colonial Brazzaville* (Cambridge University Press, Cambridge, 1995).

12. I elaborate on this term in my book, forthcoming from Duke University Press and tentatively titled *A Colonial Lexicon: Hygiene and Birth Work in Upper Zaire.*

13. The vocabulary of differential identities, power relations, and principles of mutuality and exclusivity comes from Frank Mort, 'Crisis Points: Masculinities in History and Social Theory', *Gender & History*, 6 (1994), pp. 124–9.

14. Patrick Harries, 'Symbols and Sexuality: Culture and Identity on the Early Witwatersrand Gold Mines', *Gender & History*, 2 (1990), pp. 318–36; T. Dunbar Moodie, *Going for Gold: Mines, Men and Migration* (University of California Press, Berkeley, 1994). Not that gay studies will not have their day in African history. *Defiant Desire: Gay and Lesbian Lives in South Africa*, ed. Mark Gevisser (New York, Gevisser and Edwin Cameron, 1994), includes some historical work, and other projects are in progress or in press. Nuanced and sensitive field work is also beginning, as, for example, that of linguist-ethnographer Rudolph Gaudio on Hausa men who act, and speak, like women.

15. For example, Carroll Smith-Rosenberg's germinal essay, 'The Female World of Love and Ritual', reprinted in her *Disorderly Conduct: Visions of Gender in Victorian America* (Oxford University Press, New York, 1985), pp. 53–76.

16. For an excellent history of colonial and metropolitan identity formation within Europe, see Laura Tabili, *We Ask for British Justice: Workers and Racial Difference in Late Imperial Britain* (Ithaca, Cornell University Press, 1994).

17. See, for example, Jan Vansina's *Living with Africa* (University of Wisconsin Press, Madison, 1994). These questions are aligned, at least in North America, with those of authorship and academic appointment and of multiculturalism and separatism within the field of African studies, questions which erupted in heated and not especially constructive debate at the African Studies Association meeting in Orlando, Florida, in 1995. Similar conflicts emerged at the first public meeting of the 'Women Writing Africa' project organized by The Feminist Press in Accra, Ghana, in 1994. In this case, it seems thus far that the conflicts animated a constructive debate; subsequent planning has considered how to organize the project so that it recenters the production of knowledge about Africa within Africa itself. African women scholars, writers, and leaders of grassroots and mainstream organizations are expected to take on much of the work and report their findings at regional conferences. The project also hopes to support women's studies programs throughout the continent, microfilming projects, regional archival centers, and presses specializing in African women's writing.

18. I borrow this term from Douglas Holmes. See also George E. Marcus, 'Ethnography in/of the World System: The Emergence of Multi-sited Ethnography', *Annual Review of Anthropology*, 24 (1995), pp. 95–117.

19. The linguistic and ethnic complexities of Belgian identity have perhaps facilitated work on metropolitan hybridities on colonial terrain; the Belgian Congo was also particularly rich in such mixtures. See, for example, Jean-Luc Vellut, 'La communauté portugaise du Congo belge', in *Flandre et Portugal: Au confluent de deux cultures*, ed. J. Evaraert and E. Stols (Fonds Mercator, Antwerp, 1991), pp. 315–45.

20. Mrinalini Sinha, *Colonial Masculinity: The 'Manly Englishman' and the 'Effeminate Bengali' in the Late Nineteenth Century* (Manchester University Press, Manchester, 1995), esp. p. 11. See also Graham Dawson, *British Adventurer, Empire, and the Imagining of Masculinities* (Routledge, London and New York, 1994); the term 'soldier-hero' is Dawson's.

21. See Shirley Ardener, 'Sexual Assault and Female Militancy', *Man*, 8 (1973), pp. 422–50. The theme has recently been re-introduced, notably by David William Cohen; see Cohen, *Combing of History* (University of Chicago Press, Chicago, 1994).

22. Notably, Thomas's essay takes on the representational violences reproduced, too often in obscene caricature, by Fran Hoskens's newsletter, *WIN News*, and her lectures on 'female genital mutilation'. See also Fran P. Hosken, *The Hosken Report: Genital and Sexual Mutilation of Females* (Women's International Network News, Lexington, 1994 [1979]).

'Ngaitana (I will circumcise myself)': The Gender and Generational Politics of the 1956 Ban on Clitoridectomy in Meru, Kenya

LYNN M. THOMAS

Those of the iron-wedge knife (*ciorunya*), stay at the side, you.
Do not abuse those of the razor blade (*ciokaembe*), you.
A circumcised girl without water on the stomach when guarded by the Government.
A circumcised girl without water on the stomach when guarded by the Government.[1]

In the mid-1950s, recently excised girls in Meru, an administrative district on the northeastern slopes of Mt. Kenya, sang this song as they performed punitive hard labor for defying a ban on clitoridectomy.[2] The *Njuri Ncheke* of Meru, an officially sanctioned local council of male leaders, unanimously banned clitoridectomy in April 1956.[3] Today, people in Meru recount how news and defiance of the ban spread quickly and widely. Ex-Chief M'Anampiu of Mikinduri remembered returning in the evening from the *Njuri Ncheke* council meeting only to find that 'all the girls had been circumcised'.[4] In the three years following the passage of the ban, over 2,400 girls, men, and women were charged in African Courts with defying the *Njuri's* order.[5] Interviews suggest that thousands of others who defied the ban paid fines to local *Njuri* councils and headmen.

As adolescent girls defied the ban by attempting to excise each other, their initiations marked a profound departure from the past. They also differed from earlier practices by foregoing the preparations and celebrations associated with initiation and the instruments typically used. While *atani* (s. *mutani*), the older women specialists who performed excisions, had previously used special triangular iron-wedge knives, *irunya* (s. *kirunya*), these girls of the mid-1950s simply used razor blades purchased at local shops. These departures caused some from Meru, both then and now, to doubt the legitimacy of these initiations.[6] The song is, in part, an appeal by these girls to older age groups, 'those of the iron-wedge knife', to stop abusing them and to recognize their initiation as proper. Similarly, *Ngaitana*, 'I will circumcise myself', the Meru name given to these girls by older groups of men and women, mocks the girls' determination and highlights these elders' sense of the absurdity of their undertaking. Today, mention of the name in Meru draws chuckles or, on occasion, head-shakes of knowing disapproval from those who can recall the time of *Ngaitana*. For those younger than forty-five years, however, the name most often elicits perplexed faces and queries.[7]

The song and the name of *Ngaitana* also suggest the political exigencies of the mid-1950s, during the Mau Mau rebellion and ensuing State of Emergency. While the ability to remain calm and brave—'without water on the stomach'—when being detained in a headman's camp or police station would have been a feat for an adolescent girl at almost any time during the twentieth century, such courage took on special significance during the Mau Mau rebellion, when Africans were often tortured and killed by government personnel. The name of *Ngaitana* also conveys many adults' reluctance to defy the ban for fear that their homes would be burnt or they would be fined or imprisoned. In the face of parents and *atani* who refused to assist them, some members of *Ngaitana* apparently proclaimed 'I will circumcise myself'. Others who received assistance from parents or *atani* refused to implicate their co-conspirators, claiming before headmen and African Court personnel that they had 'circumcised themselves'.

Current international debates about clitoridectomy and infibulation[8] originated during conferences organized as part of the United Nations Decade for Women (1975–85).[9] Some feminists denounced these practices as 'female genital mutilation'. Fran Hosken, for example, claimed that clitoridectomy and infibulation ravaged women's health and underpinned patriarchal structures, while Mary Daly posited these practices as one instance of the 'Sado-Ritual Syndrome' structuring 'planetary patriarchy'.[10] Human rights activists and feminist medical doctors Nawal El Saadawi and Asma El Dareer exposed clitoridectomy and infibulation as medically dangerous practices intended, among other things, to control female sexuality.[11] At international conferences, however, some African women protested these calls for eradication as a neo-colonial intrusion that drew attention away from more pressing development issues.[12] Anthropologists, accused by Hosken and Daly of a 'patriarchal cover-up', responded by drawing attention to the racist underpinnings of earlier campaigns against both male and female circumcision,[13] and by elaborating how processes surrounding excision and infibulation often are 'the primary context in which women come together as a group, constituting a ritual community and a forum for social critique'.[14] Drawing on post-structuralist theory, others criticized eradicationists for their discursive construction of a de-contextualized, passive and oppressed 'third world woman'.[15] Eradicationists responded to these critiques by strengthening networks with African women's and health organizations engaged in anti-clitoridectomy campaigns.[16] The controversy continues in Europe and North America today as debate turns to the threat of clitoridectomy and infibulation as grounds for political asylum, and the legality of these practices among African immigrant populations.

A historical analysis of the 1956 ban in Meru, one of the few attempts to outlaw clitoridectomy or infibulation in twentieth-century Africa,[17] demonstrates the limitations of universalist discourses of sexual oppression, human rights, and women's health, as well as post-structuralist deference to 'the Other', for an understanding of the social complexities of clitoridectomy. Whereas the international controversy has largely cast girls and women as victims, examination of adolescent girls' efforts to excise each other situates girls and women as central actors. Patriarchy, 'the manifestation and institutionalization of male dominance over women and children in the family and the extension of male dominance over women in society in general',[18] clearly structured familial and community relations in 1950s Meru. Yet to reduce adolescent girls' belief that clitoridectomy would transform them into adult women to patriarchal conspiracy would be to ignore how the institution of female initiation regulated relations among women as well as between men and women. Observers of female initiation have long noted that girls and women tend to defend the institution more vigorously than their male counterparts. While colonial officials and missionaries attributed female adherence to clitoridectomy to the inherent 'conservatism' of women,[19] contemporary anthropologist Janice Boddy, more insightfully, has explained such adherence as women's efforts to preserve 'bargaining tools with which to negotiate subaltern status and enforce their complementarity with men'.[20] In Meru in the 1950s, where adolescent initiation of males and females constituted the pivotal moment in the construction of an influential age group system,[21] female defense of clitoridectomy must also be viewed as an effort to maintain processes which differentiated females of various ages. Initiation transformed girls into women, and mothers of initiates into figures of authority within the community. Evidence suggests that while members of *Ngaitana* associated female initiation with the disciplining of sexual desires as well as notions of fertility and cleanliness, they did not fully anticipate the physical severity of clitoridectomy. The reluctance of older age groups to accept *Ngaitana* initiation as legitimate thus added insult to injury.

Within African, and particularly Kenyan, historiography, it would be tempting to situate a history of the 1956 ban on clitoridectomy within the now familiar paradigm of resistance to colonialism. Passage, defiance, and enforcement of the ban took place amid the Mau Mau rebellion, the most virulent period of anti-government protest in Kenyan colonial history.[22] Moreover, historians have interpreted the controversy surrounding clitoridectomy during the 1920s and 1930s as crucial to the emergence of nationalist politics within Kenya.[23] Yet the Mau Mau rebellion provided the context, not the causes, for passage and defiance of the ban. As Frederick Cooper, in a recent critique of resistance historiography, has argued: 'the dyad of resister/oppressor is isolated from its context; struggle within the colonized population—over class, age, gender or other inequalities—is "sanitized"; the texture of people's lives is lost; and complex strategies ...

of multi-sided engagement with forces inside and outside the community, are narrowed into a single framework.'[24] Like current international debates over clitoridectomy and infibulation, the resistance paradigm reifies dualities, obscuring the tangled layers of political relations which animate social protest. Within Kenyan historiography, the resistance paradigm reduced clitoridectomy disputes to political contests among men about women.[25]

In addition to situating girls and women as important participants in debates over clitoridectomy, examination of the 1956 ban through oral and written sources illuminates how relations of gender and generation structured the elaboration of a more interventionist and authoritarian colonial state in rural Kenya after World War II. Studies have revealed that the burdens of post-war development and welfare initiatives, particularly soil conservation campaigns, often fell disproportionately on women.[26] Similarly, historians have noted that women and young men comprised the bulk of Mau Mau fighters and supporters and, consequently, became the prime objects of rehabilitation campaigns inside prison camps and beyond through state-sponsored women's groups, *Maendeleo ya Wanawake*, and Youth Training Schemes.[27] No scholar, however, has explored how relations of gender and generation determined the limits of this 'second colonial occupation'.[28] A few young Africans with advanced formal education and close ties to the mission societies assisted in the formulation of the 1956 ban. Older men of the *Njuri Ncheke* and African District Council unanimously supported the passage of the ban, if only nominally. For these older men whose local authority had become increasingly tied to the colonial regime during the 1930s and 1940s,[29] a vote for the ban demonstrated their loyalty to the colonial government and their political distance from 'the Kikuyu'. For colonial officers, the ban became a test of older men's ability to control women and young men. Oral sources which present adolescent girls and older women as the organizers of *Ngaitana* suggest that older men did not possess the authority to transform institutions of womanhood. Headmen's and Home Guards'[30] failure and/or reluctance to deter transgressors reveals that even at the height of interventionist and repressive policies, colonial officials lacked the intermediaries to remake gendered social relations. In punishing those who defied the ban, headmen and Home Guards pursued their own political interests.

Clitoridectomy first became an object of official concern in central Kenya in the 1920s. At the prodding of Protestant missionaries, administrators in Nairobi encouraged Local Native Councils, bodies of elected and appointed African men presided over by a British district commissioner with veto powers, to pass resolutions restricting clitoridectomy.[31] In 1925 and 1927, the Meru Local Native Council, among others, passed resolutions prohibiting excision without a girl's consent, limiting the severity of the 'operation', and requiring the registration of all female 'circumcisors'.[32] These resolutions proved largely ineffectual. As one administrator noted, 'public opinion does not seem to be in sympathy with the cause'.[33] Believing that clitoridectomy, as part of female initiation, transformed girls into women, most Africans ignored these resolutions. According to Mary Holding, a British Methodist missionary with anthropological training, people in inter-war Meru viewed female initiation as preparation for marriage and procreation: it marked the end of sexual freedom, affirmed parental authority and filial duty, protected one against the dangers of sexual intercourse, and ensured fertility as well as ancestral blessings.[34]

The years 1929 to 1931 mark what has been termed within Kenyan historiography as the 'female circumcision controversy'. During this period, renunciation of clitoridectomy became the subject of declarations of Christian loyalty at some mission stations, while support of the practice became a platform issue for the Kikuyu Central Association. The Methodist Church of Meru, for example, instituted a loyalty declaration in early 1930; within weeks its membership dropped from seventy to six.[35] Popular protest of the missionaries' anti-excision campaigns spread with young men's and women's performance of *Muthirigu*, a dance-song which chastised missionaries, government officers, and African elders by name for corrupting custom, seducing young women, and stealing land. While the Nairobi administration moved quickly to ban performance of this critique of colonial authority,[36] they were reluctant to enact colony-wide anti-excision measures. Intervention did continue at the local administrative level.

Considered to be on the political margins of central Kenya, Local Native Councils in Meru and Embu Districts passed further resolutions in 1931, restricting the severity of the operation and providing instruction for 'circumcisors' in the newly authorized procedures.[37] Administrators in Meru, in an effort to eradicate the 'widespread' practice of pre-initiation abortion, also worked to lower the age of female initiation.[38] The impact of these interventions varied. District Commissioner Lambert recorded personally instructing the 'operators' in the new procedures, and interviewees Esther M'Ithinji and Julia Simion recalled how, in the late 1930s and early 1940s, *atani* carried permits on their walking sticks certifying that they had undergone such training.[39] A Methodist missionary, though, recorded witnessing the illegal and more severe form of excision in 1939.[40] Administrative efforts to lower the age of initiation proved more effective than efforts to regulate the severity of excision, as government police organized mass excisions for pre-pubescent girls.[41] Compared with the Methodist and Catholic missions, the Presbyterian mission in Meru maintained a more strident opposition to clitoridectomy, expelling all school girls who underwent initiation.[42] During the early years of the Mau Mau rebellion, administrators in Meru restricted initiation ceremonies and, in some cases, required that 'fees' of five shillings or fifty rat tails—in contribution to public health campaigns—be paid.[43] Between the 1920s and 1950s, the timing and form of initiation underwent significant change. Not only did most initiations occur at puberty rather than just prior to marriage, but few initiates chose to have abdominal tattooing (*ncuru*) performed or large ear holes pierced.[44] Apart from a few dozen girls from strong Christian families, though, all girls in post-World War II Meru anticipated excision as the transformative moment in their passage to womanhood.

The administrative context within which officials attempted to regulate clitoridectomy in the 1920s and 1930s differed markedly from that in which the 1956 ban was instituted. During this time, administrative ideology shifted from one of 'indirect rule',[45] in which indigenous male authorities were appointed to guide the participation of 'pristine' African societies in the colonial order, to a post-war development agenda which mandated British technocrats and mission-educated African men to remake African societies through the elaboration of economic and social reforms.[46] By 1956, Africans with close ties to mission societies held greater sway in administrative circles and British officers shared a more expansive vision of the colonial mandate. Yet, given the resources devoted to quelling the Mau Mau rebellion and the political volatility of earlier efforts to regulate clitoridectomy, it is still remarkable that administrators in Meru attempted a ban in 1956.

Documentary evidence suggests it was District Commissioner J. A. Cumber who first introduced the topic of a ban on clitoridectomy at a meeting of the African District Council (formerly the Local Native Council) in March 1956. He opened the meeting by stating how the Governor's recent decision to create a Meru Land Unit, apart from the Kikuyu Land Unit, meant that the 'Meru people had now gained independence from the Kikuyu'. He proceeded to suggest two measures by which the Meru African District Council could express its appreciation and affirm its cooperation with the Government: the introduction of a coffee tax and a prohibition on 'female circumcision'. Cumber contended that in passing such a ban, 'the Meru would be setting a good example to other Tribes in Kenya who persist in the enforcement of this iniquitous Tribal Tradition'. Later in the meeting, the Medical Officer of Health explained how he could not, in good conscience, give permits to 'circumcisors', as none of them practiced the 'operation' in a clean and hygienic manner. The Medical Officer argued that boys should be circumcised between the ages of six months and one year, instead of at adolescence, and 'female circumcision' should be abandoned entirely as it resulted in complications during childbirth. Reportedly, the Council 'wholeheartedly welcomed the suggestion' as regarded female initiation and referred the matter to the *Njuri Ncheke* for a final decision.[47] The following month, the *Njuri Ncheke* issued an edict forbidding clitoridectomy within Meru and the African District Council passed a by-law endorsing it.[48]

While the precise origins of the proposal to ban clitoridectomy in 1956 are unclear, District Commissioner Cumber's support was crucial to its passage and enforcement. Cumber repeatedly defended the ban against doubts raised by provincial and central government officials. Provincial

Commissioner Lloyd, Cumber's immediate superior with whom he was on acrimonious terms, pressured the Meru African District Council and the *Njuri Ncheke* to exempt the more 'backward' locations of the District from the ban.[49] The central government also prohibited the ban from being publicized in either the vernacular press or Meru-language broadcasts for fear that it would incite further unrest in areas of Mau Mau activity.[50] By 1957, with widespread transgressions of the ban apparent, the Provincial Commissioner firmly distanced the central government from 'this purely local... measure' by stating, 'the solution to this problem [clitoridectomy] lies in the progressive education of public opinion over a considerable time rather than in attempting to overcome any prejudice by sudden action'.[51]

An explanation of Cumber's support for the ban lies in his effort to establish Meru as a loyal and progressive district, distinct from the Kikuyu districts of central Kenya. In preparation for the March 1957 elections for the Legislative Council, Cumber orchestrated the registration of the largest number of voters in Central Province. As predicted, voters cast their ballots on a 'tribal basis' and the Meru candidate, Bernard Mate, nicknamed 'Cumber's Mate' in administrative circles, became the African member for Central Province.[52] Cumber also sought to reform local administration by recruiting younger men with higher levels of school education to replace retiring headmen.[53] In his progressive administrative program, Cumber even envisioned a role for the *Njuri Ncheke*, the central institution of 'indirect rule' policy as developed in Meru. He believed that this male council, with guidance from British officers, could maintain control 'over the young and undisciplined elements in the District'.[54]

The history of the *Njuri Ncheke* in the twentieth century is a complex one. While the earliest colonial officers in the District persecuted the *Njuri Ncheke* as a 'secret society', arresting members and burning their meeting places, later officers sought to work with it.[55] H. E. Lambert, stationed in Meru during the 1930s and renowned in official circles for his anthropological studies, was the first officer to recognize the *Njuri Ncheke* as the supreme indigenous council of Meru.[56] Lambert argued that, unlike other areas of central Kenya where such councils had been destroyed during the installation of colonialism, the *Njuri Ncheke* of Meru remained largely intact, commanding popular allegiance. Lambert sought to incorporate the *Njuri Ncheke* in local administration by securing its approval on issues of 'native law and custom' and requiring that all government employees become members. The *Njuri Ncheke* also chose all of the elected members of the African District Council from among its ranks. In collaboration with W. H. Laughton, a Methodist missionary, and Philip M'Inoti, the first African Methodist minister from Meru, Lambert devised a Christian oath so that mission adherents could join the *Njuri Ncheke*. Though the Presbyterian and Catholic mission stations remained skeptical of the ability of a 'heathen' institution to accommodate Christians, Methodist mission adherents became influential liaisons between the *Njuri Ncheke* and district administration.

Such close links with the administration caused some in Meru to doubt the authenticity of the *Njuri Ncheke*, deriding it as the 'white man's *Njuri*' and questioning the qualifications of young mission-educated members. Other young men, who were not members, resented the administrative authority accorded to the 'old illiterate men' of the council. In spite of these criticisms, the collaboration between the *Njuri Ncheke* and colonial officers proved mutually beneficial throughout the 1940s: officers heeded the *Njuri Ncheke*'s counsel on 'customary' and land matters, most notably rejecting 'Kikuyu' claims, while the *Njuri Ncheke* proved effective at instituting government policies.[57]

Early during the Mau Mau rebellion, the *Njuri Ncheke* pledged its loyalty to the colonial government and participated in the official 'rehabilitation' process by performing 'cleansing ceremonies' on those who had taken the Mau Mau oath.[58] The *Njuri Ncheke*, according to historian Joseph Kinyua, opposed Mau Mau as a Kikuyu movement threatening Meru land interests and one in which women flouted social norms by participating in political activities. Many male elders in central Kenya viewed women's mass participation in Mau Mau as an unprecedented level of female participation in the political realm and a challenge to their authority.[59] By 1953, British officials, especially young district officers recruited during the State of Emergency, began to question the efficacy of the *Njuri Ncheke*. While they never appear to have doubted the *Njuri Ncheke*'s loyalty to the Government, they accused the members of 'whole-sale corruption' in the collection of 'cleansing fees' as well as criticized them for forcibly initiating African Christians 'under pagan rites' and charging exorbitant induction fees.[60] Following on these criticisms, the ban on clitoridectomy became a test of the *Njuri Ncheke*'s ability to function as an effective and progressive administrative institution.

Oral sources call into question whether male leaders supported the ban as uniformly as expressed in official reports and suggested by the *Njuri Ncheke*'s unanimous vote at Nchiru. On the one hand, Ex-Senior Chief M'Mwirichia, a former Methodist teacher and member of *Njuri Ncheke* who worked very closely with colonial officers and missionaries, contended that the *Njuri Ncheke* strongly supported the ban. Similarly, Ex-Chief M'Iringo recalled favoring the ban, after hearing a presentation by a British medical doctor on the dangers of clitoridectomy. But Ex-Chief M'Anampiu and Ex-Subarea Headman David M'Naikiuru remembered that many at Nchiru disagreed with the ban. M'Naikiuru explained: 'you know, it was during the bad times of the Emergency. No one could argue with the authority then. Because the rule came through the District Commissioner to *Njuri*, they could not oppose it … in my opinion, they decided to ban it during Emergency because they thought, then, no one would go against it.'[61] A letter complaining of the ban written by Gerald Casey, a white settler of Timau, to a Member of Parliament, Barbara Castle, corroborates the *Njuri Ncheke*'s ambivalent position. Casey wrote, 'the ordinary tribesmen

I talk to say: "It is not our will. If we ask the *Njuri* they say it comes from the Government. If we ask the District Commissioner he says it comes from the *Njuri*."[62]

Casey also claimed that African mission adherents working for the Government, if not European missionaries themselves, played central roles in the orchestration of the ban.

> I would agree that it [the ban] may represent the will of the Government servants and mission-influenced Africans: who are a minority and separated by a psychological gulf from the more primitive and illiterate tribesmen. I was assured by officers of the administration that the missions have taken no part in the matter. The ordinary tribesman tells me the missions have very much to do with it: but keep in the background. It is at least certain that the great majority of Africans holding any position of authority in the Reserve are mission-trained and under strong missionary influence.[63]

Corroborating Casey's assertion, interviewees with the closest ties to the Methodist mission station, Stanley Kathurima and Naaman M'Mwirichia, expressed the strongest support for the ban. As Methodist mission-educated young men in the 1950s, Kathurima and M'Mwirichia served, respectively, as secretary of the *Njuri Ncheke* and a headman, and played crucial roles in the formulation of the ban.[64] Although no documentary evidence yet reveals the direct involvement of missionaries in the formulation of the prohibition, they could not have been far removed from official discussions. The Presbyterian and Methodist mission societies, though with varying approaches, had long been interested in the elimination of clitoridectomy. During the 1950s, the Presbyterians once again began to focus attention on the practice. In 1953, Dr. Clive Irvine of the Presbyterian hospital at Chogoria undertook his own initiative against clitoridectomy, only to provoke, in the words of the District Commissioner, 'a violent re-action in the Reserves'.[65] And in 1955, Irvine argued against the administrative policy that all government employees become members of the *Njuri Ncheke* on the grounds that the *Njuri Ncheke* still condoned the practice of clitoridectomy.[66] When the *Njuri Ncheke* passed the ban in 1956, the Presbyterian and Methodist mission societies received the news with prompt congratulations.[67]

Women's voices were notably, if not surprisingly, absent from discussions surrounding the passage of the 1956 ban. Methodist missionary Mary Holding's 1942 ethnographic account situated female initiation in Meru as an affair of women. Holding contended that women's councils, namely *kiama gia ntonye* ('the council of entering'), organized the years of preparation, celebration, and seclusion which comprised female initiation. Female initiation, according to Holding, not only remade girls into women, it transformed adult women into figures of authority within the community. Only a woman whose eldest child was ready for circumcision could gain admittance to *kiama gia ntonye* and, thus, a 'position of authority within the tribe'.[68] By the time of the Mau Mau rebellion, the presence of women's councils, as described by Holding, had begun to fade in most parts of Meru District. Nonetheless, as defiance of the ban demonstrated, female initiation was still a women's concern and did not easily fall within the purview of the all-male *Njuri Ncheke.*

The African District Council, unlike the *Njuri Ncheke,* was not an all-male institution in 1956. In line with post-World War II policies to broaden and professionalize the group of Africans engaged in administrative rule, officials in Meru appointed the first woman Councilor in 1951.[69] Martha Kanini of Chogoria joined the Council at the age of twenty-six years, after completing a year of study at Makerere University. She was, most likely, among the first women from Chogoria not to be initiated. Kanini remembered how the District Commissioner asked her not to participate in discussion of the ban: 'I was there alone [the only woman] and I did not even speak, the District Commissioner told me not to speak ... He wanted men to discuss it. Because I am concerned, I should keep quiet ... So long as I felt it was for their [women's] benefit, I had to keep quiet, to hear what men say.'[70] While Kanini recalled being present but silent at the meeting when the ban was proposed, the minutes of the two meetings at which the ban was formulated record Kanini as absent with apologies.[71] In either asking Kanini to remain silent or to refrain from attending the meetings, the District Commissioner sought to place the banning of clitoridectomy within the control of men.

Most adolescent girls responded to the 1956 ban on clitoridectomy by defying it. Following the *Njuri Ncheke* meeting at Nchiru, headmen held *baraza*s to inform people of the ban. Ex-Chief M'Anampiu's recollection that girls had begun to 'circumcise themselves' even before he returned from Nchiru suggests that news of the ban, in some places, preceded such meetings. Caroline Kirote remembers that, in Mitunguu, girls purchased razor blades and went to the bush to 'circumcise each other' while their parents sat listening to the Headman announce the ban. Though women of the *Ngaitana* age group recollect, in vivid detail, their defiance of the ban, few can recount the official reasons given for the passage of the ban or remember their defiance as having any connection to the Mau Mau rebellion. Between 1956 and 1959, *Ngaitana* spread from one area of the District to another. Most areas of the District experienced two or three separate episodes or 'waves' of girls, of increasingly younger ages, 'circumcising themselves'. Charity Tirindi, of the second 'wave', remembers how *Ngaitana* came to her home area of Mwichiune: 'it began from Igoji [to the south] and then went to Mwiriga Mieru [to the north] so we were left in the middle alone. They used to call us cowards, abusing us, and calling us *nkenye* (uncircumcised girls) so we sat down and we decided how we will circumcise ourselves.' This statement reveals how groups of recently excised girls exerted peer pressure, often through song, on unexcised girls in other parts of the District to join *Ngaitana*. While the first members of *Ngaitana* were probably around thirteen to fourteen years old, the proper age for female initiation in the 1950s, the age of initiates decreased to eight years old or younger as the practice spread. Very few resisted *Ngaitana*. Elizabeth Muthuuri, the first girl in the Methodist schools to attain a standard seven education in 1945, stated that school girls did not participate in *Ngaitana*. While some school girls and their families, such as Martha Kanini, had repudiated clitoridectomy by 1956, other interviews suggest that such people were a small minority.[72]

Ngaitana initiations were a marked departure from most previous female initiations in Meru. First of all, they took place secretly, in the bush, forest, or maize fields. In the past, girls were initiated in large open fields, surrounded by crowds of women and peering children. Initiation in the bush was reserved for those who became pregnant before they were excised. *Ngaitana* initiations also lacked the attendant ceremonies and celebrations. In the 1920s, female initiation spanned three or four years, with an initiate having her ears pierced the first year, abdominal tattooing performed the next, and clitoridectomy the following year. Feasts and dances accompanied these physical procedures. A several-month seclusion followed during which older women fed recent initiates large amounts of food and taught them how to behave as women. Initiates emerged from seclusion to travel to their new matrimonial homes. While by the 1950s female initiation had become a pre-pubescent rather than pre-nuptial rite and practices such as abdominal tattooing and prolonged periods of seclusion had faded, people in Meru remember *Ngaitana* as a time of profound change, when female initiation was driven 'underground', stripped of its attendant celebrations and teachings, and reduced to the clandestine performance of excision.[73]

Moreover, unlike previous female initiations, *atani*, the older women who formerly practiced excision,[74] performed few of the initial *Ngaitana* procedures. A Methodist missionary working in Meru at the time wrote that *Ngaitana* went 'against all previous custom, some circumcised themselves, others one another and others were circumcised by their own mothers'.[75] Charity Tirindi, Caroline Kirote, and Agnes Nyoroka remembered how girls, in groups of three to twenty, excised each other, and later, when healing at home, were examined by *atani* and, if necessary, cut again. Isabel Kaimuri of Giantune recounted that she excised her own daughter. Isabella Kajuju, who became a *mutani*, recalled that she first performed the operation of clitoridectomy during *Ngaitana* when the experienced *mutani*, fearing prosecution, failed to come to excise Kajuju's niece and others. In some cases, *atani* participated clandestinely in the initial operations. Elizabeth M'Iringo remembered that while she and her age mates had wondered how they would be able to 'circumcise themselves', when they arrived in the forest they found a *mutani* waiting for them.[76]

The form of clitoridectomy performed during *Ngaitana* also differed from previous initiations. In 1957, the Governor of Kenya reported the findings of a Medical Officer in Meru to the Secretary of State for the Colonies.

He [a Medical Officer in Meru] has examined girls who have been circumcised by friends, from which it is obvious that they have no idea what female
circumcision entails. Most are content to make simple incisions on either
side of the vulva or through the skin only on the labia major... He has never
seen a clitoris removed, which is the object of female circumcision when
performed by a professional. The only damage done in cases he has examined has been some bleeding and occasionally secondary infection, but this
is surprisingly rare, and of course pain and discomfort vary with the size of
the incision. In his opinion such damage would not compare with the actual
removal of the clitoris as performed by professional circumcisers.[77]

While the Medical Officer attributed the less severe forms of clitoridectomy
he viewed to girls' ignorance of the previous practice, *Ngaitana* members
may also have been unwilling or unable to perform excision. Agnes Kirimi
recounted how members of her *Ngaitana* cohort were unable to finish the
operation themselves: 'we could not complete, we just tried a little by
cutting just the clitoris ... there was this other part, the remaining part to be
circumcised and we did not know. None of us knew to that extent ... when
they [our mothers] saw we had already tried, they decided to do the
finishing.' The amount of cutting done by the initiates may also have been
determined by the instruments they used. Whereas *atani* possessed iron-
wedge knives, members of *Ngaitana* only had access to razor blades.
Monica Kanana recounted that the *Ngaitana* operations were less severe
because of the fragility of razor blades. Kanana also recalled her mother
requesting her aunt to perform a less severe form of excision on Kanana
and her cohort because of their unusually young age.[78]

People were reluctant to accept the excisions which *Ngaitana* members
performed on one another as proper female initiation. Selina Kiroki, who
was initiated in the late 1940s, claimed that *Ngaitana* had 'spoiled' female
initiation by omitting the meaningful teachings and celebrations and reduc-
ing it to the practice of clitoridectomy. Members of *Ngaitana* challenged
processual understandings of female initiation by positing clitoridectomy
as the crux of the matter. The incisions which they performed on one another, though, revealed that they did not understand and/or accept what
excision entailed. The second set of excisions which *atani* performed on
Ngaitana members appear as an effort to complete the procedure and to
reassert older women's control over the process of transforming girls into
women.[79]

Drawing on their interpretations of the Mau Mau rebellion in Meru,
officials explained defiance of the ban as a conflict between young and old
men. In 1957, District Commissioner Cumber wrote, 'it is considered that
this recurrence of female circumcision is attributable to the activities of the
young men, many of whom resent the varying degree of control exercised
by the *Njuri* elders'.[80] Similarly, before a meeting of the *Njuri Ncheke*,
Cumber claimed that young men were encouraging girls to 'circumcise
themselves' so as to undermine the authority of the *Njuri Ncheke*.[81] Young

men were a potent source of colonial anxiety during the mid-1950s. Colonial officers and Methodist missionaries in Meru established a 'Youth Training Centre' to turn young men into 'responsible citizens', 'develop their characters', and 'instill a respect for discipline and agricultural work'.[82] Most young men in Meru probably did oppose the ban. According to Charity Tirindi, even school-educated men in the 1950s refused to marry unexcised women.[83] No evidence suggests, though, that they organized defiance of the ban. In situating young men as the 'real force' behind *Ngaitana*, Cumber upheld a long tradition of colonial officers interpreting female political protest as male-instigated.

Njuri Ncheke members cited ethnic and gender as well as generational insurrection in explaining defiance of the ban before District Commissioner Cumber. Using the meeting, in part, as another opportunity to denounce their political rival within central Kenya, they claimed that it was people of 'non-Meru origin', presumably 'Kikuyus', who were encouraging excision. Moreover, they contended that the 'tendency had sprung up recently among the women and among the government officials to disregard the *Njuri's* authority and its existence'. Turning Cumber's critique of young African men around, *Njuri* members denounced the insolence of Cumber's junior officers, many of whom were more skeptical than the District Commissioner of the *Njuri Ncheke's* political worth. *Njuri* members also identified the prime organizers of *Ngaitana*: women.[84]

While most men favored clitoridectomy, interviewees suggested that young women, mothers, and grandmothers were the organizers of *Ngaitana*. Monica Kanana recalled how she and her age mates were 'beaten thoroughly' by the first group of *Ngaitana* until they too decided to 'circumcise themselves'. Agnes Kirimi attributed her decision to join *Ngaitana* to her grandmother: 'I remember why I got motivated. It's because my grandmother used to tell me, "you're left here alone with your dirt" ... You see the grandmothers were the motivators.'[85] Grandmothers' stronger advocacy for clitoridectomy than mothers' was attributable to the historic role which older women played as the organizers of initiation as well as to the special relationship which existed between grandparents and grandchildren, enabling them to discuss intimate topics considered inappropriate for discussions between parents and children.[86] In households in which parents had differing opinions on the ban, mothers most often favored excision. The fathers of both Monica Kanana and Lucy Kajuju were Home Guards who supported the ban. Kanana remembered her father beating her mother after he learned of her initiation, while Kajuju recalled how her mother fled following her initiation to escape her father's anger. Ex-District Officer Richard Cashmore recounted older women protesting the ban outside of his office in Chuka. Reiterating many themes of the dance-song *Muthirigu* performed during the 1929–31 controversy, these women sang of the ban as a government plot to make young women infertile, eliminate the 'Meru tribe', and steal their land.[87]

For adolescent girls, though, *Ngaitana* was about more than maintaining a valued practice. It became a test and demonstration of their strength and determination as an age group. Amid people being forced to live in 'villages', detained and tortured in prisons, and killed in the forest, adolescent girls too confronted the colonial state. Caroline Kirote recalled how her *Ngaitana* group, on their way to turn themselves in at the headman's camp, feared the worst: 'if it happened that we would be wiped out, girls would be wiped out together … you know because of the way the Government carried out executions at that time.' Many interviewees contended that the ban encouraged, rather than deterred, excision. Ex-Subarea Headman David M'Naikiuru recalled, 'were it not for the ban they would not have circumcised such a large number because Christianity was spreading rapidly'. Similarly, recollections by Monica Kanana and Charity Tirindi of being taunted and beaten by older *Ngaitana* to join their ranks suggest how *Ngaitana* became a movement, gathering even unsuspecting girls to its cause.[88]

While nearly all interviewees, when asked specifically, denied any direct connection between defiance of the 1956 ban and the Mau Mau rebellion, broader evidence suggests parallels, if not connections, between these two struggles. Those social groups which most vigorously participated in and supported Mau Mau—young people and women—were most open in their opposition to the 1956 ban. Official documents suggest that in Meru 'the unmarried girl class' was particularly active in supporting Mau Mau.[89] Interviewee Charity Tirindi illustrated how Mau Mau fighters themselves opposed the ban by recounting a gruesome tale of forcible excisions: 'if you were not circumcised, they [Mau Mau fighters] came for you at night, you [we]re taken to the forest [and] circumcised, and you [we]re roasted for what you have been circumcised [the clitoris] and you are told to eat it.' Those who publicly supported the ban—strong mission adherents and male elders serving as African District Council and *Njuri Ncheke* members, headmen, and Home Guards—ranked as government loyalists during the Mau Mau rebellion.[90] Furthermore, the punishment for those who defied the ban mirrored, in part, punishments meted out to those who had taken the Mau Mau oath, with Home Guards rounding up suspects, burning their homes and confiscating livestock, and detaining them in headmen's camps. Veronica Kinaito recounted a song performed by her *Ngaitana* group in which they compared their one month detention in a headmen's camp to young men's imprisonment at Manyani, the main camp for Mau Mau detainees.[91]

Enforcement of the ban on excision varied tremendously over its three-year duration, 1956–59, and from one area of Meru to another. In 'backward' areas of the District such as Tharaka, the ban was not enforced. In other areas such as Igembe, Tigania, and North and South Imenti, *Ngaitana* cases consumed the attention of district officers, headmen, Home Guards, *Njuri* members, and African Court staff for months on end. While all suspected transgressors were supposed to be charged before African Courts with contravening the *Njuri*'s Order authorized under section 17(a) of the African Courts Ordinance 65/51, oral evidence suggests that headmen and Home Guards often defied official policy, imposing and collecting fines themselves without forwarding cases to African Courts.[92] Of the 2,400 individuals charged before African Courts, fathers of initiates accounted for approximately 43 per cent; initiates, 33 per cent; mothers of initiates, 20 per cent; and 'circumcisors', 3 per cent of those accused.[93] Fines ranged from 50/- to 400/- shillings and sentences from one month in detention camp to six months without hard labor, depending on the accused's wealth and status. Settler Casey explained the scale of these fines: 'my shepherd earns Shs. 50/- a month cash wage. He will have to work eight months to realize Shs. 400/-. He is one of the lucky ones. Very few old men earn half as much as he does. Some would have to work eighteen months to two years to find the money.' One district officer reportedly remarked that the African Courts were 'making more [money] out of it [*Ngaitana* fines] than out of all the rates put together'.[94] Thousands of others paid fines outside of the African Courts.

The swiftness of girls' response to the ban appears to have caught administrators unprepared. The first group of *Ngaitana* in North Imenti paid no fine; 'nothing was done, even the daughters of Chiefs, *askaris* [Home Guards]... had circumcised themselves'. Ex-Chief M'Anampiu recalled sending home all the girls whom he met on his return from Nchiru and later fining their fathers. Ex-Home Guard Moses M'Mukindia remembered arresting initiates as they came from the forest and taking them to the Meru Civil Hospital to be examined by a British Medical Officer. At Ntakira, Monica Kanana recounted how Home Guards burnt the homes of an early *Ngaitana* group found healing in seclusion. Later cohorts, fearing that such punishment would be inflicted on their homes, turned themselves in at headmen's camps. Charity Tirindi recounted why her group presented themselves for arrest: 'we had heard that those who were caught from Igoji were beaten so we might make ourselves to be beaten for no good reason [unnecessarily] so we decided to take ourselves.'[95]

The walk to the headman's camp, according to Monica Kanana, was not easy as she tried to keep her legs apart and her head shrouded in a cloth. Upon their arrival, *Ngaitana* members responded to Home Guards' and headmen's queries by claiming that they had 'circumcised themselves'. They remained in headmen's camps from a few days to a few weeks, until their parents paid their fines. During their stay, they ate food brought by their mothers and slept in simple shelters or on dried banana leaves. Caroline Kirote and Evangeline M'Iringo remembered that at times the camps were filled with one hundred or more girls.[96]

Headmen and Home Guards along with local *Njuri* members, who served as judicial councilors within headmen's camps, consumed all of the livestock paid in fines. Fines paid varied across time and from one individual to the next. Lucy Kajuju recounted that as a headman, her father was forced to pay a double fine of two bulls and two he-goats. Evangeline M'Iringo recalled that she and her sister decided to be excised together, even though they were five years apart in age, so their parents would only have to pay a single goat. Ex-Subarea Headman David M'Naikiuru remembered a gradual decrease in the fines charged: 'they started with imprisoning and destroying the houses, they went down to fining cows ... as the number of circumcised girls increased they saw the bulls that were suppose to be eaten were too many so they started fining goats.' [97]

Fines in kind were not the only punishment meted out in headmen's camps. Many Ngaitana members, after healing, performed several weeks of punitive manual labor ranging from digging roads and drainage trenches through planting trees and clearing weeds to plastering floors in Home Guard houses. In some areas of the District, punishment involved attendance at Maendeleo ya Wanawake, state-sponsored women's groups which taught the values and practices of home craft.[98] A Methodist missionary recorded that most headmen regarded participation in Maendeleo ya Wanawake as a privilege and therefore, as punishment, forbade Ngaitana members from attending meetings for seven to ten weeks. One Christian headman, though, viewing such meetings as rehabilitation, insisted that 'all these girls should attend classes instead of doing manual work for the location'.[99] Defiance and enforcement of the ban also became entangled with sexual and marital access to initiates. Caroline Kirote recalled the following song chastising a headman named M'Mbuju for enforcing the ban and proclaiming that he would never have sex with—'cover'—a member of Ngaitana:

Yes, yes, M'Mbuju, you will die before you cover a circumcised girl.
Yes, yes, M'Mbuju, circumcised girls have been made to dig up a road.
Yes, M'Mbuju, circumcised girls have dug up a road, yes.

James Laiboni of Igembe recounted stories of two Ngaitana members who were betrothed to a headman and Home Guard, respectively, as their parents could not afford the fines imposed.[100]

Interviewees remembered that individuals taken to African Courts were those arrested by Tribal Police, as opposed to Home Guards, or those who refused to pay fines to the local Njuri. According to interviewees, people refused to pay the local Njuri either because they thought that by furthering their case to the African Court, they would avoid paying a fine altogether, or, more often, because they did not want to provide Njuri members, headmen, and Home Guards with more livestock to eat.[101] During the Mau Mau rebellion, such consumption had taken on a particular salience as headmen and Home Guards confiscated and ate the cattle of suspected Mau Mau sympathizers, depriving households of wealth as well as sources of milk and meat. In collecting fines of livestock and, possibly, young brides beyond the purview of British officers, these African men pursued local political interests and masked their inability and/or unwillingness to prevent defiance. Some of those accused of defiance subverted these political interests by choosing to pay relatively high monetary fines in African Courts rather than provide headmen, Home Guards, and *Njuri* members with meat.

While largely ignorant of politics within headmen's camps, many European observers voiced concern over the work of African Courts. Following his investigation of a *Ngaitana* case involving his shepherd, Ngarui Kabuthia, settler Casey criticized African Court personnel for not allowing witnesses and arrogantly refusing appeals: 'He [the court clerk] implied that the Court was infallible and no good would come of challenging it. Such a thing, he said, had never happened before.'[102] In reviewing the court registers, British district officers often reduced the size of fines imposed. Central government officials were wary of the ban from its inception. Monthly court returns from Meru reporting hundreds of people charged with defying the ban only added to their unease. In response to the April 1957 returns listing over two hundred *Ngaitana* cases, the African Courts Officer Rylands wrote to the District Commissioner of Meru: 'are [you] satisfied with the number of such cases so suddenly taken as a result of the Njuri's order and the severity of the fines imposed? The P[rovincial] C[ommissioner] has stressed the matter is basically one for education of public opinion.'[103] Following this memorandum, the number of cases and size of fines only increased. In July 1957, the African Courts Officer wrote to the Provincial Commissioner: 'the avalanche does not slow up.... If this is not "mass action through the courts" I don't know what is.'[104] Central government officials, though, did not halt 'the avalanche'. That took a settler's letter of complaint and two Parliamentary questions.

In July 1957, settler Casey wrote a letter to a Member of Parliament, Barbara Castle, drawing her attention to the inappropriateness of the ban and the injustices perpetuated in enforcing it. He requested Castle to secure from the Colonial Office statistics on prosecutions relating to the ban. On 1 August 1957, Castle raised the issue of the Meru ban in the House of Commons before the Secretary of State for the Colonies. Unsatisfied with his response, Castle requested a further inquiry into the matter. In this correspondence, Castle sided with Casey: 'I abhor the practice of female circumcision and certainly want to see it stamped out, but I do not think this is the right way to do it.'[105] While awaiting the Governor of Kenya's comments on the subject, the Secretary of State made a preliminary response to Castle's critique of the ban. He contended that if, as 'it seems obvious', the ban has reduced the incidence of clitoridectomy, it was justified.[106] In late December, the Governor of Kenya wrote to the Secretary of State, distancing central administration as well as officers in Meru from the formulation and enforcement of the ban.

The state of affairs brought to your attention by Mrs. Castle is the result of an excessive outburst of zeal on the part of the tribal authorities and African

Courts of Meru to stamp out female circumcision, which the more enlightened leaders of the tribe have come to abhor ... the Administration has, however, already taken steps to curb this enthusiasm and to reduce not only the
number of cases being brought to court, but also to temper the sentences
imposed ... the decision of the *Njuri Ncheke*, the indigenous tribal authority
and the arbiters of tribal law and custom, to ban female circumcision, was
taken without any influence being brought to bear on them by Government
or the Missions.[107]

The Governor explained that the anti-clitoridectomy campaign in Meru
had shifted focus from prosecutions in court to education and health
propaganda. Moreover, he stated that chiefs and headmen, as government
employees, would no longer prosecute cases in court; that task would be
left to local *Njuri* members. This represented a major retrenchment in
enforcement of the ban. The Secretary of State forwarded the Governor's
letter to Castle along with notification that, on appeal, Ngarui Kabuthia's
sentence was reduced from 400/- to 50/- shillings.[108]

In November 1957, the *Njuri Ncheke* held a meeting to discuss the position of the ban. They had already begun to feel the effects of the new policy
of enforcement reported by the Governor. Members of the *Njuri Ncheke*
agreed that while the incidence of excision had only increased of late, 'courts
had tended to disregard hearing of circumcision cases'. They proceeded to
complain of the *Njuri Ncheke*'s inefficacy as a colonial institution:

Njuri had means of enforcing its rules in the past, but since the advent of the
British Rule, Njuri has had to modify its punishments most of which were
cruel. In the old days no one dared disobey Njuri but these days the British
Government has tended to replace the indigenous authority, and
maintenance of law and order is a responsibility of Government.[109]

Before British officers, *Njuri Ncheke* members blamed the ban's failure on
the weakening of their authority under colonial rule. They did not acknowledge that the ban was a largely unprecedented extension of male authority
into women's affairs. Nor did they reveal how some headmen, Home
Guards, and *Njuri* members used enforcement of the ban to pursue more
immediate political interests.

After October 1957, the number of *Ngaitana* cases in African Courts
decreased dramatically throughout the District. By March 1959, they had
ceased entirely.[110] As even young girls defied the ban, it is unlikely that by
1959 there were many adolescent girls left in Meru who had not already
been excised.

Discourses of sexual oppression, human rights, women's health, and neo-
colonialism structure current international debates over campaigns to eradicate clitoridectomy and infibulation. Analysis of the 1956 ban, though,
demonstrates the significance of gender identities and generational relations

to understanding the continuance of these practices. In 1950s Meru, most people believed that clitoridectomy, as a part of female initiation, remade girls into women. Through female initiation, adolescent girls learned how to behave as young women as well as future wives and daughters-in-law. The 1956 ban was at least as much of a challenge to relations of seniority among women as to relations of subordination between men and women. Adolescent girls, some afraid of being denied adulthood and others feeling peer pressure, attempted to excise each other, not appreciating and/or accepting the severity of the practice. While older women reasserted control over the process by performing a second excision, *Ngaitana* permanently altered female initiation in most parts of the District. In appearing as a travesty of previous initiations, it lent support, in some areas and households, to a growing sentiment that female initiation was no longer necessary. In other places where the practice persisted, *Ngaitana* helped to reduce the process of female initiation to clitoridectomy; 'they are still circumcised secretly, the one who wants'.[111]

Analysis of the 1956 ban also reveals how relations of gender and generation shaped and limited the more interventionist policies of the post-World War II colonial state. Various scholars have examined how during the inter-war period colonial officers and older African men colluded to exert control over women and young men.[112] During the post-World War II period, the weakness of this collusion became increasingly apparent. Women and young men protested labor policies, soil conservation campaigns, and the denial of economic opportunities and political rights.[113] Officials responded to these protests by attempting both to strengthen the authority of headmen and elders and to incorporate women and young men more fully in colonial rule. The 1956 ban was, in part, an affirmation of the social vision of a small but increasingly influential group in administrative circles, young Africans with advanced school education. Colonial officers also viewed the ban, like the appointment of Martha Kanini to the African District Council, as a step towards elevating women's status. According to District Commissioner Cumber, 'women of Meru' as well as 'future generations of the Tribe as a whole' would appreciate the ban's passage.[114] As part of a broader strategy of affirming their loyalty to the colonial government and protecting Meru land from 'Kikuyu' claims, the African District Council and the *Njuri Ncheke* unanimously passed the ban.

Mass defiance of the ban revealed that the colonial state's intermediaries lacked the political authority and will to remake social relations. District Commissioner Cumber interpreted widespread defiance of the ban as young men's loss of respect for the authority of older men. While most young men probably opposed the ban and preferred excised brides, girls and women organized the defiance. Cumber assumed that male elders of long ago could have eliminated clitoridectomy; he never considered that female initiation lay beyond the jurisdiction of men's councils. Headmen and Home Guards, many still favoring clitoridectomy, exhibited tremendous discretion in punishing those who defied the ban. In accordance with the African District Council's resolution and the *Njuri Ncheke*'s proclamation, they charged some offenders in African Courts with contravening the *Njuri*'s order. Interviews suggest, though, that many cases never made it to African Courts. In fining offenders beyond the purview of colonial officers, headmen and Home Guards sought to conceal their inability and/or un-willingness to prevent defiance as well as to turn the meting out of punish-ment into personal gain. During *Ngaitana*, headmen, Home Guards, and *Njuri* members consumed extraordinary amounts of meat and, perhaps on occasion, took initiates as wives. Post-World War II interventionist state policies, even in their failures, enlarged the administrative space in which such men could pursue other, more immediate, political concerns.

Notes

I would like to thank Henry Mutoro and David Anderson and participants in their history seminars at the University of Nairobi and the School for Oriental and African Studies in November 1995, as well as David William Cohen, Frederick Cooper, Nancy Rose Hunt, John Lonsdale, Kenda Mutongi, Agnes Odinga, and Keith Shear for comments on earlier drafts. Research for this article was funded by a Fulbright-IIE Foreign Scholarship Board fellowship and an International Doctoral Research fellow-ship sponsored by the Joint Committee on African Studies of the Social Science Research Council and the American Council of Learned Societies in 1994–95.

1. Interview: Veronica Kinaito, 7/5/95, tapes no. 64–65. I am grateful to Carol Gatwiri, Doreen Jackson, Grace Kirimi, Richard Kirimi, Rosemary Kithiira, Thomas Mutethia, Nkatha Mworoa, Charity Nduru, and Diana Rigiri who provided translation assistance during interviews and transcribed and translated them afterwards. All tapes and transcripts are presently in my possession; they will be deposited at the Kenyan National Archives.

2. The terms 'clitoridectomy' and 'excision' both denote the removal of the clitoris and the whole or partial excision of the labia minora. Unlike 'female circumcision', these terms do not suggest equivalency between these genital practices performed on women and male circumcision. Throughout this paper, the term 'circumcision' is used in quoting oral sources, as it is the most widely accepted translation from the Meru language.

3. The African District Council in neighboring Embu District adopted the ban in late 1956. Kenyan National Archives (KNA): DC/MRU/1/1/12/1, Meru District Annual Report, 1956.

4. Interview: M'Anampiu, 5/10/95, tapes no. 41–42.

5. KNA: African Courts, Monthly Returns, Meru, 1956–58, ARC(MAA)/2/9/27/II, ARC(MAA)/2/10/27/III, MAA/7/282, and MAA/7/283.

6. Interview: Selina Kiroki, 6/30/95, tapes no. 62–63.

7. The incidence of clitoridectomy is still high in many areas of Meru: *Harmful Traditional Practices that Affect the Health of Women and Children in Kenya* (Maendeleo ya Wanawake, Nairobi, 1992); *Qualitative Research Report on Female Circumcision in Four Districts in Kenya* (PATH, Nairobi, 1993). My interviews are

biased towards areas of the former Meru District (now Meru, Nyambene, and Tharaka/
Nthi Districts) accessible from Meru town by public transportation and/or a five-
kilometer walk. Compared to more remote areas, the areas where I conducted interviews have better infrastructure, participate more fully in the cash economy, and have
a longer history of engagement with Christianity and school education. Within Meru,
these areas are reputed to have lower incidences of excision. Many of the women of the
Ngaitana age group whom I interviewed reported that they choose not to have their
daughters excised because they felt it to be an unnecessary and/or harmful practice.
Clitoridectomy is not illegal in Kenya today. In 1982, Kenyan President Daniel arap Moi
issued an administrative decree against clitoridectomy, but it did not entail legal sanc-
tion. Only cases of 'forcible circumcision', when a girl or woman is excised against her
or her parents' or guardians' will, are punishable under the penal code as physical assault.

8. 'Infibulation' refers to the 'excision of all or part of the mons veneris, the labia
majora, the labia minora, the clitoris, the raw wounds adhering or having been sewn
together to leave only a small aperture for the urinary and menstrual flows'. Lilian
Passmore Sanderson, *Against the Mutilation of Women* (Ithaca Press, London, 1981),
p. 2.

9. Efua Dorkenoo, *Cutting the Rose: Female Genital Mutilation, The Practice and
Its Prevention* (Minority Rights Publications, London, 1994), pp. 61–82.

10. Fran P. Hosken, *The Hosken Report: Genital and Sexual Mutilation of Females*
(WIN News, Lexington, 1979); Mary Daly, *Gyn/Ecology: The Metaethics of Radical
Feminism* (Beacon Press, Boston, 2nd ed., 1978). Both Hosken and Daly are Americans.

11. Scilla McLean, *Female Circumcision, Excision, and Infibulation: The Facts and
Proposals for Change* (Minority Rights Group, London, 1980); Nawal El Saadawi, *The
Hidden Face of Eve* (Beacon Press, Boston, 1980); Asma El Dareer, *Women, Why Do
You Weep?* (Zed Press, London, 1982).

12. Dorkenoo, *Cutting the Rose*, pp. 62–3.

13. Harriet Lyons, 'Anthropologists, Moralities, and Relativities: The Problem of
Genital Mutilations', *Canadian Review of Society and Anthropology*, 18 (1981),
pp. 499–518; Corinne A. Kratz, 'Appendix A: Initiation and Circumcision', in *Affecting
Performance: Meaning, Movement, and Experience in Okiek Women's Initiation*
(Smithsonian Institution, Washington, D.C., 1994), pp. 341–7.

14. Kratz, 'Appendix A', in *Affecting Performance*, p. 347.

15. Vicki Kirby, 'On the Cutting Edge: Feminism and Clitoridectomy', *Australian
Feminist Studies*, 5 (1987), pp. 35–55; Sondra Hale, 'A Question of Subjects: The "Female Circumcision" Controversy and the Politics of Knowledge', *Ufahamu*, 22 (1994),
pp. 26–35.

16. In Kenya, the Network to Combat Harmful Practices Affecting Women
(NCHPAW), formed in 1994, is an association of local health and women's organizations working, largely through education campaigns, to eradicate clitoridectomy. A
range of international funders support NCHPAW's work. On health-based plans of
action, Olayinka Koso-Thomas, *The Circumcision of Women: A Strategy for Eradication*
(Zed Books, London, 1987); and Dorkenoo, *Cutting the Rose*.

17. See Sanderson, *Against the Mutilation of Women*, for an account of the unsuccessful 1946 outlawing of infibulation in Sudan. The Meru ban is mentioned, though
not examined, in Sanderson, *Against the Mutilation of Women*, p. 68, and Rev. Canon
Ephantus Josiah, *Female Circumcision* (Uzima Press, Nairobi, n.d.), p. 15, cited in
Dorkenoo, *Cutting the Rose*, p. 9.

18. Gerda Lerner, *The Creation of Patriarchy* (Oxford University Press, 1986), p. 239.

19. E. Mary Holding, 'Women's Institutions and the African Church', *International Review of Missions*, 31 (1942), pp. 291–300.

20. Janice Boddy, *Women and Alien Spirits: Women, Men, and the Zar Cult in Northern Sudan* (University of Wisconsin Press, Madison, 1989), p. 319.

21. On the significance of age groups to initiation, see E. Mary Holding, 'Some Preliminary Notes on Meru Age Grades', *Man*, 30–31 (1942), pp. 58–65; Claire Robertson, 'Grassroots in Kenya: Women, Genital Mutilation, and Collective Action, 1920–90', *Signs*, 21 (1996), pp. 615–42; Bernardo Bernardi, *Age Class Systems: Social Institutions and Polities Based on Age* (Cambridge University Press, Cambridge, 1985).

22. For a review of Mau Mau historiography, see Bruce Berman and John Lonsdale, *Unhappy Valley: Conflict in Kenya and Africa, Book Two: Violence and Ethnicity* (James Currey, London, 1992).

23. For example, Carl G. Rosberg and John Nottingham, *The Myth of "Mau Mau": Nationalism in Kenya* (Praeger, London, 1966), pp. 105–35; Susan Pedersen, 'National Bodies, Unspeakable Acts: The Sexual Politics of Colonial Policy-Making', *Journal of Modern History*, 63 (1991), pp. 647–80. An exception to this paradigm is John Lonsdale, 'The Moral Economy of Mau Mau: Wealth, Poverty, and Civic Virtue in Kikuyu Political Thought', in Berman and Lonsdale, *Unhappy Valley*, pp. 315–504.

24. Frederick Cooper, 'Conflict and Connection: Rethinking Colonial African History', *American Historical Review*, 99 (1994), p. 1533.

25. On how colonial debates over *sati* similarly silenced the women at the center of that practice, Lata Mani, 'Contentious Traditions: The Debate on Sati in Colonial India', *Cultural Critique*, 7 (1987), pp. 119–56; Gayatri Chakravorty Spivak, 'Can the Subaltern Speak?' in *Marxism and the Interpretation of Culture*, ed. Cary Nelson and Lawrence Grossberg (University of Illinois Press, Urbana, 1988), pp. 271–313.

26. David W. Throup, *Economic and Social Origins of Mau Mau, 1945–53* (James Currey, London, 1988), pp. 140–70; Bruce Berman, *Control and Crisis in Colonial Kenya: The Dialectic of Domination* (James Currey, London, 1990), pp. 303, 308.

27. J. T. Samuel Kamunchuluh, 'The Meru Participation in Mau Mau', *Kenya Historical Review*, 3 (1975), pp. 193–216; Tabitha Kanogo, *Squatters and the Roots of Mau Mau, 1905–63* (James Currey, London, 1987); Luise White, 'Separating the Men from the Boys: Constructions of Gender, Sexuality, and Terrorism in Central Kenya, 1939–59', *International Journal of African Historical Studies*, 23 (1990), pp. 1–25; Cora Ann Presley, *Kikuyu Women, the Mau Mau Rebellion, and Social Change in Kenya* (Westview Press, Boulder, 1992).

28. D. A. Low and J. M. Lonsdale, 'Introduction: Towards the New Order, 1945–63', in *History of East Africa*, ed. D. A. Low and A. Smith, vol. 3 (Oxford University Press, London, 1976), pp. 12–16.

29. Throup, *Economic and Social Origins of Mau Mau*, pp. 144–8; Berman, *Control and Crisis in Colonial Kenya*, pp. 208–17.

30. Home Guards were 'loyal' Africans recruited by the colonial government and supplied with arms to eliminate passive support for Mau Mau fighters; they became notorious for their 'reign of terror'. Berman, *Control and Crisis in Colonial Kenya*, p. 357.

31. KNA: DC/KBU/7/3, N.A.D. Circular No. 36 of 9/21/25, reproduced in Jocelyn Murray, 'The Kikuyu Female Circumcision Controversy, with Special Reference to the Church Missionary Society's "Sphere of Influence"' (Ph.D. diss., University of California, Los Angeles, 1974), pp. 122–3.

32. Meru County Council Office (MCC): Meru Local Native Council Book No. 1, meetings of 10/12/25 and 6/2–3/27.

33. KNA: PC/CP8/1/1, District Commissioner (D.C.), Fort Hall, to Provincial Commissioner (P.C.), Kikuyu, 1/4/29 and D.C., Embu, to P.C., Kikuyu, 12/27/28, quoted in Murray, 'The Kikuyu Female Circumcision Controversy', p. 114.

34. Holding, 'Women's Institutions and the African Church', pp. 296–7.

35. Zablon John Nthamburi, *A History of the Methodist Church in Kenya* (Uzima, Nairobi, 1982), p. 72.

36. Murray, 'The Kikuyu Female Circumcision Controversy', pp. 136–44. For an account of the corresponding debates in the House of Commons, Pedersen, 'National Bodies, Unspeakable Acts'.

37. KNA: DC/MRU/1/2, Meru District Annual Report, 1931; and PC/CP8/1/2, D.C., Embu, to P.C., Kikuyu, 5/14/31.

38. Lynn M. Thomas, 'Reading Clitoridectomy Campaigns as the Constitution of Authorities: Meru District, Kenya, c.1918–38', paper presented to the African Studies Association, Boston, December 1993.

39. KNA: PC/CP8/1/2, D.C., Embu, to P.C., Kikuyu, 5/14/31; and Interview: Esther M'Ithinji and Julia Simion, 10/14/90, tape no. 3.

40. Bertha Jones, *Kenya Kaleidoscope: The Story of Bertha Jones for 28 Years a Servant of the Church in Kenya* (Devon, 1995), pp. 22–5.

41. Thomas, 'Reading Clitoridectomy Campaigns'.

42. Robert Macpherson, *The Presbyterian Church in Kenya* (Presbyterian Church, Nairobi, 1970); and Nthamburi, *A History of the Methodist Church in Kenya*.

43. Interview: Tarsila Nikobwe and Margaret Mwakinia, 9/20/90, tape no. 10.

44. For descriptions of these procedures, Daniel Nyaga, *Mikarire na Mituurire ya Amiiru* (Heinemann, Nairobi, 1986).

45. The classic formulation is Frederick Lugard, *The Dual Mandate in British Tropical Africa* (Blackwood, London, 1922). On Meru, see H. E. Lambert, *The Use of Indigenous Authorities: Studies in the Meru in Kenya Colony* (Communications from the School of Africa Studies, No. 16, Cape Town, 1947). On how all colonial rule is inevitably 'indirect', Karen Fields, *Revival and Rebellion in Colonial Central Africa* (Princeton University Press, Princeton, 1985), pp. 30–60.

46. Frederick Cooper, 'From Free Labor to Family Allowances: Labor and African Society in Colonial Discourse', *American Ethnologist*, 16 (1988), pp. 745–65.

47. KNA: CS/1/14/100, Minutes of the Meeting of the African District Council (A.D.C.), 3/8–9/56; and MCC: Meru A.D.C. Book No. 6, meeting of 3/8–9/56.

48. MCC: Meru A.D.C. Book No. 6, meeting of 4/12/56; and KNA: DC/MRU/1/1/ 12/1, Meru District Annual Report, 1956.

49. KNA: CS/1/14/100, 'Notes of a Special Meeting of the Meru A.D.C. held 7/3/56'.

50. KNA: DC/MRU/1/1/12/1, Meru District Annual Report, 1956.

51. KNA: MAA/1/5, Central Province Annual Report, 1957.

52. KNA: DC/MRU/1/1/12/1, Meru District Annual Report, 1956; and DC/MRU/1/ 1/13, Meru District Annual Report, 1957. Interview: Richard Cashmore, 12/6/95. On Mate's election, B. A. Ogot, 'The Decisive Years, 1956–63', in *Decolonization and Independence in Kenya, 1940–93*, ed. B. A. Ogot and W. R. Ochieng' (James Currey, London, 1995), pp. 54–8.

53. KNA: DC/MRU/1/1/13, Meru District Annual Report, 1957; and DC/MRU/1/1/14, Meru District Annual Report, 1958. Interview: Naaman M'Mwirichia, 9/18/95, tapes no. 74–75.

54. KNA: DC/MRU/1/1/13, Meru District Annual Report, 1957.

55. KNA: PC/CP/1/9/1, Meru Political Record Book, 1908–21; and DC/MRU/1/1/1 and DC/MRU/1/1/2, Meru District Annual Reports, 1910–28.

56. H. E. Lambert, *The Use of Indigenous Authorities*.

57. Joseph I. Kinyua, 'A History of the *Njuri* in Meru, 1910–63' (B.A. diss., History, University of Nairobi, c.1969–70).

58. MCC: ADM/15/16/6/I-II, *Njuri Ncheke*. Men and women joined and advanced through the ranks of the Mau Mau movement by participating in a series of oaths.

59. Kinyua, 'A History of the *Njuri* in Meru', p. 46; Presley, *Kikuyu Women, the Mau Mau Rebellion, and Social Change in Kenya*.

60. KNA: DC/MRU/1/3/12, Meru District, Handing Over Report, 1953; and MCC: ADM/15/16/6/II, *Njuri Ncheke*.

61. Interviews: Naaman M'Mwirichia, 9/18/95; Daniel M'Iringo, 6/25/95, tapes no. 59–60; and David M'Naikiuru, 4/29/95, tapes no. 34–35.

62. Following a request by an employee for a loan of 400/- shillings to pay a *Ngaitana* fine, Casey investigated the ban, interviewing officers, headmen, African Court staff, and 'ordinary tribesmen'. Public Record Office (PRO): CO/822/1647, letter written by Casey, Timau, to Castle, MP, London, 7/1/57.

63. PRO: CO/822/1647, letter by Casey to Castle, 7/1/57.

64. Interviews: Stanley Kathurima, 9/15/95, tapes no. 72–73; and Naaman M'Mwirichia, 9/18/95.

65. KNA: DC/MRU/1/3/12, Meru District, Handing Over Report, 1953.

66. MCC: ADM/15/16/6/II, *Njuri Ncheke*.

67. KNA: DC/MRU/1/1/12/1, Meru District Annual Report, 1956.

68. Holding, 'Women's Institutions and the African Church'.

69. Low and Lonsdale, 'Introduction', *History of East Africa*, p. 15. Three years later, officials appointed the first female 'headman', Ciokaraine M'Barungu, in Meru. See Rebeka Njau and Gideon Mulaki, *Kenya Women Heroes and Their Mystical Power* (Risk Publications, Nairobi, 1984), pp. 16–26.

70. Interview: Martha Kanini, 9/16/95, tapes no. 73–74.

71. KNA: CS/1/14/100, Meru A.D.C. Minutes, 1955–57.

72. Interviews: M'Anampiu, 5/10/95; Caroline Kirote, 6/9/95, tapes no. 52–53; Isabel Kaimuri, 3/20/95, tapes no. 24–25; Charity Tirindi, 2/10/95, tapes no. 21–22; Agnes Kirimi, 6/12/95, tapes no. 54–55; and Elizabeth Muthuuri, 1/3/95, tapes no. 8–9. For the young age of *Ngaitana* initiates, also see KNA: MSS/7, E. Mary Holding, 'Notes of Girls' Circumcision'.

73. Interviews: Moses M'Mukindia, 1/11/95; Jacobu M'Lithara 2/6/95; Isabella Ncence, 10/19/90; Margaret M'Ithinji, 10/17/90; Elizabeth Kiogora, 10/18/90; Charity Tirindi, 2/10/95; Caroline Kirote, 6/9/95; and Agnes Kirimi, 6/12/95.

74. Missionary Holding outlined the following qualifications for a *mutani*: she must be post-menopausal, sexually abstinent, and elected by the women's council, and she must perform her first excision on her own child. KNA: MSS/7, E. Mary Holding, 'The Functions of Women's Institutions in Meru Society'.

75. Methodist Mission Society Papers at St. Paul's Offices, Meru (MMS MSP): 1, Merle Wilde, 'Meru Women's Work Report, Synod 1958'. None of my oral material supports Wilde's statement that some girls 'circumcised themselves', as opposed to each other.

76. Interview: Charity Tirindi, 2/10/95; Caroline Kirote, 6/9/95; Agnes Kirimi, 6/12/95; Isabel Kaimuri, 3/20/95; Isabella Kajuju, 3/20/95, and her niece, Monica Kanana, 3/23/95, tapes no. 25–26; and Elizabeth M'Iringo, 3/16/95, tape no. 23.

77. PRO: CO/822/1647, Ag. Governor of Kenya to the Secretary of State for the Colonies, 12/27/57. Another medical doctor noted the continuing dangers of excision, reporting how one thirteen-year-old girl 'died of hemorrhage following on the operation of female circumcision'. Dr. Clive Irvine, Presbyterian missionary, to the Secretary of State for the Colonies, 12/21/57.

78. Interviews: Charity Tirindi, 2/10/95; Caroline Kirote, 6/9/95; Agnes Kirimi, 6/12/95; and Monica Kanana, 3/23/95.

79. Interviews: Selina Kiroki, 6/30/95; Charity Tirindi, 2/10/95; Caroline Kirote, 6/9/95; and Agnes Kirimi, 6/12/95.

80. KNA: DC/MRU/1/1/13, Meru District Annual Report, 1957.

81. MCC: ADM/15/16/6/III, Minutes of Meeting of *Njuri Ncheke*, 4/15/58.

82. KNA: DC/MRU/1/1/11/2, Meru District Annual Report, 1955; DC/MRU/1/1/13 Meru District Annual Report, 1957; and AB/16/16, Youth Schemes Meru, 1956.

83. Interview: Charity Tirindi, 2/10/95.

84. MCC: ADM/15/16/6/II, 'Minutes of a Special Meeting of *Njuri* Committee held in the A.D.C. Office on 11/6/57'.

85. 'Dirt' appears to allude to the uncleanness associated with unexcised women as well as the clitoris itself.

86. Holding, 'Women's Institutions and the African Church'; KNA: MSS/7, E. Mary Holding, '*Nthoni*: Respect, Deference, Good Manners'.

87. Interviews: Elizabeth Muthuuri, 1/3/95; Moses M'Mukindia, 1/11/95; Monica Kanana, 3/23/95; Agnes Kirimi, 6/10/95; Lucy Kajuju, 3/23/95, not recorded; and Richard Cashmore, 12/6/95. They also chided Cashmore as the district officer with 'skin like a pig'.

88. Interviews: Caroline Kirote, 6/9/95; David M'Naikiuru, 4/29/95; Monica Kanana, 3/23/95; and Charity Tirindi, 2/10/95.

89. KNA: AB 2/51, P.C., Central to Minister for African Affairs, 'Female Rehabilitation Centre, Meru', 9/23/54.

90. Kamunchuluh, 'The Meru Participation in Mau Mau'.

91. Interviews: Charity Tirindi, 2/10/95; and Veronica Kinaito, 7/5/95.

92. Of the two dozen or more people whom I interviewed who were charged with defying the ban, all paid their fines at headmen's camps, not African Courts.

93. These percentages are estimates, as it was sometimes difficult to determine an individual's status from the court registers. KNA: African Courts, Monthly Returns, Meru, 1956–58, ARC(MAA)/2/9/27/II, ARC(MAA)/2/10/27/III, MAA/7/282, and MAA/7/283.

94. PRO: CO/822/1647, letter by Casey to Castle, 7/1/57.

95. Interviews: M'Anampiu, 5/10/95; Moses M'Mukindia, 1/11/95; Monica Kanana, 3/23/95; and Charity Tirindi, 2/10/95.

96. Interviews: Monica Kanana, 3/23/95; Caroline Kirote, 6/9/95; and Evangeline M'Iringo, 3/16/95.

97. Interviews: Lucy Kajuju, 3/23/95; Evangeline M'Iringo, 3/16/95; and David M'Naikiuru, 4/29/95.

98. Audrey Wipper, 'The Maendeleo ya Wanawake Movement in the Colonial Period: The Canadian Connection, Mau Mau, Embroidery, and Agriculture', *Rural Africana*, 29 (1975–76), pp. 195–214.

99. MMS MSP: 1, Merle Wilde, 'Meru Women's Work Report, Synod 1958'.

100. Interviews: Charity Tirindi, 2/10/95; Monica Kanana, 3/23/95; Caroline Kirote, 6/9/95; and James Laiboni, 7/23/95, tape no. 67.

101. Interview: Samuel Nkure, 5/7/95, not recorded.

102. PRO: CO/822/1647, letter by Casey to Castle, 7/1/57.

103. KNA: (ARC)MAA/2/9/27/III, letter from African Courts Officer, R.F.D. Rylands, to D.C., Meru, regarding African Court Returns, 5/29/57.

104. KNA: (ARC)MAA/2/9/27/III, letter from African Courts Officer, J.B. Carson, to P.C., Central, regarding African Court Returns, 7/16/57.

105. PRO: CO/822/1647, letter written by MP Castle to the Secretary of State for the Colonies, Lennox-Boyd, 10/16/57.

106. PRO: CO/822/1647, letter written by Secretary of State for the Colonies, Lennox-Boyd, to MP Castle, 10/20/57.

107. PRO: CO/822/1647, letter written by the Governor of Kenya to the Secretary of State for the Colonies, 12/27/57.

108. PRO: CO/822/1647, letter written by the Secretary of State for the Colonies to MP Castle, 1/20/58.

109. MCC: ADM/15/16/6/II, 'Minutes of a Special Meeting of Njuri Committee held in the A.D.C. Office on 11/6/57'.

110. KNA: African Courts, Monthly Returns, Meru, 1956–58, ARC(MAA)/2/9/27/II, ARC(MAA)/2/10/27/III, MAA/7/282, and MAA/7/283.

111. Interviews: Isabella Kajuju, 3/20/95; Lucy Kajuju, 3/23/95; and Jacobu M'Lithara, 2/6/95.

112. Martin Chanock, *Law, Custom and Social Order: The Colonial Experience in Malawi and Zambia* (Cambridge University Press, London, 1985); Margot Lovett, 'Gender Relations, Class Formation, and the Colonial State in Africa', in *Women and the State in Africa*, ed. J. Parpart and K. Staudt (Lynne Rienner, Boulder, 1989), pp. 23–46; Elizabeth Schmidt, *Peasants, Traders, and Wives: Shona Women in the History of Zimbabwe, 1870–1939* (Heinemann, Portsmouth, 1992).

113. E. S. Atieno-Odhiambo, 'The Formative Years, 1945–55', in *Decolonization and Independence in Kenya*, ed. Ogot and Ochieng'.

114. MCC: Meru A.D.C. Book No. 6, meeting of 4/12/56.

'Cocky' Hahn and the 'Black Venus': The Making of a Native Commissioner in South West Africa, 1915–46

PATRICIA HAYES

This study draws upon research into processes of state construction in the mandated territory of South West Africa (present-day Namibia) from 1915. Unlike central and southern South West Africa (SWA), the so-called Police Zone which had been affected by German colonial efforts to dominate and dispossess since 1884, the northern areas of the territory faced colonization for the first time. The most populous region which straddled the northern SWA border with Angola was called Ovamboland, 'Ovambo' being the generic name given to a cluster of kingdoms and polities located in this floodplain area (see Figure 1). Germany had not attempted to occupy this region, for the eastern kingdoms of Ondonga and Oukwanyama were well-armed and powerful. But during the First World War the forces of the Union of South Africa had defeated Germany in SWA, and South Africa proceeded to send officials to occupy Ovamboland. At the same time, a Portuguese army effected military control over the northern Ovambo areas located in Angola. Thus, in Ovamboland, the year 1915 represented a radical break with the autonomy of the past.[1]

The new political and structural features in Ovamboland—colonial occupation, the demarcation of a boundary between Angola and SWA, and the development of a system of colonial overrule—raise questions about the mapping and remapping of power between the colonizers and the African societies undergoing colonization. This study will be confined to those areas of Ovamboland which came under the control of South Africa, an unusual colonial power since it had achieved a degree of autonomy from Britain with the Act of Union in 1910 but was still a semi-colony.

Recent scholarship has argued that these processes of state construction in Namibia were profoundly gendered, involving 'alliances' between colonial officials and African men to prevent the mobility of women and to ensure the labour migration of younger men.[2] This article shifts the focus to explore how gendered meanings were constructed through colonial violence, administration and ethnography. How, for example, was the promotion of male labour migration and the fixing of women in a subsistence

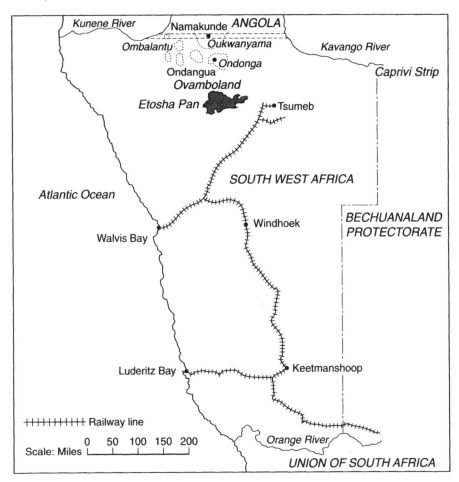

Figure 1: Map of South West Africa (Namibia) 1915–1917. Adapted from National Archives of Namibia, Map Collection, H3841; and Royal Commonwealth Society, Cambridge University Library (UK), 'The Conquest of GSWA. A Chronological Map'.

rurality linked to the physical force employed to displace centralized royal power in Ovambo polities? How was 'indirect rule' established under colonialism, and what were its gender politics? How do these processes connect with colonial representations of the Ovambo, their stereotyping and objectification as 'Ovambo' men and women, and how do Ovambo self-representations and historical (re)constructions differ from colonial ones? These questions arise from the convergence of two different worlds: Ovamboland, pre-modern though deeply affected by merchant capitalism; and South Africa, an expanding sub-imperial power with modernizing pretensions. What sorts of gendered politics and relations emerged on this new colonial frontier?

Central to all these questions is the figure of the Native Commissioner of Ovamboland, who served for three decades in a region encompassing roughly half of the population of SWA: Carl Hugo Linsingen Hahn, dubbed 'Cocky' Hahn by whites but known universally to the Ovambo as 'Shongola' (the whip). Hahn played a crucial, mediating role in constructing the colonial state in Ovamboland and in constructing 'the Ovambo' for consumption by officials and wider audiences. Hahn wrote ethnographic texts on 'the Ovambo', and for thirty-two years he authored the administrative reports on Ovamboland from which present-day historians, anthropologists and researchers of customary law must garner *their* knowledge. Given SWA's unusual circumstances as a mandated territory, with South Africa accountable first to the League of Nations and later (briefly) to the United Nations, the roles assumed by Hahn take on very important dimensions.

Collecting and compiling a coherent body of knowledge on the Ovambo was integral to South African efforts to construct a colonial state in northern Namibia. Hahn's was the most authoritative voice in these intellectual and administrative initiatives. This study will show the highly ambivalent means by which Hahn's voice became that of the expert and explore its powerful legacy. This expanding voice incorporated selective Ovambo viewpoints that were in fact extremely conservative and increasingly contested during his career and long afterwards, culminating in militant rejections of Hahn's version of history by many *oshiWambo*-speakers in the liberation struggle some decades later.

This article focuses on a moment when the ambivalence lying at the heart of Hahn's project was briefly laid bare and then subsequently smoothed over. The Native Commissioner's name was raised in a set of legal investigations in the 1920s, which took the form of an Official Complaints Enquiry prompted by the allegations of a junior officer based in Ovamboland. Here we find evidence that Hahn used violence in his dealings with the Ovambo at the same time as he gathered information about them, and that he did not confine these power dynamics to his interactions with men but extended them to women as well.

In effect, this study focuses on the *préterrain* of Hahn's ethnographic production. The *préterrain* has been described as 'the local milieu from which the ethnographer departs'.[3] Hahn was the type of non-academic ethnographer who embarked upon practical 'administrative anthropology' which often fed the academic but which more immediately serviced and shaped colonial administration.[4] Conceptually, it is helpful here to draw on the expanded and more politicized definition of the term *préterrain* developed by Pels.[5] Here the emphasis is on breaking down the process through which ethnographic writing emerges as a product. Pels points to the stages by which the ethnographer becomes immersed, first in local *milieux*, and then in the politics of the 'ethnographic occasion' in which material is garnered, both of which are profoundly revealing but which are glossed over as the final product is written up, usually removed in space and time from the site of research. In Pels's definition, the *préterrain* refers to the power relationships in which the ethnographer is caught up, which include both indigenous relationships and those brought in by the colonizers.[6] I should like to tease this out still further, to emphasize firstly that we are dealing with a gendered Ovambo *préterrain* and secondly that violence was an intimate part of the landscape in which the ethnographer Hahn was moving, just as it was an intimate part of his own past. It is to the formation of Cocky Hahn, South African official in Namibia, that we now turn.

Hahn came from a family with a long and prominent association with SWA. His grandfather was Hugo Hahn, amongst the first Rhenish missionaries from Germany to enter the territory in 1842 and the first Protestant mission-ary to visit Ovamboland. The family had gravitated towards the Cape, where Hahn's father served as the Lutheran minister in Paarl. Hahn's mater-nal grandfather, Baron von Linsingen, had died in dramatic and romantic circumstances in one of the Eastern Cape frontier wars.[7]

Hahn was born in 1886 and raised in the Cape, where he attended Paarl Boys' High School. The school in Paarl took pride in imparting 'discipline of body and mind', and later claimed to have always given absolute equal-ity to English- and Dutch- (later Afrikaans-) speaking students.[8] Physicality was an integral feature of Paarl Boys' High; indeed, this was a spiritual home of both sport and flogging.[9] Such influences suggest a great deal about 'becoming a man' at that time.[10] This ethos had some similarities with the 'Muscular Christianity' that emerged in English public schools from the 1830s, which was designed to inculcate a sense of 'discipline, service and authority'[11] and included paternalistic overtones of male responsibility towards the 'weaker sex' and the 'weaker races'.[12] The starting point was the disciplining of the body, which through sport could be 'by turns orderly and extraordinary, competent and excellent' but which also offered a sub-limation of the sexual energies and the simultaneous encouragement and discipline of violence.[13]

Hahn developed considerable sporting prowess, especially in rugby.[14] After leaving school to take up work in the Transvaal, including bank em-ployment in Johannesburg and a spell as a mine compound manager, Hahn enjoyed a flourishing rugby career. He played for Pirates Rugby Football Club and was selected as wing for the Springboks in their three test matches against England in 1910. In one of these test games, in the same year that the Act of Union made South Africa a nation, Hahn scored a try for his country.[15] Right up to the end of his life, Hahn's rugby skills were recalled by his admirers,[16] and they became inextricable from sympathetic representations of his brutality.

In the culturally mixed context in which he was raised, speaking Ger-man at home, Cape Dutch at the school in Paarl, and English in broader Cape society, Hahn seems to have been flawlessly trilingual, but as an adult identified most strongly with an 'English' culture. The process by which this

Photograph 1: 'Cocky' Hahn with Ndapona (centre), the mother of Mandume ya Ndemufayo, and her attendant in Oukwanyama, *c.*1915–21. Dickman Collection, South African Museum; reproduced courtesy of the South African Museum, Cape Town.

anglicization took place is not entirely clear, but neither Hahn nor his siblings had any problem with offering their services to the Union Government and to Britain against Germany in both world wars. In the inter-war years his pungent criticisms of German nationalism in South West Africa were well-known. In 1926 he married Alcye Fogarty, daughter of the Anglican Bishop of Damaraland. And Hahn most attached himself to the small but elite coterie of English-speaking administrators in SWA.[17]

Hahn joined the Imperial Light Horse when South Africa entered the First World War.[18] He first went north in 1915 as part of Pritchard's expedition to Ovamboland following the German surrender to General Botha. Judged to be 'skilful in handling Africans',[19] Hahn then served as Intelligence Officer to Charles Manning, the Resident Commissioner, and was crucial in gathering information and mustering the support of Kwanyama headmen against their king, Mandume ya Ndemufayo, between 1915 and 1917. He participated in the military action against Mandume in 1917.[20] In 1920, when Manning transferred to Windhoek and became Chief Native Commissioner, Hahn became Native Commissioner of Ovamboland and remained in that post until 1946. He then served one year on the Public Service Commission in Windhoek, and retired to his farm in Grootfontein where he died in 1948.[21]

Photograph 2: 'Cocky' Hahn in Ondangua, Ovamboland, c.1915–21. Dickman Collection, South African Museum; reproduced courtesy of the South African Museum, Cape Town.

As part of his mediation of the Ovambo to the outside world, Hahn represented SWA at a 1937 meeting of the Mandates Commission of the League of Nations in Geneva. In 1942 Hahn accompanied Lawrence, the South African Minister of Justice, to the League of Nations to advise on the 'treatment of natives' in the territory, and he performed the same service for Smuts at the UN Conference in New York in 1946, at a time of intensifying international criticism of South Africa's handling of the mandate.[22] Hahn's attraction to South African politicians was his exceptional image as an enlightened administrator, successfully controlling one hundred thousand Ovambo under his brand of indirect rule and preserving their tribal ways to boot. This view of Hahn appeared to be validated internationally. Lord Harlech reportedly described Hahn, after an official visit to address Ovambo leaders during World War II, as 'one of the ablest Native administrators in the whole of Africa'.[23]

Beyond the accolades of administrative colleagues, the man attained legendary proportions. Hahn embodied the popular romance of the 'Lords of the Last Frontier'.[24] His personal attributes appealed to a wide white southern African audience. Because of his location in the north, rugby anecdotes were superseded by hunting exploits which 'required all the most virile attributes of the imperial male'.[25] It was not only his sporting prowess, vigour and air of command that fed the imagination of Hahn's admirers; it was also the location of the handsome former Springbok player in the remotest wilds of 'Old Africa'. Ovamboland's distance from the South African metropole was an important factor in the cultural elaboration and romanticization of Cocky Hahn, and it offered a new cultural frontier for South African masculinity. South Africa had perpetuated the old division in SWA between the Police Zone, characterized by a settler-state type *modus operandi*, and 'the north', where 'Native Administration' now operated and where whites needed permits to enter. Hahn's place on this northern periphery, distant even from SWA's capital, Windhoek, allowed him to exercise enormous independence as Native Commissioner. This autonomy reinforced Hahn's voice as mediator of the Ovambo to the outside world as much as it did his authority, which in turn facilitated the smooth functioning and positive public image of what he later came to term 'indirect control'.

Indirect rule has been described as 'that hybrid compound of formal, bureaucratic power above and of orderly and cooperative traditional power below'.[26] This concept of local government in Africa was originally developed in Nigeria and then formally applied in British colonies elsewhere, notably Tanganyika. From the outset in Ovamboland, the South African administration had taken what seemed the most practical and economical route, and sought to rule indirectly through the embodiments of African power: those kings, headmen and sub-headmen who already held position in Ovambo polities. Lugard's book on the 'dual mandate',[27] which Hahn assimilated in the late 1920s, provided the Native Commissioner with a language through which practice could be crystallized into policy and the *de facto* situation elevated into principle.

The very success of what came to be formulated as the Ovamboland model of indirect rule owed much to the pre-existence of centralized and stratified social organizations. In order to work effectively, indirect rule needed 'tribes' and hierarchical political structures. In many areas, one or both of these had to be created. Ombalantu, a decentralized clutch of kin-based groupings in western Ovamboland, was a case in point.[28] Indirect rule, as it became more systematized in British tropical Africa and in northern SWA, was designed to prevent or at least control social breakdown.

The point was 'to develop the native on lines which will not Westernize him and turn him into a bad imitation of a European', and to consolidate 'tribal organisation' which would in turn preserve 'the African atmosphere, the African mind, the whole foundations of his race'.[29]

One of the problems inherent in systems of indirect rule (or the fore-runners of these systems) was that colonial officials wanted to appropriate to themselves the awe in which subjects held their chiefs, yet found the most awe-inspiring chiefs inconvenient allies.[30] In Ovamboland this led to the removal of two kings, Mandume ya Ndemufayo in Oukwanyama in 1917, and Iipumbu ya Shilongo in Uukwambi in 1932, and their replacement by councils of headmen. In both these cases of severe tampering with political systems, Hahn was directly involved. Despite this fact, much was made officially of Hahn's skill in preserving the Ovambo in their 'raw tribal state'.

Hahn made high claims for the special features of Ovambo history. He took particular pains to dwell on their historical longevity, asserting that the Zulu were 'newcomers' compared with the Ovambo, who were 'the oldest settled people in Southern Africa'.[31] An Ovambo identity was served up for outside consumption, most literally so in the case of the Ovambo home-stead constructed in Windhoek under Hahn's co-ordination for the 1936 trade fair exhibition. In Ovamboland itself, the large homestead of the cooperative Kwanyama headman, Nehemia, at Omhedi was the tourist or ethnographic destination for many a white visitor.[32] A relatively homogen-ous 'traditional' identity was presented in these show-places; Ovamboland's isolation and Hahn's lengthy period as Native Commissioner lent it cred-ibility to most outsiders.

In Hahn's view, the mechanisms of social and ideological control by Ovambo ruling groups, while making life at times hidebound for the sub-ordinate, were healthy and admirable. Hahn argued that where western-izing influence was least apparent, 'the natives are virile, well-ordered and progressive'. The term 'virile', which Hahn frequently applied both to Africans and to animals in the Etosha Game Reserve, implied the opposite of domestication and arose from his belief in letting 'nature' run its course.[33] Hahn doubtless also drew from his pre-war exposure to mine compound discourses on the problems posed by the 'detribalized' or 'dressed natives'. There was an instrumentality to these opinions, as Hahn frankly admitted: 'The "raw" native is also generally preferred at labour centres.'[34]

The encouragement of migrant labour was of course the primary purpose of native administration in Ovamboland, and this was the only contact the Ovambo were allowed with the outside world. It was hoped (unrealistic-ally, as it would prove) to prevent 'detribalization' by keeping labour contracts short. No commercial traders were permitted into the area from 1915, and animal disease control ensured that the Ovambo had no access to markets elsewhere in the territory.[35] As a result, agriculture remained of the subsistence rather than the peasant order, and women's labour remained crucial in cultivation. Women who attempted to go south and escape this role were summarily punished if caught, usually being handed over to their headman for a beating.[36] Women's mobility was seen as highly threatening to the 'traditional' order, which highlights the fact that African women were designated not only as the bearers of agriculture but also as the bearers of culture. Such thinking was not simply imposed from above. It was reinforced through temporary alliances between officials and conservative male elders and leaders, who in their turn drew selectively on African cultural precedents concerning gender norms.[37]

Hahn as a matter of course also defended polygyny. In his view numerous wives in a homestead ensured plenty; the headman Nehemia's thirteen wives in Omhedi were a case in point. Hahn pointed disparagingly to the relative poverty of monogamous Christian homesteads in Ondonga, the historical core area of mission work in Ovamboland.

Official anxiety over rapid Christianization was inevitable, and showed itself in the slowness with which the administration opened up the region to new mission denominations and the stringent conditions imposed on all mission work, including that of the Finnish Mission which had been in Ovamboland since 1870. Tensions came to a head in the 1930s. While missions typically argued that the administration was backward in facilitating education and training, that 'Natives are most useful to the Europeans as raw labour, and they must be encouraged to "stay put"',[38] Hahn typically complained that the large-scale Christianization and education of the Ndonga by the Finnish mission in particular had made it 'an uphill fight to get Christianised natives to regard themselves as tribal natives'.[39] This had 'practically destroyed the authority of the chiefs and headmen; so much so that little tribal discipline is left and it becomes more obvious that the tribe is retrogressing'.[40] 'Retrogression' in this case was accompanied by a very unsatisfactory Ndonga labour migration rate, particularly compared with the numbers of migrants from Oukwanyama. Hahn ominously raised the spectre of social unrest: 'The Union Government is today tasting the bitter fruit of past mistakes in allowing the breaking up of native areas and tribal organisation'.[41]

Nowhere was the division over tribal 'integrity' between Hahn and Ovambo traditionalists on the one side, and missions and Christian subjects on the other, more obvious than over the *efundula*, the female initiation rite. These often massive ceremonies occurred every few years in all areas, and ritualized the passage of young women into full maturity after which they were entitled to marry. Rigorous physical endurance sessions were undergone to test both stamina and illicit pregnancy, but fertility was a major emphasis in the overall ritual. The Finnish Missionary Society complained that Hahn glamorized *efundula* by having its dances performed for his official visitors. As for what took place during *efundula*, the Finns insisted that no decent person could even speak of it.[42] In the less reserved Anglican view, the whole *efundula* ritual was tainted because of its 'phallic flavour'.[43] Hahn brushed this prudery aside and argued that the main objective of the missionaries was 'to have the "efundula", the most important of all Ovambo rites, smashed up and wiped out'.[44]

It is easy to see how Hahn's creation of a body of ethnographic knowledge provided him with ammunition against missionaries. He frequently responded to their criticisms concerning administrative reinforcement of local power structures with the rejoinder that their knowledge of the putative Ovambo mentality was faulty. Hahn sought to show that he enjoyed the monopoly of expertise amongst white people.

Hahn was by no means unique among colonial administrators in having a reputation for expertise on 'the customs' and history of the Africans he governed. But neither was he unique among administrators in combining this with an apparent readiness to resort to force.[45] When I first researched Hahn, I thought that the whiff of brutality that clung to him and emerges from much oral history was prominent in his early years as an official, and that intellectual attainments came later in life. He engaged in academic exchanges with noted anthropologists such as Winifred Hoernlé, co-published the important ethnography, *The Native Tribes of South West Africa*, with Vedder and Fourie, and conducted a distinguished international correspondence in which from the late 1920s he elaborated his conception of indirect rule in Ovamboland.[46]

The initial question, then, was to explain the apparent transition from unthinking to thinking man. On closer reading, however, it was not as simple or as chronological as it had initially seemed. Within the first few years of his arrival in Ovamboland, Hahn was eliciting information from his father in Paarl, sending him to consult German mission ethnographic accounts of the Ovambo and their rituals and political institutions.[47] The date of publication of *Native Tribes* is also revealing: 1928, only three years after a Staff Complaints Enquiry in which he is depicted as particularly brutal by the complainant, a junior officer. Hahn therefore had a curiosity and a desire to know from the very outset. Far from being in transition from physical to mental exertion, as it were, Hahn integrated both throughout his career in Ovamboland. As one official admirer euphemistically expressed it, Hahn always combined 'both brains and pluck'.[48]

The simultaneity of the exercise of power through physical force and the exercise of power through the production and dissemination of ethnographic knowledge concerning the Ovambo is the anchoring argument in this article. Africanists have become increasingly concerned recently with the more abstract forms of exercising power, and at times with their own sinister role in reproducing this phenomenon.[49] While this concern is well placed, it has gone so far that historiography now faces two dangers. The first is that the decrease in emphasis on questions of enforcement, the quotidian practice from which violence (both systemic and contingent) is not excluded, means that power associated with modernity is given precedence. For example, 'the African' is constructed as an object of knowledge around which systems and practices are elaborated that are intrinsic to colonial power. But forms of power associated with pre-modern regimes, which act through repression and prohibition, which act on the body,[50] are de-signified in some of the new historiographies. The second danger that we run here is of overlooking the consequences for those among the colonized whose bodies were at the receiving end of violence, 'de-traumatizing' their history.[51]

Questions need to be asked concerning the origins of violent practices, the wider aetiologies of violence in both white and African histories, and how these are constructed and portrayed. The effects on both perpetrators and victims also need scrutiny, and should be related to issues of domination, control and resistance. We should not assume, moreover, that colonial violence in Ovamboland was simply functional. Studies of violence elsewhere have argued that it goes beyond 'the search for profits, the need to contract labour'. What must be taken into account are those 'inextricably construed long-standing cultural logics of meaning—structures of feeling—whose basis lies in a symbolic world and not in one of rationalism'.[52]

Popular white literature and favourable official discourses surrounding Hahn are challenged by oral accounts of Ovambo subjects and by the detailed set of enquiries following an official complaint against Hahn in the 1920s. An initial complaint lodged in 1923 against Hahn had been dismissed, but when related accusations were made against a fellow-officer, Harold Eedes, by the Postmaster in the nearby town of Tsumeb in 1925, both cases were thrown open for full investigation. The ensuing Ovamboland Enquiry constituted a counterpoint in colonial discourse. In itself, it represented some of the conflicts within coloniality at a time in the early 1920s when there was still a degree of space to question the practices of senior officers. In this brief moment before the consolidation of South African colonialism in Namibia, dissensions amongst those in the administration could become public transcripts.[53]

The main enquiry against Hahn was brought on the complaint of an aggrieved junior officer, a clerk serving in Ovamboland between 1921 and 1923. Percival Chaplin was an Englishman in his early forties who had been sent out to South Africa late in 1914. He was deployed in the mechanized transport service and occupied several clerical posts upon leaving the military.[54] Personal differences between himself and Hahn abounded, and it was plain these existed between other officers too. Anglicized he might have been, but Hahn 'had no time for an Englishman born in England'.[55] It seems that the cultural production of an 'Englishman' in the Union of South Africa, imitative though it was in some respects, was quite specific to this colonial periphery and probably appealed to an earlier and more manly Imperial age.[56]

While Chaplin had apparently worked competently in Native Affairs in Windhoek,[57] criticisms of his service record elsewhere were dragged out during the Enquiry. These highlighted much that was antithetical to the ideals of masculinity held amongst white southern Africans at the time. The Magistrate at Okahandja described Chaplin as 'very childish and weak', 'neurotic' and 'out of his element here', while Manning judged him to be 'peculiar' and 'particularly unsuitable for camp and veld life'.[58] His poor hunting and riding skills were widely deplored. Hahn revealed his own means of surviving the isolation of Ovamboland when he put Chaplin's discontentedness down to the fact that he 'had no hobbies except playing a mandolin and never used to do any reading'.[59] Chaplin was no sportsman, being rather inclined to 'brooding' instead. He was not physically vigorous, having received a bayonet wound in war service which still troubled him and in a sense feminized him. As Chaplin explained: 'Whenever I sat down anywhere I had to fold my handkerchief into a knob and sit on it. I was not always fit as my wound would sometimes bleed and when I was in this condition I could not ride.'[60] He also claimed that a blow to the head from a tree whilst driving through thick bush during the Ovamboland Expedition in 1917, not to mention the odd fever and the worry caused by the Enquiry, had contributed to the ruin of his health.[61] He alleged that he had been mistreated by the administration, being passed over for positions because he did not belong to the necessary patronage networks. Chaplin seems to have had something of a persecution complex, and was not always consistent in the statements he made. A less heroic figure and a greater contrast to the confident and manly Cocky Hahn would have been difficult to find.

In several sets of documents, we hear accusations of illegal trading activities and hunting by Hahn and his predecessors, and Hahn's explanation of relevant procedures and how they had been misinterpreted; we hear allegations of beatings administered on the orders of or personally by Hahn, resorting to kicking when his fists grew tired, and his admission of one case where whipping took place but denial of any other occasion on which he used force; we hear of a disturbing assault by Hahn on an Ovambo woman, and Hahn's categorical rejection that any such incident ever took place.[62]

This bald summary of the different voices emerging from the Ovamboland Enquiry demonstrates that emotions were riding high. As Hahn was officially exonerated of trading for profit, of gratuitous beatings and the assault on the woman, merely taken to task for not keeping proper records of his transactions in goods with chiefs,[63] one may ask, what is the point of exploring the accusations against him? It is impossible to verify whether Hahn abused the Ovambo woman, whether he beat men as frequently as some witnesses testified, or even whether he preferred tinkering with machinery to writing reports in his office, as the complainant alleged.[64] Verification would be desirable in all these cases, but it is not the point. It is what the report raises as issues, what was deemed to be officially and publically acceptable and unacceptable in the northern administration, what dissident colonial discourse emerges and how it is dealt with, that is so suggestive here.

Photograph 3: 'Hahn and his spoil,' a giraffe he had slain during a hunting trip in Angola whose legality was questioned in the Ovamboland Enquiry. Dickman Collection, South African Museum; reproduced courtesy of the South African Museum, Cape Town.

The issue of trading dominated the first investigation in 1923 and also occupies most of the pages of the Enquiry proceedings in 1925. Rumours had become rife that Hahn and others were trading for profit with the Ovambo, which was strictly against official policy in the north. Timber was allegedly brought in illegally from Angola, and goods sold to Portuguese officers on the border. Chaplin reported another officer's estimate that Hahn made £5,000 to £6,000 over and above his salary by selling goods over a period of years to the Ovambo.[65] Manning too was accused of having pocketed proceeds from such trade in his time as Resident Commissioner. In their defence, both Manning and Hahn argued that it was government policy in Ovamboland to 'increase the wants of the natives' in the absence of trading stores in the north beyond Tsumeb. Their activities came under this official rubric and were argued to be necessary, given the commercial vacuum. Thus goods such as clothing and horses were said to be passed on to headmen and kings at cost price, through the offices of the Native Commissioner.[66] Hahn also handled King Martin of Ondonga's savings for the purchase of a motor-car. It was acknowledged that blankets were often purchased and then exchanged with Ovambo for 'curios', as most people had little use for cash at this time. This unusual public transcript provides a revealing glimpse of how colonial officials created alliances with Ovambo headmen and kings and cemented them with objects of exchange, and documents one very important way leading officials, especially Hahn, controlled the north.

Both investigations of 1923 and 1925 cleared Hahn and Manning of all charges of illegal trading. The Enquiry moved on to a range of less serious accusations, including illegal hunting in Angola and failure properly to record the death of government horses. Hahn pointed out that his official counterparts in Angola had invited him to hunt while a distinguished guest visited Ovamboland, and the hunting question was dropped. But the problems of his record-keeping were taken more seriously, to the extent that he was ordered to adopt more rigorous methods in future.[67] This was the only area in which the Native Commissioner received any rebuke.

The Ovamboland Enquiry of 1925 brought in a set of charges which had not been raised in 1923 and related to flogging and mistreatment of 'natives'. This subject produced widely divergent testimonies, which fell either into the category of violence represented by Chaplin or the category of officially-sanctioned enforcement represented by Hahn. Chaplin presented a vivid picture of Hahn's use of force, both calculated and seemingly random. He described one case in Namakunde in Oukwanyama, where Hahn ordered a Kwanyama man to be held down by his hands and feet and made the 'police boy' flog him. Chaplin also alleged that when Hahn grew tired of beating, he used to resort to kicking.[68]

The response that emerged was an official admission of the limited use of floggings, but only in the unstable, post-confrontational conditions of 1915–17. Hahn acknowledged the administration of floggings to Kwanyama 'troublemakers' immediately after Mandume's demise and to bandits in Ombalantu in western Ovamboland.[69] The Native Commissioner argued that floggings had been administered in Oukwanyama because after Mandume's death it was 'a most difficult matter for one official new to the work to keep the balance and affairs in order'. He stated that he had had to dissuade headmen who advocated more severe punishments, which were 'very drastic indeed'. He argued that 'caning' was never administered except after an open trial in which headmen were present and approved the sentence. He alleged that since 1921–22 he had succeeded in prevailing on these headmen to abolish all corporal punishment.[70]

This admission of regulated and sanctioned violence is very revealing in the context of colonial occupation. The Ovambo region constituted a strong exception to the trend elsewhere in SWA to do away with flogging completely, to build a case for South African humaneness and superiority to the German system in which flogging was very widespread. The Germans had endorsed flogging practices by settlers in the Police Zone, who were allowed the right to 'parental chastisement'. The apogee of the South African arguments against the brutality of German rule was the Blue Book of 1918,[71] which included photographs of flogging atrocities. Tony Emmett argues that in the years of martial law until 1920, South Africa had to prove to the League of Nations that it was a better colonizer than Germany in order to win the mandatory award.[72] Thus, just as floggings were commencing in Ovamboland, which was being occupied for the first time, floggings were ceasing in the centre and south. Flogging in fact resumed in certain parts of SWA,[73] being by far the cheapest and least 'inconvenient' form of punishment, but acknowledgement of its practice after 1917 virtually disappeared from official records in Ovamboland.

An important measuring stick for South African officers in Ovamboland was the conduct of their counterparts across the border in Angola. Portuguese soldiers were said to be brutal and undisciplined; they and officials openly cohabited with black women;[74] they were ill-supplied from their regional centres and at times depended on the South Africans for medicine and supplies. There was a very high turnover of senior officials. Any sign of sliding down to Portuguese standards, particularly regarding inter-racial sexual relations, was stiffly and officially rebuked. For example, a South African soldier who served with Manning found himself transferred from Ovamboland when he began a liaison with an Ndonga woman and fathered her child.[75]

South Africans prided themselves on being much less violent than the Portuguese. There were certainly differences between them, but these should be seen in their respective contexts. For example, while Manning and Hahn inflicted floggings on the Kwanyama after Mandume's death in 1917, General Pereira de Eça had inflicted hangings after the Portuguese conquest of northern Oukwanyama in 1915 as part of the imposition of martial law in southern Angola.[76] Moreover, South African claims to being more enlightened with regard to forced labour should be treated with caution. On both sides of the border road-building was undertaken by unpaid and reluctant Ovambo men.[77]

Ovamboland in 1915 had just emerged from a high phase of merchant capitalism through trade mainly in guns and cattle, but now on the SWA side was connected to the capitalist economy in a very restricted way, through labour migration to the south. Forms of control were often symbolic and physical, signalling a pre-modern ethos. For example, the show of unity between Hahn and Kwanyama headmen after the death of Mandume was achieved through floggings of 'radicals', with all parties present at the spectacle. This ritualized sharing of authority represented a displacement to a new central power far away, mediated through the bodies of young Kwanyama men undergoing this punishment. Power was now dispersed from king to headmen, some of whom had been victimized by Mandume for tugging centrifugally at the core of the precolonial kingship.[78] The display cemented the bond between the administration represented by Hahn and the headmen. New colonial nuances accompanied this gendered and generational form of disciplining the young men who had been Mandume's fighters and were now expected to insert their bodies into the channels of the migrant labour system.

Chaplin's testimony covering the early 1920s, however, depicted violence which spilled over from any regulated framework constructed by officials. It is not necessary to labour the point concerning whether Hahn admitted instances of gratuitous brutality; he may have denied this in 1925, but he did not always do so during the twenty-one years that remained to him as Native Commissioner. The report of a meeting which followed disturbances at the jubilee celebration in 1936 in the Windhoek location, for instance, tells us that 'Major Hahn, who was present, had stated that in his sphere of work he would have used the sjambok [rhino-hide whip] on any natives who behaved as the location natives did on that day'.[79] Furthermore, references are sprinkled through oral history regarding Hahn's beatings of Ovambo men, particularly at road and other construction sites.

Most white literature and forms of discourse had ways of representing Hahn's violence that rendered it less disturbing by projecting it in sporting terms. For example, an incident during the 1915–16 famine is embellished in literary form in Negley Farson's popular and suggestively entitled account, *Behind God's Back*. Hahn is said to have rugby-tackled young men and laid about him with a *sjambok* in the case of queue-jumpers during famine relief distribution. This account states that the approving Ovambo audience, in gratitude for Hahn's forceful and protective action, bestowed on him the name 'Shongola'.[80]

Sporting metaphors abounded in colonial discourses in Africa.[81] In Cocky Hahn's case, the rugby metaphor projected humour on to brutality, distancing those observers who shared his cultural background from the trauma of actuality, defusing the impact of violence for white onlookers and later writers who packaged these incidents in sporting terms. Hahn's jaunty nickname among whites, bestowed on him at least as early as his Springbok days, would also have helped to reduce the distance between him and his audience[82] and increased the distance between such white audiences and the Africans who suffered him.

A specific case of unregulated or gratuitous violence against an Ovambo woman is related in the 1925 Enquiry report. The woman in question was given no name. In front of at least two witnesses, so Chaplin alleged, Hahn came up behind this woman as she was on her hands and knees smearing polish on the *stoep* (veranda) of the residence. She was probably wearing the *omihanga*, the short leather apron which, apart from ropes of beads around the hips, constituted the dress of most Ovambo women at that time. One officer described her as being 'without clothes'. Hahn came up from behind and kicked the woman straight 'in her private parts'.[83] According to Chaplin, 'Hahn took a running kick at the girl'.[84] The conjunction of the sporting metaphor and brutality appears to have been too disturbing to be humorous in this case. Chaplin reported that his fellow officer Anderson, who witnessed the scene, said it was 'disgraceful' of Hahn.[85] In his rebuttal of the accusation of kicking this woman 'between her legs', Hahn stated that the whole incident had been fabricated.[86]

It is impossible to ascertain whether the incident occurred. When the Enquiry made its conclusions known, it was not even mentioned. Instead, Chaplin was found to have behaved improperly, making accusations that were motivated by malice rather than public duty, and his allegations (except for certain instances of Hahn's bureaucratic ineptitude) were judged to be unfounded.[87] Chaplin stood alone in the gravity of the accusations made; he argued that other officers shared his complaints but chose to say nothing to impugn Hahn in the Enquiry. Judging from the verdict that Chapin's conduct was 'improper and unbecoming', bringing accusations against Hahn would have seriously damaged officers' careers.[88]

Since a variety of evidence corroborates that Hahn did personally use physical violence against Ovambo, it is not inconceivable that he may have abused an Ovambo woman in this way. While no oral accounts by women have been elicited which relate to assaults of this kind, evidence of gendered violence—let alone sexual violence—is notoriously difficult to gather. Whatever the case, the episode involving the assault on the woman stands in this essay as a symbol and a pivot around which to pose a variety of questions about Hahn, about the socio-cultural system that produced him, about the administration in the north, and about the documentation this administration has produced and on which we rely for historical research. It tells us a tremendous amount about constructions of gender and race.

The incident involving the woman occupies remarkably little space in the report of the Enquiry. It emerges in the late stages of Chaplin's final testimony, and he stated that he had only just remembered it in the course of presenting his final case against Hahn.[89] This in itself could be seen as compelling evidence of a colonial ethos in which African women were so unimportant that their mistreatment could be forgotten or repressed almost completely. It calls to mind the argument made about sexual violence more generally in history, that frequently all that we are left with in sifting through the material is 'a conspicuous absence: a configuration where sexual violence against women is an origin of social relations and narratives in which the event itself is subsequently elided'.[90] I have argued elsewhere that the apparent invisibility of women in Ovamboland is largely a product of androcentric attitudes and archives, and that 'the often silent and hidden operations of gender ... are nonetheless present and defining forces' in these societies.[91] In this instance, the highly visible and vocal Hahn came into contact with what was usually invisible, and we are left with an inkling of how that invisibility was reproduced, both through the action which would make any woman keep her distance and through the official attempts to dismiss the episode.

But Chaplin did remember its occurrence; and instead of dismissing him as no more than the victim of his own illusions and the possessor of a unreliable memory, as the Magistrate conducting the Enquiry opined, there could be another type of explanation for him personally inserting the incident at a particular point in his testimony. A simple but effective argument has been advanced by Halbwachs, to the effect that memory is collective, that the social collectivity shapes the way human beings remember.[92] What may well have prompted Chaplin to remember the case of Hahn's abuse against the woman was the combative public position in which he found himself during the Enquiry. Once he recalled the incident, he returned to it again and again. He had little else to lose.

While her existence was not quite lost to memory, the woman described in the Enquiry never had any name. It is her anonymity and inaudibility, coupled with the nature of her transient visibility, which has prompted the title 'Black Venus' in this essay. There is no documented mention of a 'Black Venus' or 'Hottentot Venus', as the phenomenon is more popularly known in southern Africa, by any of the officials serving in Ovamboland. This is purely an authorial intervention. But it is taking no liberty to call this anonymous woman the Black Venus, for the archive shows that Cocky Hahn was familiar with this form of representing women. Indeed, in the midst of his photograph collection is a postcard showing a naked woman in the Kalahari, posed for the camera to show the extent of her 'Bushman' steatopygeia. The postcard dates from the 1930s when Nazi activities in SWA emerged, for this figure has a swastika engraved on one buttock.[93]

The image of the 'Hottentot Venus' was a trope that was very thick on the ground in the Cape where Hahn was raised. From high-brow publications such as Galton's to well-advertised exhibitions, newspapers and popular magazines, this celebrated marker of racial and sexual difference had been in very wide circulation for a very long time.[94] The name became synonymous with Saartjie Baartman, the Khoi woman who travelled to Europe in the early nineteenth century to be exhibited by her keeper and then later pathologized by the French scientist, Cuvier.[95] But Saartjie Baartman was only the most famous of numerous women who were thus objectified. In South Africa itself, an ongoing process of producing images and knowledge on the subject during and well beyond Hahn's lifetime fed into the development of human and social sciences in academic institutions.[96]

European ideas about African women focused on their supposedly excessive sexuality. Buttocks and private parts (particularly of Khoisan women) were represented as unusual and were made the subject of both scientific enquiry and, as Carmel Schrire puts it, 'covert pornography'.[97] Like other categories of women marked out as different, if not freakish, the ironic negation or inversion of the classical connotation of 'Venus' leaves us with a painful juxtaposition. The values loaded into the term 'Black' (or 'Hottentot') and the values loaded into 'Venus' are diametrically opposed, constituting a paradox at the very heart of things. Because of her race, the Black Venus is objectified and denigrated, and should not be desired. But because of her gender, she also stands to be sexualized by men. Hahn was surely conscious of these ironies when he referred to those Ovambo women he photographed as 'dusky belles'.[98]

Representation aside, the text of the Enquiry presents a very immediate Black Venus: the pseudo-scientific detachment of a Cuvier is not what we are dealing with here. Hahn was in the field, where the Ovambo numbered over a hundred thousand and white men probably twelve. Though there were white women working on several mission stations, the first decade of administration in Ovamboland saw no white woman gracing any official residence and Hahn himself was not yet married. The Ovambo woman's body and sexuality, made vulnerable by the combination of 'traditional' clothing and the posture of servitude while polishing the *stoep* of the colonial residence, were visible and available to a man raised in the Victorian Cape in a missionary household, and who had rounded out his life to date in the masculine worlds of boys' school, mine, bank, army and administration.[99] His repertoire of behaviour was indeed limited.

The concept of a Black Venus is used here to go beyond historical fascination with the 'production of knowledge' and the textual objectification of African females and to show the link between representation and physical violence. This Black Venus should remind historians that Africans were not only having knowledge about them produced, they were also being assaulted. In Namibian history, as elsewhere, violence has been gendered and at times sexualized. The statement from a study of Cuvier and the Venus Hottentot, that '[w]e should no longer be surprised to find Africa represented by the genitalia of its women',[100] should be lifted out of its purely representational paradigm to embrace the corporeal. Cocky Hahn was confronted with the immediate embodiment of the tribal Ovambo woman, and we should not be surprised that she was the object of physical abuse.

Most of the African staff working in the official quarters in Ondangwa came from outside Ovamboland. A southern woman called Frederica was in charge of housekeeping, and she recruited local women to work in the domestic quarters and kitchens of the officials. At times old clothes were passed on to domestic workers,[101] but it would appear that in this case and maybe in others, women still carried out their duties in 'tribal' gear. Unlike the elaborate 'domestication' of women performing tasks for whites in the Belgian African case analysed by Nancy Rose Hunt,[102] the woman in the text was in a dangerous limbo between the wild/tribal and the domestic. She represented feminized 'raw labour', transposed suddenly into a white masculine space. This kicking incident shows that the intellectual Hahn was also a physical Hahn acculturated to violence against blacks. On this frontier it was a short step from the violence of representation to the violence of action. There was a direct connection between the ethnographic images of the African woman with which Hahn was familiar, whose defining feature was her buttocks, and the opportunity for abuse that was presented to him by the 'unclothed' woman labouring on the *stoep*.

Photograph 4: '*Efundula* dancing', photograph taken by 'Cocky' Hahn, Ovamboland, n.d. Hahn Collection, Basler Afrika Bibliographien; reproduced courtesy of Basler Afrika Bibliographien, Switzerland.

Both the treatment meted out to this woman and the representation of her 'social skin'[103] had a bearing on everything else going on in newly colonized Ovamboland. Hahn was a vocal supporter of the *efundula* and attended its ceremonies regularly, where numbers of young women would be in various stages of dress marking their change in status, none of which missionaries would have deemed decent. Hahn is recalled by female oral informants as attending the ceremonies and taking many photographs of the dancing.[104] The woman in the text was 'without clothes' on the *stoep* of the Residence. Hahn was at odds with missionaries who were trying to clothe and Christianize the Ovambo: 'As soon as a native is christianized he thinks he must wear European clothes.… In his natural state he manufactures his garments from the produce of the country … he need not be ashamed to appear everywhere in them; and above all he retains his caste.'[105] One of the implications of Hahn's project to maintain 'tribal health' in Ovamboland was that he sought to maintain rituals which kept the bulk of the tribe 'unclothed'.

One way of regarding nakedness in such contexts is through its associations with innocence. Looked at through the lens of the white administrator with a 'European' and Christian outlook, such a view would have infantilized Africans and placed them in a continuum of civilization below the

acquisition of 'knowledge' and 'shame', with connotations of backwardness and weakness. This may have fitted in with the educational background of men such as Hahn, coming from schools which sought to imbue
some sense of paternalistic responsibility towards the 'weaker races'.
Moreover, corporal punishment such as flogging would have appeared in
the light of 'parental' chastisement. The trouble with this argument, however, is that the concept of paternalism implies the eventual development
of the 'child'. In this respect, missionaries in Ovamboland were far more
paternalistic than Hahn because they sought to influence and Christianize
the Ovambo in their own mould. Hahn was an agent of reification rather
than of progress.

Anthropologists have rightly described nakedness as a more complex
trope, suggesting darkness, disorder and pollution to missionaries and proclaiming 'savagery' more generally. A more convincing way to approach
Hahn's assault on the Ovambo woman and gratuitous beating of other
people in Ovamboland is to recall Michael Taussig's comment from his
study of genocide in the Putumayo rubber forests, that 'it is not the jungle
but the sentiments men project into it that is decisive in filling their hearts
with savagery'.[106] Unlike missionaries who sought to take the Ovambo out
of their culture, Hahn in some ways tried to step into Ovambo culture. He
reportedly dressed himself in the leather apparel worn by Kwanyama men
when he attended *efundula*,[107] a refashioning of himself which could be
read as an appropriation, to deepen his knowledge of 'the native' through
participation. It is also possible to argue that in doing so he took on some
of the 'savagery' imputed to the Ovambo. Such propensities certainly need
much further examination than can be given here,[108] but we should note
that Hahn also set careful limits on how far he stepped into Ovambo-ness.
For example, despite being fluent in the two main languages of eastern
Ovamboland he always took care to conduct official business through an
interpreter. White people who romanticized Hahn might have referred to
him as 'a real live Ovambo' or the 'Super-Ovambo',[109] but the Ovambo
themselves were highly conscious of the ways he maintained distance and
kept them in their place. In sum, the notion of paternalism cannot encompass the complexity of a Native Commissioner whose own brother-in-law
Cope, the labour recruiter based in Ondangwa, dubbed Hahn 'the
Paramount Chief'.[110]

There are other questions besides whether Hahn saw innocence or savagery in the nakedness of the 'tribal' Ovambo. We can, after all, only
speculate as to the influences at work. The most crucial point here is that
Hahn vigorously worked to keep the Ovambo cut off from outside influences and trade, without radios[111] and 'without clothes'. Arguably it was in
this condition that people could be more easily controlled and more easily
abused.

This violence had implications far beyond its functionality in enforcing
dominance and hierarchy, especially in its excessiveness. Allen Feldman

argues that violence acts to bifurcate the self of the other.[112] Literature on the effects of violence suggests that one of the outstanding symptoms is for the subject affected simply to vacate space, especially the space where the violence might have occurred.[113] This displacement may last until those affected by violence can reconstruct a world for themselves, be it through the counter-violence of cult movements in Mozambique suggested in the work of Ken Wilson[114] or the sacrifice of the body through hunger striking by IRA prisoners in Northern Ireland described by Feldman. These turn violence back on to the perpetrators, and no small part of the process is the production of a wholly different cultural construction of violence from that of the aggressors. Integral to the process of this reconstruction is the narration and recasting of events through oral history. Oral history has the capacity to recreate subjectivity after the process of objectification and domination. Feldman goes so far as to say that 'in oral history, the body fragmented is reassembled, and this act, the weaving of a new body through language, as much as any act of violence, testifies to the emergence of political agency'.[115] We should be asking not only 'what history does to the body but what subjects do with what history has done to the body'.[116] There may well be the outward appearance of submission but the inward development of politicization and attitudes of resistance.

The Ovambo created and reproduced histories orally that showed the impact of colonization over time but also signalled forms of integrity which were resistant to colonial force and cultural manipulation. Hahn exercised power on a variety of levels in Ovamboland, but the figure of Shongola himself has been incorporated, blamed and processed in sites where the Ovambo have relied on their own forms of knowledge.

This was shown in an entirely different set of court hearings from those conducted in the 1920s. At the height of nationalist struggle against South African colonialism, the name of the late Native Commissioner in Ovamboland came up once again in court. The years 1973–74 saw South Africa attempt to enforce full-blown apartheid policies in Namibia, which met with widespread resistance. Masses of striking contract workers returned to Ovamboland and elections which were intended to establish a bantustan government were boycotted.[117] In the midst of this ferment, public floggings had been staged. Many Ovambo who were perceived to be opponents of the South African regime and its 'tribal' system in the north (founded by Hahn) were beaten with the *epokolo*, a lethal whip made from the central rib of the *makalani* palm tree. Others were sent away to prison. In an attempt to end the public humiliation of respected teachers, leaders and nurses being stripped and flogged in the open, an urgent application was brought in court by church figures sympathetic to the nationalist movement, SWAPO. The South African authorities argued that the floggings were legitimate because they were traditional and were being administered by the new bantustan power based on precolonial custom. But the victims and their supporters refused to accept what they saw as an invented tradition.

Instead, affidavits were submitted which argued that the flogging system originated not with their forebears, but with 'Shongola'.[118]

During the two decades following the Ovamboland Enquiry's official exoneration of Cocky Hahn, his career as Native Commissioner flourished. This period roughly coincided with the greater consolidation of South African rule in SWA and the decreasing likelihood, especially in the north, that colonial practices might be called into question from within. Likewise, Hahn's personal life settled into a new phase in 1927 with his marriage to Alyce Fogarty, the tomboyish daughter of the Anglican bishop of Damaraland.[119] They had one son and occupied the Residency in Ondangwa as a family. The Ovamboland Enquiry became no more than a bad memory, part of a troubling *préterrain* whose ambiguities could now fade in the light of Hahn's growing fame as an administrator and the stabilization of his domestic life. He broadened his intellectual interests to include botany, zoology and game conservation, and continued his amateur photography. His visual representations of public occasions, especially in his favourite region, Oukwanyama, projected a consensus over indirect rule and were considered so persuasive that they were regularly included in the official *Annual Reports to the League of Nations.*[120]

The questions raised by the Ovamboland Enquiry remain crucial to Namibian historiography and to an understanding of the processes of state construction in Ovamboland from 1915. That these processes were connected to projections of white male identity must be obvious. But the most important point made in this article is that colonial power worked simultaneously through the production of knowledge and the exercise of physical force, and both were gendered to the core. The smooth image of Hahn and 'native' administration in the first decades of South African rule is disrupted, which broadens the possibilities for those other histories which arise from individual and collective memory in Ovamboland.

Some questions of course will never be answered. There remains a tremendous difficulty in understanding exactly what happened to the Ovambo woman whose presence erupts and then disappears from the text of the Enquiry, and why she appeared and vanished from the historical record. Her suffering prefigures the fate of many more women in the war zone that Ovamboland became in the 1970s and 1980s. And can resistance strategies, including those nationalist historical reconstructions which critique the colonial system inaugurated by Hahn, ever address the wrongs arising from gender?[121]

Notes

Thanks are due to many colleagues and friends who offered insights, references and inspiration in the writing of this essay, to those who attended presentations of earlier drafts in Boston, Basel and the Western Cape, and to *Gender & History*'s editors and anonymous readers. I am indebted to the South African Museum (Cape Town) and the

Basler Afrika Bibliographien (Switzerland) for the photographs; the views expressed about them are my own.

1. A full account of the simultaneous colonization by South Africa and Portugal in Ovamboland can be found in Patricia Hayes, 'A History of the Ovambo of Namibia, ca 1880–1930' (PhD thesis, Cambridge University, 1992).

2. See Jeremy Silvester, Patricia Hayes and Marion Wallace, 'Introduction', in *'Trees Never Meet': Mobility and Containment in Namibia, 1915–1946*, ed. Patricia Hayes, Jeremy Silvester, Marion Wallace, Wolfram Hartmann with Ben Fuller (Windhoek, 1996 forthcoming); also Marion Wallace, '"A Person is Never Angry for Nothing": Women, Venereal Disease and Windhoek'; Patricia Hayes, '"The Famine of the Dams": Gender, Labour and Politics in Colonial Ovamboland, 1929–1930'; and Meredith McKittrick, 'Generational Struggles and Social Mobility in Ovambo Communities, 1915–1954', all in *'Trees Never Meet'*.

3. Peter Pels, 'The Construction of Ethnographic Occasions in Late Colonial Uluguru', *History and Anthropology*, 8 (1994), p. 322.

4. Peter Pels and Oscar Salemink, 'Introduction: Five Theses on Ethnography as Colonial Practice', *History and Anthropology*, 8 (1994), pp. 1–34, especially p. 4.

5. Pels, 'The Construction of Ethnographic Occasions', p. 322.

6. Pels, 'The Construction of Ethnographic Occasions', p. 322.

7. Cape Archives Depot, A2048 Vol. 13 MS 12/986, Hugo Hahn, biographical notes and drafts 'Baron von Linsingen', n.d.

8. Paarl Boys' High School, *Hoër Jongenskool Paarl Eeufees* (Paarl, 1968).

9. Patrick Harries, personal communication, July 1994.

10. This phrase is borrowed from Paul Monette's suggestive autobiographical work on the development of male identity, *Becoming a Man* (London, 1994).

11. Toby Miller, 'A Short History of the Penis', *Social Text*, 43 (1995), p. 4.

12. Patrick Harries, personal communication.

13. Miller, 'Short History of the Penis', pp. 1–2, 4.

14. Paarl Boys' High School, *Hoër Jongenskool*.

15. Teddy Schnapps, *A Statistical History of Springbok Rugby: Players, Tours and Matches* (Johannesburg, 1989), pp. 39, 170.

16. See obituaries in the *Cape Times* and *Cape Argus*, 28 September 1948.

17. On the rivalries and cliques among white settlers and officials in this period of Namibia's history, see *'Trees Never Meet'*, ed. Hayes et al., Introduction.

18. Hayes, 'History of the Ovambo', pp. 291–2.

19. Eric Rosenthal, *Southern African Dictionary of National Biography* (London and New York, 1966), p. 155.

20. Excellent primary sources on this episode include Union of South Africa, *Report on the Conduct of the Ovakuanyama Chief Mandume and on the Military Operations Conducted against him in Ovamboland* (Cape Town, 1917); National Archives of Namibia (NAN) A450, Vol. 23, Intelligence Diary Ovamboland Expeditionary Force, 1916–1917; and Hayes, 'History of the Ovambo', Vol. 2, Interview with Vilho Kaulinge, Ondobe, 30 September 1989, pp. 27–86.

21. National Archives of Namibia (NAN), NAO 1 1/2 v 1, C.H.L. Hahn, 1919–36.

22. Nissan Davis, '"Shongola": Cocky Hahn, "The Whip"', *South West Africa Annual*, 1977, p. 33; see NAN A450 Vol. 15 8/1–8/5 for Hahn's record of these proceedings.

23. Cited in Davis, '"Shongola"', p. 33. For details of Harlech's and Hailey's tours to Ovamboland in the 1940s, see NAN NAO 27, 22/1, Tours to Ovamboland: itinerary Lord Harlech; itinerary Lord Hailey.

24. Lawrence G. Green, *Lords of the Last Frontier* (Cape Town, 1952).

25. John M. Mackenzie, 'The Imperial Pioneer and Hunter and the British Masculine Stereotype in Late Victorian and Edwardian Times', in *Manliness and Morality. Middle-Class Masculinity in Britain and America 1800–1940*, ed. J. A. Mangan and James Walvin (Manchester, 1987), p. 179.

26. Gwyn Prins, 'The Battle for Control of the Camera in Late Nineteenth Century Western Zambia', *African Affairs*, 89 (1990), p. 97.

27. Lord Lugard, *The Dual Mandate in British Tropical Africa* (London, 1922).

28. Hayes, 'History of the Ovambo', pp. 245–50, and McKittrick, 'Generational Struggles and Social Mobility', in *'Trees Never Meet'*, ed. Hayes et al.

29. John Iliffe, *A Modern History of Tanganyika* (Cambridge, 1979), p. 321, citing the Tanganyikan administrator, David Cameron.

30. Steven Feierman, *Peasant Intellectuals. Anthropology and History in Tanzania* (Madison, 1990), p. 153.

31. Green, *Lords of the Last Frontier*, p. 234.

32. See Negley Farson, *Behind God's Back* (London, 1941, 10th impression), pp. 91–101; Green, *Lords of the Last Frontier*, p. 238; NAN NAO 27, 22/1, Tours to Ovamboland, Itinerary General Holcomb 1946; Itinerary Lord Hailey 1946; Itinerary Lord Harlech 1944.

33. On Hahn's theories concerning 'balance' in nature, see NAN NAO Vol. 39 33/1, NC Ovamboland—Secretary SWA, 15 February 1938.

34. NAN NAO Vol. 13 6/2/5 v 1, NC Ovamboland—Secretary SWA, 11 January 1935; Vol. 13 6/3/1, NC Ovamboland—Secretary SWA, 28 July 1936. On 'dressed natives' and the influence of mining discourses on Native Affairs, see Randall M. Packard, 'The "healthy reserve" and the "dressed native": Discourses of Black Health and the Language of Legitimation in South Africa', *American Ethnologist*, 16 (1989), pp. 686–703.

35. One store run by the mining concerns was opened in Ondonga from the mid-1920s.

36. For analysis of the contradictions inherent in allowing men to migrate while attempting to maintain a 'tribal' system, see McKittrick, 'Generational Struggles and Social Mobility', in *'Trees Never Meet'*, ed. Hayes et al. Attempts to control the movement of women from Ovamboland are covered in Hayes, '"Famine of the Dams"', also in *'Trees Never Meet'*.

37. See the Introduction and articles by Hayes, Wallace and McKittrick in *'Trees Never Meet'*, ed. Hayes et al.

38. Bishop Tobias, *Ovamboland Mission Quarterly Paper*, July 1935.

39. NAN NAO Vol. 13 6/4/1 v 1, NC Ovamboland—Secretary SWA, 16 March 1936.

40. NAN NAO Vol. 13 6/2/5, NC Ovamboland—Secretary SWA, 27 August 1935.

41. NAN NAO Vol. 13 6/4/1 v 1, NC Ovamboland—Secretary SWA, 16 March 1936.

42. NAN NAO Vol. 11 6/1/1, Kivinen—Secretary SWA, 8 March 1937.

43. NAN NAO Vol. 13 6/3/1, NC Ovamboland—Secretary SWA, 28 July 1936.

44. NAN A450, C. H. L. Hahn papers, Vol. 4, Minute No 32/5, Hahn, 17 April 1947.

45. A similar case is broached in Hilary Sapire, 'Apartheid's "Testing Ground": Urban "Native Policy" and African Politics in Brakpan, South Africa, 1943–1948', *Journal of African History*, 35 (1994), pp. 99–123.

46. C. H. L. Hahn, L. Fourie and H. Vedder, *The Native Tribes of South West Africa* (Cape Town, 1928). The Medical Officer of the territory, Louis Fourie, solicited and edited this and other writings by Hahn for the League of Nations and local publications such as the *Journal of the South West Africa Scientific Society*. NAN A450, personal correspondence, Fourie to Hahn, 27 April 1928.

47. NAN A2048, Vol. 13, Carl Hugo Hahn—C.H.L. Hahn, 15 June 1919.

48. Farson, *Behind God's Back*, p. 99.

49. For one example of such interrogation, see Robert Gordon, *The Bushman Myth. The Making of a Namibian Underclass* (Boulder, 1992), pp. 216–20.

50. An analysis of such processes in the production of medical knowledge about Africans can be found in Megan Vaughan, *Curing Their Ills: Colonial Power and African Medicine* (Cambridge, 1991), esp. pp. 8–12. Material from Namibia suggests that the view of Engels and Marks that *violence directe* was the exception rather than the rule (at least in the British Empire) is not quite correct; see Dagmar Engels and Shula Marks (eds) *Contesting Colonial Hegemony. State and Society in Africa and India* (London and New York, 1994), esp. Introduction.

51. Luise White, 'Vampire Priests of Central Africa: African Debates About Labour and Religion in Colonial Northern Zambia', *Comparative Studies in Society and History*, 1993, p. 756, citing Hayden White, 'Historical Text as Literary Artifact', in *Tropics of Discourse: Essays in Cultural Criticism* (Baltimore, 1978), pp. 86–7.

52. Michael Taussig, 'Culture of Terror—Space of Death. Roger Casement's Putumayo Report and the Explanation of Torture', *Comparative Studies in Society and History*, 26 (1984), p. 483.

53. See James C. Scott, *Domination and the Arts of Resistance. Hidden Transcripts* (New Haven and London, 1990), pp. 55–6. This periodization of the consolidation of South African rule is argued in *'Trees Never Meet'*, ed. Hayes et al., Introduction.

54. Percival Cameron Chaplin was born in Colchester, Essex, in 1880. NAN SWAA 1893, 406/4/103.

55. NAN SWAA 2/19/3, Complaints against Ovamboland Officials, Exhibits: P. Chaplin, 'My Experiences in the South West Africa Administration', n.d. (*c.*1923–25).

56. See Mackenzie, 'The Imperial Pioneer and Hunter', and Allen Warren, 'Popular Manliness: Baden Powell, Scouting and the Development of the Manly Character', both in *Manliness and Morality*, ed. Mangan and Walvin, pp. 176–98 and 199–219.

57. NAN NAW 7/1919/10, Officer in Charge Native Affairs Windhoek—P. Chaplin, Clerk in Charge Location Office Windhoek, 26 February 1919.

58. NAN SWAA 2/19/3, Ovamboland Enquiry, Manning to Secretary SWA, 27 November 1923.

59. NAN SWAA 2/19/3, Ovamboland Enquiry, Hahn statement, Ondonga, 26 October 1923.

60. NAN SWAA 2/19/3, Ovamboland Enquiry, Proceedings, p. 17. The notion that this wound feminized Chaplin is influenced by recent scholarship on male sexuality in prisons and mine compounds in southern Africa; see for example Zackie Achmat, '"Apostles of Civilised Vice": "Immoral Practices" and "Unnatural Vice" in South African Prisons and Compounds, 1890–1920', *Social Dynamics*, 19 (1993), pp. 92–110.

61. NAN SWAA 2/19/3, Complaints against Ovamboland Officials, Exhibits: P. Chaplin, 'My Experiences in the South West Africa Administration', n.d (*c.*1923–25).

62. NAN SWAA 2/19/3, Ovamboland Enquiry, Proceedings, p. 138.

63. NAN SWAA 2/19/3, Ovamboland Enquiry, Scott—Administrator SWA, 15 September 1925.

64. NAN SWAA 2/19/3, Ovamboland Enquiry, Proceedings, p. 9.

65. NAN SWAA 2/19/3, Ovamboland Enquiry, Proceedings, p. 9.

66. NAN SWAA 2/19/3, Ovamboland Enquiry, Proceedings, pp. 99–105 and 126–7.

67. NAN SWAA 2/19/3, Ovamboland Enquiry, Scott—Administrator SWA, 15 September 1925.

68. NAN SWAA 2/19/3, Ovamboland Enquiry, Proceedings, pp. 1–24.

69. NAN SWAA 2/19/3, Ovamboland Enquiry, Proceedings, p. 137.

70. NAN SWAA 2/19/3, Ovamboland Enquiry, Proceedings, pp. 137–8.

71. Union of South Africa, *Report on the Natives of South West Africa and their Treatment by Germany*, Command Paper 9146 (Pretoria, 1918).

72. Anthony Brian Emmett, 'Popular Resistance in Namibia', in *Namibia 1884–1984: Readings on History and Society*, ed. Brian Wood (London, 1988), pp. 224–58. See also David Killingray, 'The "Rod of Empire": The Debate over Corporal Punishment in the British African Colonial Forces, 1888–1946', *Journal of African History*, 35 (1994), pp. 201–16.

73. Reference to flogging in Windhoek can be found in NAN MWI 36/1/37 Vol. 10, Advisory Board Minutes.

74. NAN RCO 10/1916/1 v 1, Fairlie, Memorandum, Omatemba, c.1916.

75. NAN RCO 1/1916/11, RC Ovamboland—Secretary Protectorate, 14 November 1916. A subtext to the Ovamboland Enquiry was the affidavit submitted to Hahn's lawyers in Windhoek in 1925, which stated that Chaplin had spread rumours concerning Hahn's sexual activities with Ovambo women but that these were unfounded. NAN A450 Vol. 1, W. Eedes affidavit, 13 October 1925.

76. NAN A 233, William Chapman Memoirs Vol. 2, p. 83.

77. Interviews with Titus Iita, Ombalantu, 3 November 1989; Simpson Ndatipo, Nakayale, 3 November 1989; and Petrus Amutenya, Ongandjera, 28 September 1989.

78. Patricia Hayes, 'Order Out of Chaos: Mandume Ya Ndemufayo and Oral History', *Journal of Southern African Studies*, 19 (1993), pp. 89–113.

79. NAN MWI 36/1/37 v 13, Deputation to the Administration of Hereros Resident in the Location on 12 June 1936.

80. Farson, *Behind God's Back*, p. 99; also in Davis, '"Shongola"', p. 33. The official interpreter, Booi, also refers to this incident in NAN SWAA 2/19/3, Ovamboland Enquiry, Proceedings, pp. 70–1.

81. One of the numerous examples can be found in Elizabeth Schmidt, *Peasants, Traders, and Wives. Shona Women in the History of Zimbabwe, 1870–1939* (London, 1992), p. 77.

82. See Albert Grundlingh, 'Playing for Power. Rugby, Afrikaner Nationalism and Masculinity in South Africa', in *Beyond the Tryline. Rugby and South African Society*, ed. Albert Grundlingh, André Odendaal and Burridge Spies (Johannesburg, 1995), pp. 106–35. The German name 'Hahn' translates as 'cock' or 'rooster'; it was common in South Africa for nicknames to be ironic derivatives of such surnames.

83. NAN SWAA 2/19/3, Ovamboland Enquiry, Proceedings, p. 113.

84. NAN SWAA 2/19/3, Ovamboland Enquiry, Proceedings, p. 109.

85. NAN SWAA 2/19/3, Ovamboland Enquiry, Proceedings, p. 113.

86. NAN SWAA 2/19/3, Ovamboland Enquiry, Proceedings, p. 138.

87. NAN SWAA 2/19/3, Magistrate Scott—Administrator SWA, 15 September 1925.

88. NAN SWAA 2/19/3, Magistrate Scott—Administrator SWA, 15 September 1925. The only other figure to bring an accusation against Ovamboland officers, Postmaster Downey in Tsumeb, was charged with misconduct. NAN SWAA 2/19/4, Ovamboland Enquiry, G.W. Downey, November 1925–March 1926.

89. NAN SWAA 2/19/3, Ovamboland Enquiry, Proceedings, p. 109. Chaplin blamed his previous lapse of memory of this incident on the 'worry and injustice' he had received at the hands of the SWA Administration over a long period of time.

90. Lynn A. Higgins and Brenda R. Silver (eds) *Rape and Representation* (New York, 1991), pp. 2–3.

91. Hayes, '"Famine of the Dams"', in *Trees Never Meet*, ed. Hayes et al., citing Joan Scott, *Gender and the Politics of History* (New York, 1988), p. 27.

92. Maurice Halbwachs, *On Collective Memory*, ed. and tr. Lewis A. Coser (Chicago, 1992), esp. p. 23.

93. NAN A450. See photograph collection, boxes P1–P4. It is unclear whether the swastika was placed on this postcard for pro- or anti-Nazi purposes, probably the latter.

94. The plenitude of this image in print comes out strikingly from the exhibition of historical representations of the Khoisan recently mounted in Cape Town, entitled 'Miscast: Negotiating Khoisan History and Material Culture' (South African National Gallery, 13 April 1996—15 September 1996, curated by Pippa Skotnes). See Francis Galton, *Narrative of an exploration in tropical South Africa being an account of a visit to Damaraland in 1851* (London, 1890, 3rd ed.), p. 54. The longevity of this fascination is discussed in Carmel Schrire, 'Native Views of Western Eyes', in *Miscast: Negotiating the Presence of the Bushmen*, ed. Pippa Skotnes (Cape Town, 1996), p. 350.

95. On Cuvier and the Venus Hottentot, see Sander Gilman, 'Black Bodies, White Bodies: Toward an Iconography of Female Sexuality in Late Nineteenth Century Art, Medicine and Literature,' *Critical Inquiry*, 1985, pp. 204–42. Griqua communities in the Northern Cape have requested the return of her remains from the Musée de l'Homme in Paris for honourable reburial; see 'Forum on Khoisan History and Material Culture', South African National Gallery, 14 April 1996, and testimonies submitted to the Truth and Reconciliation Commission hearings, South Africa, April–May 1996.

96. See Raymond A. Dart, 'The Physical Character of the Bushman', *Bantu Studies*, 11 (1937), pp. 219–26; Phillip V. Tobias, 'Bushmen of the Kalahari', *Man*, 36 (1957), pp. 33–40. (Thanks to Ciraj Rassool for these connected references.) For Hahn's correspondence with Hoernlé at the University of the Witwatersrand in Johannesburg and his receipt of lecture notes on Bantu Studies from that institution, see NAN A450.

97. Schrire, 'Native Views of Western Eyes', pp. 343–54.

98. NAN NAO 1, 1/2 v 2, NC Ovamboland—Clarke, 1 April 1937.

99. Hahn was not yet married; he shared quarters in Ovamboland with other male officers.

100. John Comaroff and Jean Comaroff, *Of Revelation and Revolution. Christianity, Colonialism, and Consciousness in South Africa*, Vol. 1 (Chicago, 1991), p. 123.

101. NAN SWAA 2/19/3, Ovamboland Enquiry, Proceedings, pp. 88–9.

102. Nancy Rose Hunt, 'Domesticity and Colonialism in Belgian Africa: Usumbura's Foyer Social, 1946–1960', *Signs*, 15 (1990), pp. 447–74.

103. Terence S. Turner, 'The Social Skin', in *Not Work Alone*, ed. J. Cherfas and R. Lewin (London, 1980).

104. Interviews with Helena Shihutuka, Oshatotwa, 28 June 1994, and Albertina Hipulenga ya Hamukoto, Onekwaya, 26 June 1994.

105. NAN NAO Vol. 19, Annual Report 1937, pp. 19–20.

106. Taussig, 'Culture of Terror—Space of Death', p. 483.

107. Interviews with Helena Shihutuka, Oshatotwa, 28 June 1994, and Albertina Hipulenga ya Hamukoto, Onekwaya, 26 June 1994.

108. Carolyn Hamilton's study of Theophilus Shepstone and the Zulu suggests that the receptivity of certain white men to African forms of power explains their performance of power and even in some cases the perpetration of violence; see Carolyn Hamilton, 'Authoring Shaka: Models, Metaphors and Historiography' (unpub. Ph.D. diss., The Johns Hopkins University, 1993), chs 5 & 6.

109. When preparing for his overseas trip in 1937, the Administrator Clarke wrote to Hahn: 'The Marquis' [Theodoli] idea, if I remember correctly, was that you were a "real live Ovambo" and you must be prepared to satisfy Mlle Dannevig's thirst for the real article.' This was with reference to presenting materials on Ovamboland to members of the Permanent Mandates Commission. NAN NAO 1/2 v 2, Clarke to Hahn, 8 February 1937. See also Davis, '"Shongola"', p. 33.

110. Jeremy Silvester provided this information from the files of the South West Africa Administration in the National Archives of Namibia in 1994.

111. Nancy Robson, personal communication, Odibo, September 1994.

112. Allen Feldman, *Formations of Violence. The Narrative of the Body and Political Terror in Northern Ireland* (Chicago, 1991).

113. See for example E. M. Ellis, B. M. Atkeson and K. S. Calhoun, 'An Assessment of Long-Term Reaction to Rape', *Journal of Abnormal Psychology*, 90 (1981), pp. 263–66.

114. Ken Wilson, 'Cults of Violence and Counter-Violence in Mozambique,' *Journal of Southern African Studies*, 18 (1992), pp. 527–83.

115. Feldman, *Formations of Violence*, p. 10.

116. Feldman, *Formations of Violence*, p. 177.

117. See Richard Moorsom, 'Underdevelopment, Contract Labour and Worker Consciousness in Namibia, 1915–72', *Journal of Southern African Studies*, 4 (1977), pp. 52–87; and Richard Moorsom, 'Labour Consciousness and the 1971–72 Contract Workers Strike in Namibia', *Development and Change*, 10 (1979), pp. 205–31.

118. The political disturbances, floggings and legal cases in Ovamboland were widely covered in the Namibian and South African press at the time. For a summary and a statement by the Lutheran Bishop Leonard Auala on Hahn's responsibility, see *The Observer*, 7 April 1974. See also David Soggott, *Namibia: The Violent Heritage* (London, 1986); Soggott was one of the lawyers employed to seek an injunction against the flogging.

119. 'A Wilderness Wedding', *Windhoek Advertiser*, 26 February 1927.

120. These photographs have been analysed in the exhibition by Patricia Hayes, Jeremy Silvester and Wolfram Hartmann, 'The Colonising Camera: Photographs in the Making of Namibian History, 1915–1946', exhibited at the University of Cape Town in May 1995, Yale University in January–February 1996, and various venues in Namibia between 1994 and 1996.

121. Ovamboland became the main theatre of guerrilla warfare in the struggle against South African rule launched by the South West Africa People's Organisation (SWAPO). For the impact of warfare on women in the region, see Soggott, *Violent Heritage*; Tessa Cleaver and Marion Wallace, *Namibia. Women at War* (London, 1990); Colin Leys and John S. Saul (eds) *Namibia's Liberation Struggle. The Two-Edged Sword* (London, 1995); Panduleni Kali and Ndamona Kali, 'SWAPO's Prisons in Angola', *Searchlight South Africa*, 4, February 1990; Paul Trewhela, 'Women & SWAPO. Institutionalised Rape in SWAPO's Prisons', *Searchlight South Africa*, 11, October 1993, pp. 23–9; and Siegfried Groth, *Namibia—the Wall of Silence* (Wuppertal, 1995).

'Not Welfare or Uplift Work': White Women, Masculinity and Policing in South Africa

KEITH SHEAR

The South African Police was an institution that few would hesitate to label 'masculine', given the centrality of organized violence in maintaining modern South Africa's deeply divided social order. One historian, with little analysis or further curiosity, describes South African policemen during the First World War as 'firmly anchored ... bastions of blue serge masculinity....'[1] Yet assuming the masculinity of the police institution forgoes an opportunity to appreciate an important dimension of the formation of a segregationist state in early twentieth-century South Africa.[2] It also suppresses the history of a significant white women's campaign to enlist in the South African Police that drew on international theories of preventive policing to articulate an alternative vision of the state and its role in shaping the colonial social order.[3]

Gender theory has taught us to interrogate decontextualized epithets such as 'masculine', and to search for concrete historical 'moments and ... circumstances' in which the seemingly self-evident content of such epithets becomes reified precisely in 'the refusal or repression of alternative possibilities....'[4] This essay argues that the development of a masculine police institutional identity was mediated by the white women's campaign to enroll in the South African Police. The exclusion of white women from the police was continually protested by white women's organizations from 1915 to 1972, when white women were at last admitted. It was in the years before 1920, however, that these organizations posed their most significant challenge. Women's inclusion was a distinct possibility at that time because their campaign was mounted during a period of unusual plasticity in South African state and policy formation, which created an opportunity for promoting competing conceptions of policing.

The South African War of 1899–1902 inaugurated an era of statebuilding in southern Africa that continued effectively into the 1920s. First the defeated Boer (Afrikaner) republics of the interior came under direct British rule as the Transvaal and Orange River Colonies. Here British officials fashioned policies and bureaucracies to reconstruct agriculture, to service the Witwatersrand gold-mining industry centered on Johannesburg, and to mobilize and discipline labor for white employers. After 1905 a Liberal ministry in Britain promoted a political settlement extending self-government to the Afrikaner leadership of the new colonies in exchange for a loyalty to empire that implied continuity in the public service and sympathetic treatment of the mining industry. In 1910 a Union of South Africa, including also the coastal colonies of the Cape and Natal to the south and east, emerged from this decade of imperial assertion as a self-governing British dominion, possessing a constitutional status comparable to that of Canada or Australia.[5]

Despite the constitutional fiction of the 'white' dominion, South Africa remained an unstable patchwork of recently unified colonies for at least a decade after 1910. White elites had evolved the idea of segregation to give overall form to a social order that already had done much in the previous decade to promote modern South Africa's defining pattern of racial domination. Yet 'as a systematic political doctrine' addressing the 'native question', segregation remained 'relatively undeveloped'.[6] In the immediate post-Union years, race relations was only one of several concerns of the state. Although officials and reformers throughout the 1910s regularly decried the 'close association of black and white' in inner-city slums, which they believed led to 'the lowering of the white race and the loss of respect by the native for the white people', the government also faced massive strikes by disaffected English-speaking workers and a rebellion by Afrikaans-speaking 'bitterender' republicans.[7]

As a hegemonic white-supremacist rallying cry, segregation fared better, but at a cost to its ideological clarity.[8] To some segregation meant simply controlling Africans. Employers and mainstream political leaders invoked the concept opportunistically to exhort their refractory white workers and followers to 'rise to the position' of 'controlling the kafir [African] and holding [themselves] entirely aloof and superior....'[9] Others, including the white middle-class women reformers who are the subject of this article, envisaged a much more interventionist role for the state in uplifting lower-class whites, preventing their figurative slippage into blackness. These differences in interpretation manifested in conflicting understandings of the police function and in a sustained dialogue between officials and white women's organizations. White women's demands for entry into the police force compelled officials at the national level to articulate otherwise unexpressed assumptions about the exercise of power and the nature of the state in South Africa's evolving segregationist dispensation. In a period of flux, the women's campaign played an important part in crystallizing ideas about what a police force should be and do.

Critical to the outcome of the debate was a growing official conviction during its latter stages that the main challenges to the social order would in future come from Africans rather than, as hitherto, from white labor or Afrikaner republicanism. 'Sparked by soaring inflation', from the end of the First World War 'black protest hitherto unprecedented in scope and intensity ... [erupted] in almost every major town as well as in numerous rural areas'.[10] Segregation envisaged as a policy for controlling Africans now took clear precedence over segregation conceived as a project for elevating lower-class whites through state intervention. Mediated by the debate with campaigners for women police, this trend led to the triumph of punitive over preventive methods within the South African Police. In this way a 'masculine' police institutional identity embodying much more starkly the racial purpose of policing emerged through rhetorical opposition to the discarded 'feminine' policing program associated with the women reformers. At stake ultimately was not the exclusively male composition of the police but the direction of state policy.

The South African movement for women police began in wartime Cape Town in worried response to the 'khaki fever' occasioned by the passage of large numbers of troops through the city. Alarmed by police reports of increases in prostitution and in 'contraventions of the morality laws generally', the Cape Women's Christian Temperance Union (WCTU), which had long pioneered reformist causes, called for policewomen. Julia Solly, a prominent suffragist and leading member of both the WCTU and the recently formed National Council of Women (NCW), sought both organizations' cooperation to set up a volunteer patrols movement. In February 1915 the executive of the WCTU assented and went further, requesting the Minister of Justice to appoint 'Policewomen to deal with female prisoners'. Officials replied that 'matrons and wardresses' already had charge of 'women prisoners confined to the Gaols'. But as Colonel G. D. Gray, the Deputy Commissioner of the South African Police in the Western Cape, pointed out when asked to comment, the WCTU's 'resolution was meant to urge the employment of police women to deal specially with prostitutes, etc.'[11]

Before the war, the WCTU had been particularly concerned with issues of 'Social Purity' and the enforcement of local 'Morality' legislation regarding prostitution and inter-racial sex.[12] In this the WCTU was representative of the many middle-class white women's reformist organizations that actively participated in producing the pervasive post-1910 anxiety over South Africa's urban social environment. Central to all were concerns about racial purity and separation, expressed in campaigns to rescue destitute white children, monitor inter-racial sexual contact, and combat prostitution and liquor consumption.[13]

Although South Africa had long hosted discourses of social reform derived from Europe and the United States, mobilization of white women around such issues gathered pace in the immediate pre-war years during a scare about a putative 'black peril' in South Africa's urban centers. White women, and hence the integrity of white society, were believed to be threatened by an ever larger black male work force.[14] Fear of rape and assault waxed. A public inquiry into this scare recommended white women's immurement.[15] Despite figuring women as passive and vulnerable, the inquiry and the discussion it generated were not simply conducted by white men about white women. A white women's movement coalesced in these years around opportunities to mobilize against the 'black peril'. Not only did Leagues for the Protection of Women and Children emerge specifically in response to urban racial scares, but 'black peril' issues attracted the range of existing women's societies into alliances such as Johannesburg's Standing Committee of Women's Organizations, which brought nineteen associations together 'first of all as a Black Peril Committee' early in 1911.[16] In debating their own protection, white middle-class women claimed greater political space.

There was no mention of policewomen at this stage; indeed, there is no evidence that women's organizations contemplated the idea before the First World War.[17] But when the scheme was mooted early in 1915, white women were well prepared organizationally and ideologically to promote it by their activity during the 'black peril' scare. Both causes drew on a broader white communal repertoire of concerns about immorality, prostitution, crime, health, and contamination, the topoi of segregationist discourse. At a public meeting in Johannesburg during the 'black peril' panic of 1912, a prominent woman reformer espoused the common theory that Africans 'take over the evils and vices of the white race'. This, she thought, was an 'inevitable result of the importation of undesirable [white] lower classes of every part of the world.... *We must and have to reform ourselves.*'[18] In calling three years later for representation within the police institution, white middle-class reformers were not so much pushing for women's emancipation as seizing an opportunity further to delimit and police a white racial morality by drawing on the powers of the state.

Concern about prostitution, the proximate motive for organizing a women's police movement, illustrates the continuing relevance of segregationist discourse to the logic of white women's mobilization in the campaign for policewomen. As in other countries, reformers oscillated between blaming prostitutes as agents of corruption and infection and viewing them as victims of male violence or material distress.[19] In South Africa, these perceptions were interwoven with notions of racial degeneration and purity. This was evident in the complaint of a Cape Town advocate of policewomen, whose fears of the unredeemable, contaminating 'hardened prostitute' (concealed in 'undesirable looking groups' of 'loud, laughing coloured girls', threatening 'many a young man, soldier or sailor … with a disease which will ruin his life') vied with her hopes to place vulnerable innocents on the path to salvation. She described leaving 'a City Hall concert' and seeing 'a very young, tall, pale & helpless looking girl (almost, or quite white).... She had on a light frock (it was a cold night) …, & there was no doubt but that her purpose was to attract, though from her awkwardness & apparent lack of experience it seemed as if it wd not be a difficult thing to save her, had there been anyone to do it.'[20] Note the parenthetic uncertainty of 'almost, or quite white': a policewoman empowered to intervene, this reformer seemingly implied, might recover not only the woman's moral but also her racial status.

Encouraged by the Cape WCTU's initial request, the sympathetic Deputy Commissioner, G. D. Gray, averring that the 'moral question … [was] becoming increasingly important every day', and perceiving 'a large scope for good policewomen', obtained the permission of police headquarters in Pretoria to employ two 'Female Detectives' as 'an experimental measure', and reported in mid-May 1915 that he was 'taking steps to procure two suitable women at once'.[21] Before long, the idea had outgrown these modest steps. In June, the National Council of Women (NCW) approached Gray with its scheme to form 'Volunteer Women Patrols' which, in his words, would 'work around the various [Military] Camps and … patrol those parts of the town which are frequented by foolish and immoral women'.[22] The prototype for the scheme had been established by the NCW's British counterpart, and it was thus to the Women's Patrol Committee in London—with whose Honorary Secretary Julia Solly corresponded—that the local body looked to recommend an organizer.[23]

Meanwhile, the NCW canvassed the idea amongst Cape Town's high society at 'private drawing-room meetings' before calling a public conference of women at the City Hall in July to elect an 'influential' Board of Control. Gray, invited to address the meeting, prophesied 'a tremendously powerful outcome of good resulting from the Women Patrols', which he labeled 'but the beginning of a great programme of social reform'. Thus, alongside a small number of women remunerated out of the allocation for 'detective services' and accountable ultimately to Gray, a considerably larger organization of unpaid patrols arose. In practice the identities of the two groups overlapped, given the common purpose and protagonists behind their inauguration. (One woman, first a Miss Barr, but later Margaret Sterling, served as Organizing Secretary of both.)[24] It is reasonable, then, to speak inclusively of a movement for policewomen, and undoubtedly women supported the Volunteer Patrols in the hope that their work would demonstrate the value of permanently enrolling a significant number of paid women in the police after the war.[25]

The Board of Control closely supervised the work of the volunteers, who within a year comprised 'some hundreds of ladies throughout [the] Peninsula' willing to do duty two or three times a week. After initial training from the organizer, the volunteers walked beats in pairs, wearing distinctive, numbered badges on their arms. Each woman received an instruction booklet together with a card authorizing her to call upon the police for assistance. The patrols were directed to 'observe and note anything bearing on the welfare and conduct of women and girls'. They took up cases of abused or destitute children, and visited the parents of children or young women they encountered on the street. Coming off duty, the volunteers submitted reports to the Board of Control, which discussed them at weekly meetings. The movement also established 'club rooms and counter-attractions to the camps and streets'. The Volunteer Patrols enjoyed no special powers of arrest. Their duties were defined as 'purely preventive', their presence intended 'to save foolish women and silly girls from moral danger, to lessen the social evils of [the] streets and other public places and to raise the moral tone of the community, particularly the female portion of it....' Leaders of the movement were careful to reassure the public that the patrols were not intended as a slur on the reputation of men serving in the army.[26]

Prevention was the pivotal concept around which the movement would construct a more global theory of policing to justify its work. A Johannesburg reformer was typical in contending that 'modern opinion has changed in regard to crime, that is, that the police should be used for the prevention rather than the punishment of crime'.[27] 'Prevention' was the serendipitously flexible term of campaigners for policewomen everywhere. Derived from medical literature, it enjoyed a prominent status in the lexicon of social reformers, eugenists, criminologists, and police theorists. Depending on its usage, 'prevention' possessed both progressive and conservative connotations. It could charter ruling-class intervention in the lives of the working and 'dangerous' classes. It could stand in as a moral equivalent for the severer concepts of control and restraint. In a period of irresolute transition from laissez-faire to state interventionism, it promised both the economy of the former and the technical efficiency of the latter. It respected the cult of domesticity and conventional ideas about women's place, but to uphold them licensed a multiplication of public roles for women.[28]

The kind of work implied by the campaigners' use of 'prevention' was not unknown in police forces internationally, but it was not accepted as regular practice. One difficulty was to delimit the activities of a differentiated police institution, even if the larger principle of state responsibility was granted. What interventionist practice, after all, might not be held to contribute to the more effective policing of society? Historically, this line had been variously drawn for the police of different countries, but leading authorities of the day routinely prescribed preventive as well as punitive functions to police forces. Police preventive work, however, necessarily existed in a continuum with punishment since it was always backed by the potential to invoke powers of pursuit and arrest. This is why women believed entering the police would further goals previously but ineffectually advanced solely through voluntary organizations. In police theory, prevention at a minimum meant walking beats, but it could also accommodate practices such as supervising street children thought susceptible to delinquency, keeping tabs on prostitutes, and other activities designed to inculcate mores. And for such work the campaigners and sympathetic men, extending the ideology of domesticity, proclaimed women 'peculiarly fitted'. This rhetoric of women's difference would prove a considerable liability for the movement because it would enable opponents to locate such work, and hence the broader vision of preventive policing, outside the bounds of their idea of the legitimate police function by defining it as 'social welfare' or 'private women's' work.[29]

State support for the Cape Town experiment was confined initially to providing office and mailing facilities, and to paying the salaries of the organizer and of another woman who patrolled 'the low quarters of Cape-town' and followed up on cases reported by the Volunteer Patrols.[30] Even this limited material support testified to the movement's social and political standing. The Board of Control was indeed influential. Members during the first two years included Hester Carter, wife of the Archbishop of Cape Town, Lady Innes, active in many women's organizations and wife of the Chief Justice, Emily Solomon, President of the Cape WCTU, and Mayoress Parker, founding President of the local Girl Guides and active in the Child Life Protection Society. All were prominent in war support work.[31] If enthusiasm for the movement seemed to wane, Lady Buxton, the Governor-General's wife, could be relied upon to host a meeting at Government House to revive it.[32] Thus, a year after the NCW first approached Gray, he felt confident of Pretoria's approving the appointment of two more paid women. 'The experiment of using women has proved successful and it is now desired to extend the work generally, especially its preventive side.' He wished to see women patrolling around the naval base at Simonstown, 'where social evils are very bad and the Magistrate, Clergy and Naval Authorities have specially asked for help'. A few months later the Cape Town Council voted funds to employ a further three women under Margaret Sterling's direction.[33]

The class position of the movement's proponents guaranteed its respectability and commanded a hearing from the state. The fluidity in the state's institutional arrangements at this time meant that the campaigners could reasonably hope to be heard sympathetically. South Africa remained a patchwork of recently unified colonies after 1910. The work of molding pre-existing into new coercive forces was approached with a combination of theory and pragmatism. The theory was provided by Jan Smuts, a former Republican State Attorney and Boer general, and now the dominant figure in the Cabinet, who argued that 'towns and districts closely populated by Europeans' required a 'purely civilian' police, whereas 'frontier or rural districts where the population is sparse or comprises a large preponderance of natives' needed a 'military police force' with 'all those special qualities which are most effective in warfare'. Accordingly, in 1913, a Permanent Force, the South African Mounted Rifles, under the Defence Department, was placed in these rural districts, while the South African Police, under a Commissioner reporting to the Justice Department, operated everywhere else.[34] The new system was hardly in place when wartime mobilization rendered it impracticable, and by 1916 it was common opinion in official circles that the state's coercive resources would have to be completely reassessed after the war.[35]

Smuts's emphasis on a civil police force in settled areas reflected an aspiration to metropolitan-style normalization that also afforded the movement considerable scope. The campaigners' claim that urban social conditions in South Africa were analogous to those of other countries where policewomen were employed was well calibrated to appeal to officials' admiration for 'modern' methods as defined by governmental practice in Europe and the United States. Gray, who in a few years would head the Criminal Investigation Department of the entire country, warmly supported the movement. The Commissioner, Colonel Truter, although not personally enthusiastic, initially countenanced Gray's experiment, and subsequently gave the idea 'serious consideration as regards South Africa' in 'view of the attention [it] has lately been receiving in Europe and other parts of the world....' A senior Witwatersrand officer likewise believed 'the matter is one for serious consideration.... It is essential that we should move with the times.'[36] The movement for women police represented a plausible vision of policing in these years, with a real possibility of success.

Cape Town's example was not lost on other urban centers. In April 1916, Theresa Lawrence, the President of the Women's Reform Club in Johannesburg, wrote to Colonel Douglas, the Deputy Commissioner of Police, citing the 'unqualified success' of the Cape experiment and communicating the Club's belief that there was 'as great a need for Police Women in Johannesburg'.[37] At the end of June, the executive of the Cape WCTU, meeting in Port Elizabeth, resolved that policewomen 'should be appointed in every large town and ... facilities for training be afforded'.[38] Further pressure from women's associations led the Mayor of Johannesburg to consult the Commissioner of Police, Colonel Truter, in late July, a month ahead of a proposed public meeting on the issue sponsored by the National Service Fund.[39] Once again, the cause profited from the interest of Lady Buxton, who agreed to chair the meeting. Also present were the Mayor, local Members of Parliament, clergymen, and Colonel Douglas. The question of policewomen, according to the *Rand Daily Mail*, which endorsed the meeting, had 'not so far been put before the [Johannesburg] public very strongly'.[40] The speeches, tailored to a largely uninitiated audience, illustrate the movement's rhetoric as it had crystallized in the Cape Town experience.[41]

Lady Buxton, who spoke first, left developments in Cape Town to Margaret Sterling to describe. Instead, she dwelt on the wartime transformation of the status of women in England, which in her view the women's police movements there epitomized. She hoped this was an irreversible transformation, but her chief emphasis was that it had happened without the rancor caused by suffragettes before the war. Although she told her listeners that objections to the idea of policewomen 'could all be answered', her principal argument was not that women were ably doing work previously the preserve of men but that, 'being different', they possessed special capacities for certain aspects of police work. 'The work of a policewoman [is] largely preventive work, and [is] chiefly concerned with women and children. In a word, they [supplement] and [complete] the work of a policeman, and the details which [escape] the observation of a man [do] not escape a woman's eye.' Those involved in the movement, Lady Buxton concluded, 'were all deeply interested in social reform', and expected that 'knowledge gained through the police ... would add immensely to their experience and to the value of their work.'

Sterling, the next speaker, also stressed that women would not usurp men's prerogatives. 'Domiciliary visiting' was as significant a part of police-women's work as patrolling the streets; 'tenderness and sympathy and tact' were 'very valuable qualities' alongside men's 'physical force'. But beyond this concession to feminine nature, Sterling developed a more vigorous theme. Policewomen, she went on, could 'shed a light on hitherto unre-vealed conditions and half-solved problems'. Their presence, she implied, augured an interventionist state in a much larger sense. The Bishop of Pre-toria supported this thesis, referring to the 'intolerable' social conditions on the Witwatersrand, 'with whites, coloureds and natives' living in proximity. It was allotted to Theresa Lawrence, however, to suggest firmly that the movement would lead not to a less virile model of policing than then existed, but rather to a more broadly policed society, thoroughly consonant with the ethos of white supremacy. Dispensing a heady compound of jingoism, social purity, and eugenics, she claimed that appointing women to the police would contribute to the war effort, not only in releasing men to fight, but in 'prevent[ing] wastage of infant life' by ensuring 'clean and healthy fathers and mothers', hence maintaining and purifying the (white) population. Speakers at Women Patrols meetings in Cape Town stressed this same point. 'Woman's standard', explained one, 'is the standard of the nation. Strong, healthy children are the nation's first asset to-day, and potential mothers should be protected from harm of any kind.'[42]

Although frequently couched in such maternalist language, the cam-paigners' vision of preventive policing needs to be distinguished analyt-ically from the rhetoric of women's difference. Certainly the movement for policewomen drew much of its energy from ideas about 'woman's stand-ard'. One reformer, for example, spoke of policewomen 'extending' the 'influence of pure women and pure homes ... beyond the four walls of the home'. 'It seems so self evident', another proclaimed in 1919, 'if immor-ality exists there must be women to investigate the cases'.[43] Apart from the opportunity that the language of domesticity afforded opponents in the way of a negative label, however, there was within the context of South Africa's emerging segregationist dispensation nothing inherently 'feminine' about the campaigners' broader statist vision, which after all was shared by im-portant male officials and reformers. The rejection to which their rhetoric exposed the women's larger vision was revealed at the Johannesburg meeting in a discordant note sounded by the Rev. J. G. Aldridge, who thought the term 'police' unnecessary because he could not see that any-thing more was being proposed than an extension of the work of such organizations as the Children's Aid Society. But that the interventionist implications of the movement were also clearly registered was evidenced two days after the meeting in a letter to the *Star* from a member of the audience who objected to the public expenditure that a breaching of the boundary between state action and voluntary welfare work would incur.[44]

The key ambiguity in the South African campaigners' rhetoric arose from its embeddedness in segregationist discourse. Segregation was an essential component of efforts to mobilize white women. But segregation would also turn out to be the chief cause of officials' rejection of the demand for policewomen. The ideal of metropolitan-style normalization retained its appeal, but inner-city slums were increasingly being studied as a specifically South African 'native problem' necessitating the control and removal of Africans.[45] The campaigners did not extend to Africans the universalizing tenets of their imported progressivism. Their own preventive program, while undoubtedly propelled by the same processes of change that created large urban black work forces, mostly ignored Africans, for their white-supremacist ethos was skeptical of the potential to transform 'native' mores. Their rhetoric, captive to the middle-class model of women's domestic role and reflecting their residential experience in affluent homogeneous suburbs, presupposed existing racial boundaries that could adequately be defended by policing the mores of lower-class whites.

The contradictions in the campaigners' vision were obscured as long as decision-makers articulated no coherent policy of urban segregation. For most of the 1910s, indeed, officials seemed immobilized by the apocalyptic language with which they vocalized their perception of South Africa's urban problems. The head of the Criminal Investigation Department impotently complained of Johannesburg 'yards', enclosing up to forty rooms 'let out to different people. A chinaman has one room, a white woman has the next, a Kaffir the next.' Police raids revealed these people 'making common cause, and the best of friends. The little children are all playing together ... in these hot-beds of vice and crime. That should not be allowed.'[46] An influential commission proclaimed 'local segregation of natives in Urban areas ... highly desirable', but simultaneously emphasized 'the imperative and urgent necessity of steps being taken to uplift the fallen classes of the white races....'[47] Administrators entertained competing approaches to segregation. Pass document checks and raiding for home-brewed liquor, emblematic of repressive racial policing, did not at this time appear incompatible with the reformers' preventive program. Only an unprecedented surge in black urban militancy in the late 1910s, comprising strikes, riots, boycotts and anti-pass demonstrations, directed officials' attention more systematically to the 'native question' and strengthened their evolving suspicion that South African urban conditions were not comparable to those of Europe or the United States, with deleterious results for the campaigners' model of policing.[48]

Despite the well-supported meeting in Johannesburg in 1916, no movement emerged on the Witwatersrand to match that of Cape Town. In part this was because police headquarters and the divisional commanding officer were not prepared to assist. In reply to the Mayor of Johannesburg's inquiry before the meeting, Colonel Truter, the Commissioner of Police, insisted that, although the Cape patrols had 'done remarkably good work', any police funds to pay women outside of Cape Town would be considered only after a local voluntary movement had proved its worth and endurance.[49] Colonel Douglas, less versed in the international literature on sociology and criminology than Gray and far less disposed to Christian moralism, pleaded 'no experience of women Police' and refused to facilitate the work.[50] Nonetheless, by late 1916, the successful establishment of the Cape Town movement had compelled Pretoria to begin defining a more coherent response. In November, Truter requested from Gray a detailed account of the work of the paid patrols so that he could 'defend the expenditure already incurred'. Citing legal opinion, the Commissioner declared that 'to call these women "Police women" is a misnomer'. The Police Act would have to be amended before women could be enrolled 'as members of the Force' with all the powers that status conferred.[51]

Gray sensed that principle was now at stake, that the issue would soon be raised in Parliament, and that 'a line of action [should] be decided upon' beforehand. He responded by elaborating a theory of policing to validate the work of the patrols, much as Margaret Sterling and Theresa Lawrence had done at the meeting in Johannesburg. 'The real question to be settled', he contended, was 'whether or not it is the duty of the State to take preventive action with regard to a social evil such as prostitution. In the past this action has been left entirely to private agencies, and very little has been done at all, the result being that the community has been injured very much by the serious growth of this evil.' Gray's 'community' was a white community and, like the reformers, he thought in terms of raising its prestige by securing its boundaries. He alluded pointedly to 'numerous cases of very young white girls leading immoral lives' for whom paid patrols had done more than 'relief societies' because 'they can watch the girls (unknown to them) when they are out on the streets, and *no other [social] workers do street work*'. If this was the state's duty, then a larger number of women should be properly trained, inducted into the police, and set to work in other urban centers. If it was not, the experiment could be halted at the end of the war, but this 'would be a great pity ... and would ultimately recoil upon the Force, as we are bound to get more and more out of touch with the "Social Evil" and accordingly fail in one of the primary justifications for our existence in the modern city'.[52]

The interventionist terms in which Gray defended the Cape Town experiment compelled the Commissioner of Police to adopt a formal position. Commenting on Gray's minute, Truter offered his 'own opinion ... that these are matters which could very well be left to the control of local bodies, such as Municipalities, social institutions, etc., and should not be administered in any way by this Department'. If the Minister of Justice thought otherwise, Parliament would have to vote additional funds and amend the Police Act to enable women to enroll. The Minister, Nicolaas de Wet, did not think otherwise, and was not prepared to sponsor an amendment. Apparently unaware that Gray would interpret their response as 'definite instructions', Truter and de Wet did not consider the consequences for the existing experiment. Margaret Sterling, the Organizing Secretary, gave six weeks' notice on learning of the decision. Gray, declaring that both the paid and voluntary work would suffer seriously without her leadership and without the protection and authority that association with his office bestowed, arranged to dismiss all the salaried patrols.[53]

Truter and de Wet also did not reckon with the Volunteer Patrols' influential Board of Control, which reacted by mobilizing reformist opinion. In quick succession de Wet received letters from Bishopscourt, the Chief Justice's Chambers and City Hall. Hester Carter, the Board's chair and the Archbishop's wife, argued that to discontinue the experiment would be a 'disaster' and urged that it receive 'full official recognition ... for the good of the community and the welfare of the town'. Innes, the Chief Justice, termed de Wet's response 'a retrograde step'. He referred to the acceptance of policewomen 'even in conservative England' to 'deal with an aspect of social work which men could hardly touch'. Mayor Hands asserted that thanks to the patrols 'the streets have never been so clean of prostitutes, and the town so free of immorality as to-day....' Their withdrawal would 'expos[e] our women folk to dangers from which they should ... be protected by the State'. A flustered de Wet, claiming not to understand why Gray had been so precipitate, committed himself to continuing the experiment 'at any rate while the war lasts', and set off a rapid exchange of telegrams between Pretoria and Cape Town to 'put the matter right'. De Wet refused, however, to 'hold out much hope of an amendment of the Police Act ... in the near future'.[54]

As Gray had predicted, reformers, no longer content with the patrols' quasi-legal status, turned next to the House of Assembly. Early in 1917, Hugh Wyndham, a long-time advocate of white women's rights, tabled a motion entreating the government 'to take into consideration the appointment of women police in the urban centres of the Union'. De Wet telegraphed Truter for an official report on the Cape Town experiment, but also wrote 'privately' requesting 'anything in the nature of ammunition against it'. The Commissioner obliged, citing 'sound argument' by Fuld and Freund, American authorities who held that 'the Police Force is not a Body to which we should look to suppress [immorality] as, by the powers given them by Law, they can in a measure only control it by taking action when outward manifestations occur'. The existing 'Special Staff' did not require women who would have no more powers than 'ordinary male members' and thus could 'do no more from a Police point of view than the Law permits'. Women who were 'anxious to assist the State', Truter added, could best do so by forming 'societies ... of an entirely private nature' to educate the public and supply officials 'with any information upon which action could be taken....' A woman might be at 'very most ... a Police Agent or Informer', he concluded, but to 'vest in [her] the powers of a Policeman ... would ... throw much and unnecessary responsibilities upon the State by reason of the fact that a woman is ... neither fitted nor is she physically capable of carrying out the duties of an ordinary Policeman which are, as is well known, often fraught with considerable dangers'.[55] The final argument was especially significant: it would be easier to proclaim the inherent unfitness of white women for police work in a colonial context than to address comprehensively all the difficult questions of policy the movement posed. In the cauldron of debate, Truter was moving to define the nature and scope of police work in distinctly masculine ways.

In the Assembly, Wyndham and other sympathizers conceptualized policing sufficiently broadly to encompass a 'preventative' program directed by women, but denied that their definition challenged received ideas about women's dependence and familial calling. H. F. Blaine argued that the motion recognized women's 'weakness ... as a sex and their disability', while Wyndham thought women best qualified to administer work that the state already had begun to wrest from overburdened homes and charities. De Wet took the lead in opposing the principle. Following Truter's advice, he invoked Fuld's authority in support of a narrower and more virile construction of the police function. 'The next thing the police [will be] called upon to do', he scoffed, is 'hold prayer meetings at street corners'. Citing a letter in the police magazine, the *Nongqai*, de Wet contended that even its 'openly favourable' author did not believe women should police 'the worst slums of Cape Town'. De Wet suggested that South African urban conditions were exceptional to the point of nullifying the relevance of metropolitan precedent. To say that policewomen were 'a success in Europe' was 'all very well', the Minister opined, but what 'class of woman' could be obtained locally to patrol areas like Cape Town's District Six at night 'without having two policemen to protect her?' He would 'not dream of sending a policewoman even in broad daylight' to 'certain districts of Johannesburg'. Since for middle-class whites District Six had long connoted 'a fusion of races', de Wet, without directly mentioning race, had echoed segregationists' horror of integration in the Union's inner cities. He had also drawn on the resources of pre-war black perilism to intimate that respectable white women would not be found to do police work.[56]

Despite publicly disparaging the reformers' cause, de Wet could not retract his earlier promise to continue the experiment for the duration of the war. He did, however, refuse all requests for policewomen in other centers.[57] Nonetheless, their institutional foothold in Cape Town sustained campaigners' hopes, as did a prevalent discourse among senior police officers about the 'very unsatisfactory class of men' (mostly rural Afrikaans-speaking poor whites, 'perhaps the lowest class in the country') offering themselves as recruits. This was the very 'class' that white women reformers believed should be policed, not police others. 'No complaints', they argued, had 'been lodged against the class of women enrolled as women police in Cape Town', and additional 'suitable women could be found for the work'.[58]

Even after the war, de Wet had to proceed cautiously in ending the experiment. Ironically, Truter himself, possibly influenced by the creation of a women's force under the new Commissioner of the Metropolitan Police in London, briefly exhibited interest in the idea. Seeing in the contemplated post-war reorganization of the Union's coercive institutions 'an excellent opportunity' to remove the existing legislative obstacle, he recommended the appointment of 'a small number' of women. He now felt 'sure' that there were 'many duties in the Police which could be success-fully undertaken by women....' De Wet replied that he would not be introducing amending legislation that year, adding that he did not believe the Cape experience had 'been a marked success'. When Truter persisted, the Minister scribbled: 'We can only inform Compol that the whole ques-tion of women employed in connection with the Police will be considered when the Police Act is overhauled.'[59]

The institutional reorganization took place during 1920 without any amendment to the Police Act or any opportunity for public discussion of the 'question of women'. By then, the defining reversal for the experiment had already occurred. H. F. Trew, Gray's replacement in Cape Town, quickly concluded that the patrols were 'useless as an adjunct to the Police Force'. In July 1919 he sent Truter comments, by the head of the city's morality branch, on a hostile article in the press relating a court case in which two white women were charged with solicitation on the strength of evidence brought by the patrols. 'This is the first case', Trew remarked, 'in which they have been called on to give evidence before a Court and the attached reports will show what a lamentable failure their efforts were. They entirely broke down under cross-examination and would not adhere to a single statement which they have [sic] originally made.' Sub-Inspector Miller believed they 'would have secured a conviction' had they 'stuck to their convictions....' Instead of inferring that the women needed training in court procedure, he decided that 'frankly [they] are of no use carrying out Police work'. Trew wanted to give them a month's notice, but warned: 'Of course any attempt to do away with these women will meet with a strong opposition from the Social Purity people in Capetown.'[60]

De Wet now had the documentation he needed to label the four-year experiment a failure without risking contradiction from the ranking divi-sional officer. The label stuck: sixty years later the police's official history asserted that the 'experiment proved unsuccessful....'[61] In a reply marked 'secret', headquarters instructed Trew that the Minister did 'not wish the movement continued' but that his 'decision should not hastily be given effect to'; he wanted Trew to dismiss the women quietly at the end of 1919.[62] By 1920, the Board of Control had dissolved. White women's associations, bruised by the defeat, increasingly focused on the franchise as a prerequisite for success in other causes.[63]

At the end of 1920 Truter gave Trew a last opportunity to reconsider. The Society for the Protection of Child Life in Cape Town, citing English successes, had urged the Justice Department to reinstate the patrols. Interestingly, Trew's comments were not entirely negative. He persisted in calling the experiment a 'failure' on the grounds that the women had been too old, poorly supervised, had lacked legal powers, and had been assigned duties 'not suitable ... for women police'. Males were needed to '[patrol] the streets and [control] hardened prostitutes'. But women would, he felt, 'be of great use' in maintenance and probation work and for dealing with abused children, because the 'male Constable' then doing this was not 'in the position a woman would be to judge if a child is properly nourished, clothed and healthy'.[64] His concluding paragraph, however, revealed a more fundamental official misgiving that, in tandem with the post-war escalation in black urban militancy, had been expressed with growing frequency. 'It is impossible in this question to make comparisons between the conditions in England and South Africa. The coloured and Kafir question here complicates the matter to a great degree.' For Truter this settled the issue: forwarding Trew's report, he commented that since de Wet had not introduced amending legislation he did 'not think the question of Women Police, in so far as the Union ... is concerned, need be further discussed....' If Gray, now based at police headquarters as chief of the Union's Criminal Investigation Department, continued to harbor a contrary opinion, he evidently kept it to himself: a 1926 commission reported that senior officers 'unanimously opposed' the idea.[65]

A consensus had been reached at the top of the police hierarchy that remained undisturbed until the 1960s, save for a brief period of renewed state institutional self-questioning in the 1940s. At the end of 1929, I. P. de Villiers, the martinet who succeeded Truter as Commissioner, told Kimberley's Women's Enfranchisement and Civic Association: 'It is considered the conditions obtaining in South Africa are entirely against the employment of Women Police.' He repeated this view in 1937: 'And in regard to women police in this country, with your mixed population here and your native population, I have only one comment to make, and that is this; "quis ipsos custodes custodiet"[sic].' A memorandum prepared in 1954 summarized the previous three decades of opinion at headquarters: 'Naturally the main object [of the police] is to combat crime and not welfare or uplift work.... Circumstances in South Africa, with its large non-white population, make it impossible to follow the same policy here as for example in Europe.... If a woman was placed on street work, she would have to be under constant observation for her own protection, especially against non-white assaults at night, and that would defeat the whole purpose....

Women could possibly be used in immorality cases, but in view of the moral danger this would place them in it is felt that the price would certainly be too high.' The police, the document asserted, could do its work 'without unnecessarily exposing the noble daughters of our country to such depravity'.[66] Throughout these decades, white women's organizations continued to protest white women's exclusion from the police, but they were unable to shift the post-1920 consensus at police headquarters or the entrenched terms in which the issue was discussed.

The leadership of the South African Police, in defining a position on the issue of policewomen after several years of debate with reformers, was simultaneously establishing the masculine institutional identity the organization would henceforth project. In a period of fluidity in state bureaucratic and policy development, the debate revealed a degree of uncertainty and contestation within the police force about the nature and scope of its work. In confronting officials with an alternative conception of the police function, the discussion compelled them to reflect upon and articulate their own assumptions about how the colonial social order was to be configured and maintained. In concluding finally that the preventive program advocated by women's associations was not police work, officials were also narrowing their definition of what did qualify.

   In their arguments with officialdom, white women's organizations did not necessarily offer a softer competing vision of the police function. Indeed, in some respects their ideas would have entailed greater levels of state-directed social engineering than did existing or subsequent practices. Yet their alternative, despite enjoying support from important male officials and reformers, came during the course of the pre-1920 debate to be labeled as 'feminine', largely because of an association with stereotypical ideas about women and 'women's work' that was reinforced by the tendency of the campaigners themselves to couch their arguments in the language of domesticity. In rejecting the idea of women in the police, and with it this competing feminine theory of policing, officials quite consciously invested the components of their own, now firmer, ideas about the purposes of policing with an opposing, positive, masculine valency.

   In advocating a theory of policing founded on the imported concept of prevention, the campaigners did not give much thought to Africans. Their refusal was part of the longer retreat from the ambitious nineteenth-century liberal imperialist project of remaking Africans in the image of 'rational', metropolitan, middle-class subjects.[67] But in weighing reformers' arguments, the white state could not fail to register their broader interventionist implications in a period of unprecedented black militancy. Whether directed at blacks or lower-class whites, preventive policing was much too ambitious. Sympathy for a perspective of 'normalization' correspondingly declined: South Africa's 'circumstances' were different. It is likely, too, that the prospect of white women in uniform provoked officials' concern that 'the loss of respect by the native for the white people' which so preoccupied them in this period would be exacerbated by bringing the authority of the state, which claimed legitimacy in sustaining indigenous patriarchy, itself into question among Africans.[68]

The image the state now strove more resolutely to project through the department that interfaced most systematically with its African subjects was one of white control maintained by repressive violence. Rather than participating in transforming social relations, policing in the emerging segregationist dispensation involved drawing rings of force around spatially isolated arenas in which these relations could operate without challenging settlers' residential security or economic interests. It was easier to define and maintain racial boundaries through the strategic application of preemptive violence than to face the consequences of intervention on the scale logically implied by the reformers' vision.

In 1920, as the debate over policewomen reached its denouement, the South African Police absorbed the bulk of the South African Mounted Rifles and assumed responsibility for policing the entire country, a decisive rejection of Smuts's original scheme for a separate, 'purely civilian' force for white-settled areas. Within a year, police massacres of striking black workers in Port Elizabeth and of a millenarian black religious community squatting on common land at Bulhoek starkly revealed the tendency of these new coercive arrangements.[69] Everyday policing now focused almost exclusively on containing the perceived symptoms of social disorder through the bureaucratized, quantifiable procedures of pass document checks and liquor raids. Convictions of Africans for pass offences rose dramatically from approximately 48,000 annually in the early 1920s to 94,000 a decade later, reaching nearly 111,000 in 1940. In 1920 there were 7,571 convictions for possession of home-brewed beer; there were 15,503 in 1922, 35,397 in 1929, 56,442 in 1934, and 82,849 in 1940.[70] These figures reflect the character of policing in the established segregationist order. Gone were the florid evocations of 'intolerable' social conditions that had created an opening for advocating preventive policing.

The women's campaign thus brought gender to a conscious level in an unfinished discussion among decision-makers about the purposes of policing and the structure and procedures of the institution which would best give effect to these purposes. The movement for policewomen disclosed connections among the internal organization of white society, the control of Africans in an emerging racial capitalist dispensation, and the nature and projection of a state that could preside over these different relations. Officials could engage discursively with white middle-class women, with whom they shared many ideological and cultural assumptions, in ways they would not have thought possible or desirable with Africans. It was via this complex, unintended historical circuitry that a 'masculine' police institutional identity emerged with respect to Africans, rather than in a direct relationship of 'feminization' that a binary colonizer/colonized framework might suggest. At stake in the debate was not simply the exclusively male composition of the police but the nature of the social order and the role of policing in its maintenance. 'Masculine' and 'feminine' represented competing positions in this debate, but the epithets themselves reveal nothing essential about the intellectual content of these positions.

The consolidation of a masculine police institutional identity by the early 1920s was mirrored in new arguments by white women's associations in subsequent years. Increasingly, campaigners for policewomen linked their rejection by the authorities as much to their status as women laboring under truncated citizenship rights as to government's refusal to assume responsibility for reformist causes conventionally construed as 'women's work'. As early as 1925, a Cape columnist reported that women's organizations had accused 'the Department of Justice of "male prejudice" because it refuses to repeat the disastrous experiment of the war period when the larger towns of the Union had women-police'.[71] This trend was even more evident following the enfranchisement of white women in 1930 and the establishment of a Department of Social Welfare in 1937. Indeed it is striking how by the 1950s, a decade of escalating police violence against Africans, organized white women had come to focus on the police as exemplifying their marginalization from the levers of power.[72]

Under consistent pressure during these decades to answer the argument about South Africa's peculiar 'circumstances', white women's organizations began seriously to consider the role that policewomen might play in black communities. They countered that since nurses and social workers went unprotected and unharmed in these areas, so could women police. Police managers' response is an instructive indication both of the triumph of the narrow conception of policing and of the image they believed the force had cultivated by then in black and slum communities. I. P. de Villiers said in 1937 that nurses 'virtually go in to succour the poor. If they went in as police women, heaven help them.' His successor as Commissioner, Brigadier Palmer, declared in 1945: 'the outlook of the native ... is that the police are fair game, and I do not think that police women will get the benefits of the chivalry extended to nurses and social workers.... they will class them with the Police in general.'[73] The sex of the person wearing the uniform had become immaterial; the uniform, even in officials' eyes, now unambiguously connoted repressive physical force. The corollary was that the enrollment of women would entail no substantial reconceptualization of the South African Police's institutional profile or purpose. When white women were finally admitted in 1972 because of male personnel shortages it was, unsurprisingly, in defence of the racial status quo rather than an acknowledgement either of their sectional claims or of the need for an alternative vision of policing.[74]

Notes

Research for this article was assisted by a grant from the Joint Committee on African Studies of the Social Science Research Council and the American Council of Learned Societies with funds provided by the Ford, Mellon, and Rockefeller Foundations. For encouragement, constructive criticism, and assistance with sources I am grateful to Keith Breckenridge, James Campbell, David W. Cohen, Micaela di Leonardo, Jonathon Glassman, Nancy R. Hunt, Tessie Liu, Stephan Miescher, James Oakes, Grey Osterud, Mervyn Shear, Christina Smith, Lynn Thomas, and two anonymous reviewers. Unless otherwise indicated archival sources are from the Central Archives Depot in Pretoria.

1. Bill Nasson, '"Messing with Coloured People": The 1918 Police Strike in Cape Town, South Africa', *Journal of African History*, 33 (1992), p. 306.

2. Linzi Manicom has challenged scholars to '[understand] South African state formation as a gendered and gendering process, [and to explore] the different institutional sites and ruling discourses in which gender identities and categories are constructed'; 'Ruling Relations: Rethinking State and Gender in South African History', *Journal of African History*, 33 (1992), p. 465.

3. Helpful reassessments of the role of white women in colonial contexts are Ann Stoler, 'Carnal Knowledge and Imperial Power: Gender, Race, and Morality in Colonial Asia', in *Gender at the Crossroads of Knowledge: Feminist Anthropology in the Postmodern Era*, ed. Micaela di Leonardo (University of California Press, Berkeley, 1991), pp. 51–101; and Margaret Jolly, 'Colonizing Women: The Maternal Body and Empire', in *Feminism and the Politics of Difference*, ed. Sneja Gunew and Anna Yeatman (Westview Press, Boulder, 1993), pp. 103–27.

4. Joan Wallach Scott, *Gender and the Politics of History* (Columbia University Press, New York, 1988), p. 43.

5. Shula Marks and Stanley Trapido, 'Lord Milner and the South African State', *History Workshop Journal*, 8 (1979), pp. 50–80; Martin Chanock, *Britain, Rhodesia and South Africa, 1900–45: The Unconsummated Union* (Frank Cass, Totowa, 1977), pp. 10–37; David Yudelman, *The Emergence of Modern South Africa: State, Capital, and the Incorporation of Organized Labour on the South African Gold Fields, 1902–1939* (David Phillip, Cape Town, 1983), pp. 52–78.

6. Saul Dubow, *Racial Segregation and the Origins of Apartheid in South Africa, 1919–36* (St. Martin's Press, New York, 1989), pp. 3, 39–40.

7. *Report of the Commission Appointed to Enquire into Assaults on Women* (Cape Town, U.G. 39-'13), para. 98 (hereafter *Report of Assaults on Women Commission*).

8. On segregation as 'profoundly ambiguous and self-contradictory', thereby facilitating its adoption by a diversity of constituencies, see John W. Cell, *The Highest Stage of White Supremacy: The Origins of Segregation in South Africa and the American South* (Cambridge University Press, Cambridge, 1982), p. 2.

9. Barlow Rand Archives, Central Mining and Investment Corporation (London), Storage Case 117/118, Johannesburg Letters, L. Phillips to F. Eckstein, 2 October 1913.

10. Helen Bradford, *A Taste of Freedom: The ICU in Rural South Africa, 1924–1930* (Ravan Press, Johannesburg, 1987), p. 2.

11. Cape Archives Depot, Accession 1696, 1/2, Minutes of [WCTU] Executive Committee held at Cape Town, 12 February 1915; Archives of the Police Inquiry Commission, 1936–1937 (K80), Vol. 4, Day 33, evidence of Julia F. Solly, p. 2307; Archives of the Secretary for Justice (JUS) 1/57/16, Secretary for Justice (SJ) to Secretary, WCTU, 5 March 1915; Archives of the South African Police (SAP) 33/2/30, Part 1, Secretary, SAP

(SecSAP), to Deputy Commissioner (DC), SAP, Capetown, 10 March 1915; SAP 33/2/30, Part 1, G. D. Gray to SecSAP, 16 March 1915. On 'khaki fever' and patrols, see *Cape Times (CT)*, 7 September 1915. On Julia Solly, see *The South African Woman's Who's Who* (Biographies (Pty.) Limited, Johannesburg, 1938), p. 353.

12. Elizabeth B. van Heyningen, 'The Social Evil in the Cape Colony 1868–1902: Prostitution and the Contagious Diseases Acts', *Journal of Southern African Studies*, 10 (1984), pp. 187–9. Ethel M. Mackenzie, 'Women's Christian Temperance Union', in *Women of South Africa: A Historical, Educational & Industrial Encyclopædia & Social Directory of the Women of the Sub-continent*, ed. Thos. H. Lewis (Le Quesne & Hooton-Smith, Cape Town, 1913), p. 305. See also Edward J. Bristow, *Vice and Vigilance: Purity Movements in Britain since 1700* (Gill and Macmillan, Dublin, 1977), p. 121. For 'Offences Connected with Prostitution' and 'Miscegenation', see Irene Antoinette Geffen, *The Laws of South Africa Affecting Women and Children* (R. L. Esson & Co. Ltd, Johannesburg, 1928), pp. 281–9.

13. For a sample of these organizations and their work, see Lewis (ed.) *Women of South Africa*, pp. 299–309.

14. On social reform in South Africa, see van Heyningen, 'Social Evil', and Charles van Onselen, *Studies in the Social and Economic History of the Witwatersrand*, Vol. 1 (Ravan Press, Johannesburg, 1982), pp. 103–62. Van Onselen does not mention women's associations in the formation of middle-class opinion, although he notes the importance of their English counterparts' example. On pre-war 'black peril', see van Onselen, *Studies*, Vol. 2, pp. 45–54.

15. *Report of Assaults on Women Commission*, paras. 139–40.

16. On Leagues, see Lewis (ed.) *Women of South Africa*, p. 303. For Standing Committee, see Chamber of Mines Archives (CMA), Assaults on European Women by Natives—No. 2, 1912, Round Table Conference with the Joint Committee held in the Town Council Chamber, 21 June 1912, pp. 14–5.

17. See testimony in Archives of the Commission to Enquire into Assaults on Women (K373), 1912–1913, a perusal of which reveals that the women members of the Commission, energetic participants in women's organizations, did not question witnesses on the issue. There was intermittent interest in women police in pre-war England, and a more established movement existed in the United States by 1914. See Chloe Owings, *Women Police: A Study of the Development and Status of the Women Police Movement* (Frederick H. Hitchcock, New York, 1925), pp. 2–6, 94–104; and Joan Lock, *The British Policewoman: Her Story* (Robert Hale, London, 1979), pp. 13, 19, 22. South Africans cited these precedents only after initiating their own campaign.

18. CMA, Assaults on European Women by Natives—No. 2, 1912, Round Table Conference, pp. 17–19 (my emphasis). See also 'The Contact of the Natives in certain Localities with Undesirable Europeans', in *Report of Assaults on Women Commission*, pp. 21–3.

19. Van Heyningen, 'Social Evil', pp. 193–5; Christine Stansell, *City of Women: Sex and Class in New York, 1789–1860* (University of Illinois Press, Urbana and Chicago, 1987), p. 191.

20. JUS 1/57/16, unsigned letter (apparently a copy) to Miss Murray, 24 September 1917.

21. SAP 33/2/30, Part 1: Gray to SecSAP, 16 March, 6 May and 18 May 1915; SecSAP to DC, SAP, Cape Town, 11 May 1915.

22. SAP 33/2/30, Part 1, Extract from Report by the Deputy Commissioner of Police, Commanding Western Division, Cape, for the Year Ending 31 December 1915, enclosed

in Commissioner of Police (Compol) to Mayor's Secretary, Johannesburg, 27 July 1916 (hereafter Extract from Report).

23. Owings, *Women Police*, pp. 9–13; Lock, *British Policewoman*, pp. 22, 32–3. Lock states that Cape Town was 'among the first cities to ask for organizers'.

24. SAP 33/2/30, Part 1: Extract from Report; Commissioner, SAP, to SJ (Telegram), 11 March 1916. For City Hall meeting, see *CT*, 20 July 1915. Sterling, who arrived from England in mid-November 1915, was recruited by Gray. On her experience in organizing patrols, see *CT*, 22 November 1915. Miss Barr, her predecessor, also had English experience: *CT*, 5 November 1915.

25. See speech of Mrs K. Stuart in *CT*, 27 July 1915.

26. SAP 33/2/30, Part 1: Extract from Report; Commissioner, SAP, to SJ (Telegram), 11 March 1916; *CT*, 20 and 27 July, 10 August and 7 September 1915; *Rand Daily Mail* (*RDM*), 29 August 1916.

27. JUS 1/57/16, Deputation to Lt.Col.Gray ..., enclosed in Compol to SJ, 20 March 1919.

28. For the broader context, see G. R. Searle, *The Quest for National Efficiency: A Study in British Politics and Political Thought, 1899–1914* (University of California Press, Berkeley, 1971), pp. 64, 241–2; and Martin J. Wiener, *Reconstructing the Criminal: Culture, Law, and Policy in England, 1830–1914* (Cambridge University Press, Cambridge, 1990), pp. 337–8, 378–80.

29. Authorities included Ernst Freund, *The Police Power: Public Policy and Constitutional Rights* (Callaghan & Company, Chicago, 1904); Leonhard Felix Fuld, *Police Administration: A Critical Study of Police Organisations in the United States and Abroad* (1909; repr. Patterson Smith, Montclair, 1971); Raymond B. Fosdick, *European Police Systems* (The Century Co., New York, 1915); Raymond B. Fosdick, *American Police Systems* (The Century Co., New York, 1920); Arthur Woods, *Crime Prevention* (Princeton University Press, Princeton, 1918); Owings, *Women Police* (p. 218 for 'peculiarly fitted'). For rhetoric of sympathetic men, see Dr Symington's speech in *CT*, 7 September 1915; and SAP 33/2/30, Part 1, J. Rose Innes to N.J. de Wet, 28 December 1916, enclosed in SJ to Compol, 3 January 1917. For helpful discussion of the 'canon of domesticity' see Nancy F. Cott, *The Bonds of Womanhood: 'Woman's Sphere' in New England, 1780–1835* (Yale University Press, New Haven and London, 1977), pp. 69–71, 97–98; and Linda J. Nicholson, *Gender and History: The Limits of Social Theory in the Age of the Family* (Columbia University Press, New York, 1986), ch. 2.

30. SAP 33/2/30, Part 1, Gray to SecSAP, 14 June 1916.

31. *CT*, 20 July 1915; SAP 33/2/30, Part 1, Hester Carter to Minister of Justice, 29 December 1916. Biographical details from Lewis (ed.) *Women of South Africa*, and *South African Woman's Who's Who*.

32. SAP 33/2/30, Part 1, Compol to Mayor's Secretary, Johannesburg, 27 July 1916.

33. SAP 33/2/30, Part 1: Gray to SecSAP, 14 June 1916; Commissioner, SAP, to Gray, 7 November 1916.

34. *Memorandum Explanatory of the South African Defence Bill* (Cape Town, S.C. 7-1912), pp. 8–9.

35. Louis Botha to J. X. Merriman, 10 October 1916, in *Selections from the Correspondence of John X. Merriman, 1905–1924*, ed. Phyllis Lewson (Van Riebeeck Society, Cape Town, 1969), p. 284.

36. JUS 1/57/16, Truter to SJ, 20 March 1919; SAP 33/2/30, Part 2, J.M.L. Fulford to Colonel Bredell, 21 October 1919.

37. SAP 33/2/30, Part 1, Theresa Lawrence to Colonel Douglas, 2 April 1916, copy enclosed in Douglas to SecSAP, 4 April 1916.

38. Cape Archives, Accession 1696, 1/3, Minutes of Executive Committee held in Port Elizabeth, 29 June 1916.

39. SAP 33/2/30, Part 1, Mayor's Secretary to Compol, 26 July 1916.

40. *RDM*, 23 and 29 August 1916.

41. For the meeting, see *RDM* and *Star*, 29 August 1916. Where the two reports are identical, I assume that speakers' exact words have been rendered indirectly.

42. *CT*, 17 December 1915.

43. *CT*, 27 July 1915; JUS 1/57/16, Deputation to Lt.Col.Gray ..., enclosed in Truter to SJ, 20 March 1919.

44. *Star*, 30 August 1916.

45. Sue Parnell, 'The Construction of Johannesburg Slums as a "Native Problem" in the 1910s', Seminar Paper No. 362, Institute for Advanced Social Research, University of the Witwatersrand, 1994.

46. K373, Volume 3, No. 168, evidence of T.E. Mavrogordato.

47. *Report of Assaults on Women Commission*, paras. 98, 151.

48. Dubow, *Racial Segregation*, pp. 3–4, 40.

49. SAP 33/2/30, Part 1, Compol to Mayor's Secretary, Johannesburg, 27 July 1916.

50. SAP 33/2/30, Part 1, DC, Johannesburg, to SecSAP, 4 April 1916. Gray, raised in a clerical family, had been ordained an Anglican minister before poor health brought him to South Africa in 1898. Interview with Douglas Awdry Gray, 19 August 1994.

51. SAP 33/2/30, Part 1, Commissioner, SAP, to DC, SAP, Cape Town, 7 November 1916.

52. SAP 33/2/30, Part 1, Gray to SecSAP, 25 November 1916 (emphasis original).

53. SAP 33/2/30, Part 1: Truter to SJ, 4 December 1916; SJ to Commissioner, SAP, 6 December 1916; Gray to SecSAP, 13 December 1916 and 9 January 1917.

54. SAP 33/2/30, Part 1: SJ to Compol, 3 January 1917, enclosing copies of J. Rose Innes to N.J. de Wet, 28 December 1916, and Hester Carter to Minister of Justice, 29 December 1916; Acting Commissioner, SAP, to SJ, 5 January 1917; Gray to SecSAP, 9 January 1917; JUS 1/57/16, H. Hands to N.J. de Wet, 5 January 1917.

55. SAP 33/2/30, Part 1: N.J. de Wet to Colonel T.G. Truter, 2 March 1917; Commissioner, SAP, to SJ, 5 March 1917; T.G. Truter to N.J. de Wet, 6 March 1917.

56. *RDM* and *CT*, 16 March 1917. On District Six's reputation, see Vivian Bickford-Smith, *Ethnic Pride and Racial Prejudice in Victorian Cape Town: Group Identity and Social Practice, 1875–1902* (Cambridge University Press, Cambridge, 1995), pp. 127, 212.

57. JUS 1/57/16, Women Police: Memorandum of Deputation to the Minister of Justice on 4 March 1918.

58. JUS 1/57/16, Organising Secretary, Women's Reform Club, Johannesburg, to Minister of Justice, 21 May 1918; JUS 1/57/16, Secretary, National Council of Women Workers of South Africa, to Minister of Defence, 27 May 1918; Nasson, '"Messing with Coloured People"', p. 308.

59. Lock, *British Policewoman*, pp. 87–9; JUS 1/57/16, Truter to SJ, 20 March 1919, with handwritten minute by the SJ, 25 March 1919; JUS 1/57/16, Truter to SJ, 22 April 1919, with handwritten instructions by de Wet, 25 April 1919.

60. JUS 1/57/16, H.F. Trew to SecSAP, 16 July 1919, enclosing 'A Woman Patrol Faux Pas', *South African Review*, 11 July 1919, and Sub-Inspector Miller, Liquor and Morality Branch, Cape Town, to DC, Cape Western Division, 14 July 1919.

61. Marius de Witt Dippenaar, *The History of the South African Police 1913–1988* (Promedia Publications, Silverton, 1988), p. 37.

62. SAP 33/2/30, Part 2, SecSAP to DC, SAP, Cape Town, Secret, 22 August 1919.

63. Cherryl Walker, 'The Women's Suffrage Movement: The Politics of Gender, Race and Class', in *Women and Gender in Southern Africa to 1945*, ed. Cherryl Walker (David Philip, Cape Town, 1990), pp. 331–88.

64. It is notable that this argument, while typing what women could not do, was as much about what men could not do and, by extension, about where policemen could not go. Keith Breckenridge suggested that this logic might be related to the twentieth-century South African state's notorious indifference to domestic violence.

65. SAP 33/2/30, Part 2, SecSAP to DC, SAP, Cape Town, 3 November 1920, enclosing SJ to Commissioner, SAP, 28 October 1920; JUS 1/57/16, Truter to SJ, 4 December 1920, enclosing Trew to SecSAP, 24 November 1920; *Report of the Commission of Inquiry to Inquire into the Organisation of the South African Police Force Established under Act No. 14 of 1912* (Cape Town, U.G. 23-'26), para. 239.

66. SAP 33/2/30, Part 1, Compol to President, Women's Enfranchisement and Civic Association, Kimberley, 4 December 1929; K80, Vol. 9, Day 104, evidence of Colonel I.P. de Villiers, p. 8911e ('who is to guard the guards themselves'); SAP 33/2/30, Part 4, Memorandum, stamped 18 May 1954 (my translation).

67. For comparative periodization of the declining interest in transforming the internal mechanics of 'native' societies, see Stoler, 'Carnal Knowledge', pp. 86–7.

68. Walker identifies this concern in analogous debates on the suffrage in 'Women's Suffrage Movement', p. 341.

69. Dippenaar, *History*, pp. 46–50.

70. *Union Statistics for Fifty Years* (Bureau of Census and Statistics, Pretoria, 1960), F-4; Union of South Africa, *Official Year Book*, No. 12, 1929–1930, p. 307; No. 16, 1933–1934, p. 325; No. 22, 1941, p. 375.

71. SAP 33/2/30, Part 1, Trew to SecSAP, 28 March 1925, enclosing cutting from the *Cape*, dated 27 March 1925.

72. See correspondence in SAP 33/2/30, Part 4; and SAP 33/2/30/1, Part 1.

73. K80, Vol. 9, Day 104, evidence of Colonel I.P. de Villiers, p. 8911f; Archives of the Public Service Inquiry Commission (K47), 1944–1947, Vol. 10, No. 166, evidence of Brigadier R.J. Palmer, p. 9897.

74. Dippenaar, *History*, p. 428.

Love Magic and Political Morality in Central Madagascar, 1875–1990

DAVID GRAEBER

This essay sets out from a simple question. Why is it that at the end of the last century, people in Imerina in central Madagascar seem to have universally assumed that it was men who used *ody fitia*, or 'love medicine', while when I was living there between 1989 and 1991, absolutely everyone I spoke to took it for granted that it was women who did so? This question is linked to another. In both periods, love medicine was the stuff of scandal, but over the last hundred years, what was scandalous about it seemed to have changed. Nineteenth-century texts dwell on the implicit violence of the medicine's effects, the harm and humiliation it could bring to its victims, but the people I knew concentrated on something very different: the fact that people under its influence would do whatever their enchanter told them, that they were, in effect, enslaved. Why? What had happened in the meantime?

The assumption, in Imerina, has always been that love medicine is widely available; just about anyone could, if they had the money or connections, get hold of the knowledge and ingredients. As a result, the danger that someone they knew might use *ody fitia* was one any reasonable person had to take account of. To talk of love medicine, then, is to talk about fears: about the dangerous powers people saw lurking in their social environment, and about how those fears found shape in startling images that in the nineteenth century centered on women driven mad by sorcery, ripping off their clothes to run through the streets, and in the twentieth century, on men ridden like horses by naked witches in the night. This is my central thesis: that such fantasies are ultimately fantasies about power, and the only way to understand them is by casting them in a broader political context.

Between the end of the last century, when Imerina was the center of an independent kingdom, and the time when I lived there lie sixty five years of French colonial occupation. The experience of colonial rule had a profound impact on popular conceptions of power and authority, by which I mean, the ways in which it was considered possible, and legitimate, to influence others. Now, the authority of ancestors and elders in highland Madagascar had long been conceived in basically negative terms: authority was seen most of all as a matter of forbidding, of binding, of restraining others from acting rather than causing others to act. True, this was not the only kind of authority people recognized; the power of kings, for instance, was conceived quite differently. But one effect of colonial rule was that this kind of authority, which I will call 'negative authority', came to be seen as the only traditional 'Malagasy' one and, as such, explicitly counterposed to relations of command, which were identified with an alien, military, government. As such, it was the only kind of authority that was considered entirely legitimate. Nor was this simply a matter of abstract ideology. It appears to have entailed a genuine change in attitudes and, especially, in the standards by which people judged each other's actions. It was this new social world which created the fears that found shape in the new images of witchcraft and love medicine.

Such an argument is a little unconventional. Feminist scholarship has long contended that traditional distinctions between 'public' and 'private' domains are profoundly deceptive, and that the forms of power and authority assumed to be characteristic of each are entirely dependent on each other. Still, there is a tendency to assume that if, say, sexual politics or the fears and fantasies surrounding imagined dangers in domestic life have any relation to national politics, it will be as a kind of infrastructure. It is easy to imagine how the appeal of a fascist regime or nationalist movement might ultimately be based in male anxieties about a threatened loss of power in the home; much more difficult to imagine how affairs of state might have an effect on people's most intimate anxieties. But this is precisely what I am arguing here.

Of course it is easier to see how things might work this way in a case like Madagascar, under a colonial regime imposed by foreign conquest and maintained by force which did not have to maintain even the fiction of the consent of the governed. But as an approach to colonial history, this is a bit unusual as well. First of all, I am not really interested in colonial policy, with what the French regime in Madagascar thought it was doing. Nor am I dealing with questions of hegemony and resistance, with the degree to which colonial institutions like schools and churches could impose their definitions of reality on the colonized or the degree to which the colonized were able to develop their own counterposed ideologies.[1] Or not exactly. By focusing on the question of authority, I am starting from an existing moral order with its own characteristic tensions and dilemmas, its own ways of arguing about right and wrong. Doing so casts the problem not so much as how people dealt with their conquerors—most, in fact, tried as far as possible to avoid having to deal with them at all—but rather how, as a result, they ended up having to reconsider their own relations with each other.

Malagasy *fanafody*, or 'medicine', consisted mainly of objects called *ody*, a word normally translated as 'charms'. Most ody consisted of bits of rare wood, preserved in an ox-horn, wooden box or similar receptacle. Different ingredients gave the owner different powers, but an ody's power was ultimately derived not from the ingredients but from the conscious agency of an invisible spirit, which the user had to invoke with prayers each time the charm was used. In ordinary conversation, though (and this is as true then as now), people do not tend to speak of ody either as objects or as spirits. They speak of them as a form of knowledge. One never says, for instance, that one suspects some person 'has an *ody fitia*'; one says that one suspects they 'know how to use' one. In common conception, ody become a kind of knowledge that extends their owners' powers to act on the world.[2] They are almost never said to act on the users, but always on someone, or something, else. Love medicine, for example, is never said to make its user more attractive or desirable but always to inspire desire directly in another. On the other hand, ody were more than mere extensions of their owners; ody, or at least the more important ones, had their own will and intelligence, and their owners had to appeal to them, sacrifice to them, and generally treat them as hierarchical superiors.

Medicine has always been governed by one absolute moral principle: to use it in order to cause harm to other people is always wrong. Such behavior can never be justified. It is witchcraft, and *mpamosavy* (witches or sorcerers) were the very definition of evil. If medicine has always had a somewhat morally dubious cast to it, then, it was because it had such a tremendous potential to cause harm. Only *fiarovana*, or medicine used for protection from harm, was entirely above suspicion. As a result, people would always try to represent their medicine as a form of protection if it were possible to do so.

Early sources speak of ody that can protect their owners from hail, crocodiles, guns, thieves, witches, knives, locusts, fire, and an endless assortment of other dangers. I heard practically identical lists myself. But then as now, the protection such charms afforded took a distinctly active form. Rather than fortifying the user or her possessions against harm, they were almost always said to intervene to prevent or disrupt the harmful actions of others, though never in such a way that they could be said to be actually attacking them. An ody that provided protection against bullets, for instance, did not make the bearers' skin invulnerable: it made those shooting at them miss, or turned their bullets into water. Charms employed in lawsuits never made the bearer's own words more persuasive, but always prevented his antagonist from arguing effectively or at all.

There is a very famous book called *Le Tsiny et le Tody dans la pensée Malgache*, written in 1957 by a young Protestant pastor named Richard Andriamanjato (who has since become a major figure in national politics).[3] In it he argued that since traditional Malagasy thought assumes that anything one might do will inevitably bring at least indirect harm to someone else, all action is intrinsically problematic. One can easily imagine the ethics of protection as a kind of corollary: if acting is so problematic, then at least in areas in which one is wielding extraordinary powers—for instance, the invisible powers of medicine—actions could only be entirely above question if meant to prevent the even more harmful actions of someone else. The same logic applied to the more public powers involved in communal authority as well. In my experience, the role of elders was never represented as a matter of initiating or even coordinating communal projects, but of imposing prohibitions and stepping in to prevent younger people from taking actions likely to shatter the solidarity of the community. Ancestors are seen as acting in much the same way, imposing taboos or rules of conduct that were always stated in the negative. This is a point which will become very important as the argument develops; for now, suffice it to say that this meant love medicine, which could hardly be represented as a form of protection, was seen as lying at least on the borders of morality.

'The love charm', one missionary wrote, 'gives the wearer control over the affections of any person he desires, and is chiefly in requisition by unfortunate ill-looking youths in search of a wife, or by profligate characters seeking to seduce their prey'.[4] The assumption here, as in all the nineteenth-century sources, is that it was typically men who made use of *ody fitia*, even if some added that women could do so on occasion.

The reigning assumption a hundred years later, when I was living in the town of Arivonimamo in western Imerina in 1990–91, was precisely the opposite. Several women in fact made a great point of this to me, suggesting it provided a profound insight into the difference between male and female psychology. If a girl, they said, is attracted to a boy but finds he has no interest in her, her instinct will be to try to make him change his mind; if she appeals to medicine, she'll try to find something that will make him love her as much as he possibly can. If a boy is turned down by a girl, he's much more likely to get angry and look for medicine that will enable him to take revenge, say, by blasting her with lightning or driving her insane. While everyone conceded that men had been known to use love medicine, this was considered an exception. On the other hand, *ambalavelona*, a form of sorcery which caused its victim to be possessed by an evil ghost and thus driven insane, was often said to be employed by men against women who had rejected their sexual advances.[5] This is useful to bear in mind while considering nineteenth-century accounts, because the *ody fitia* described in them can be seen as a combination of the two: that is, they punished women by driving them insane at the same time they were said to evoke love and desire.

The greatest source on nineteenth-century Merina medicine is a book by a Norwegian Lutheran missionary named Lars Vig, who lived in the far south of Imerina between 1875 and 1902. It was common practice for new converts to turn in their ody to the local missionaries, but Vig seems to have become an enthusiastic collector, quizzing their former owners on their ingredients and manner of use and later publishing his notes. Of the 130 charms or elements of charms Vig lists, twenty-four are described as love charms. Some of these were meant to strengthen, or disrupt, existing relationships; but the majority—and these were the archetypal ones—were meant to arouse passion in a woman who had proved resistant to the user's advances.[6]

The implicit scenario seems to have been roughly similar to the one assumed by the people I talked to in Arivonimamo: a man makes advances; the woman is 'proud' (in other words, she is not interested); he resorts to medicine. The charm Imahaka, for example,

> helped to overcome the resistance of a 'proud' woman.... [It] was supposed to have the power to render women mad, of provoking amorous madness. This is the prayer one makes to it 'Listen o Imahaka. There's a woman who is proud towards me: render her mad, demented like a rabid dog.... Make it so that her heart moves, bubbles, boils, so that she can no longer be kept back by her father, by her mother, by her kin'.[7]

The woman would thus be compelled to the caster's bed. This sort of 'amorous madness' was said to be a feature of almost all such charms, but the descriptions often suggest, not a person caught up by a frenzy of desire, but one simply torn away against her will. Often it seems as if the enchanter is acting out of a vindictive desire to humble and humiliate the woman who had rejected him. Consider for instance the prayer to another charm:

> '... even when the woman is before the eyes of her brother, or in public, may you render her so mad as to throw off her clothing to run to me. Even if the rivers are deep and the current strong, even if the day is dark and the place she lives very distant, may she be obliged to come. Even if she is hidden away and a thousand men let forth a cry of war to retain her, make it so they can do nothing'.[8]
>
> The poor enchanted woman would be like a rabid dog, like a mad thing; 'the foam would keep coming from her mouth like a rabid dog, and like a rabid dog she would fling herself about, run and run without aim or reason, and all the while raving like a lunatic. This state would continue until she came to the man who had enchanted her using the charm'.[9]

If held back or confined in her house, the woman would be overwhelmed by fits of trembling and breathlessness; she would weep uncontrollably; she would be ravaged by fevers of malarial intensity, unable to move from her bed but hearing her enchanter's voice in every rooster's crow outside; or else she might suddenly become so overpoweringly strong that it was impossible to hold her back from running off to him.[10]

Vig himself tended to downplay the punitive, sadistic overtones in these descriptions. Noting that for a woman to be too consistently 'proud' was considered an affront to sociability, he suggests that those spurned could represent themselves as acting within their rights.[11] Perhaps so: but there is little reason to think that anyone else would have taken such claims seriously. Elsewhere, Vig himself admits that love medicine was always considered to be very close to simple vindictive witchcraft, and reports that Queen Ranavalona I (1828–1861) was said to have taken such umbrage against the idea that men were driving women mad with love medicine that she sent emissaries around the country to have every known practitioner rounded up and killed.

In contrast, the one Malagasy source we have from this period, an account of the diviner's art preserved in a collection of documents called the *Tantara ny Andriana*, provides a much less ambiguous perspective. There are, says the author, two different sorts of *ody fitia*. One is a form of sorcery. Inspired by the desire for revenge, it drives its victims insane and, unless treated by a skilled diviner, will ultimately kill them. The other kind does not cause madness but enduring mutual love; this, the diviner himself can provide, for instance, for a boy who wishes to marry a girl against the wishes of her parents.[12]

This model would seem to leave little place for most of the ody Vig collected from his parishioners, all which were apparently thought to cause only temporary madness and were certainly never fatal. But the Malagasy author had biases of his own. He was, presumably, himself a diviner, and therefore would hardly have wanted to leave open the possibility that the sort of love medicine he himself could provide could possibly harm anyone. Thus his separation of love and vengeance, which he takes so far as to make it impossible to tell what his evil 'love medicine' has to do with love at all. What Vig's material suggests is that for most people, things were not nearly so clear-cut; most believed that even medicine used to inspire desire in others could have violent, punitive effects to the precise measure that the user's desires were mixed with wounded pride and desire for revenge.

This same Malagasy author provides the closest one can find to a nineteenth-century reference to women using *ody fitia* in a rather unusual moral tirade about young men from the highlands who leave their wives and families to engage in petty commerce on the coast, take local mistresses to help them with their business, and then ultimately abandon them. Often, he says, these coastal women know how to place ody on their lovers which will only begin to work once the men have returned to their wives and children in the highlands. When they do, the effects are spectacular. The victim loses all sensation in the lower half of his body, he becomes incontinent, he is impotent, he soils the floor and the bed. Eventually, he dies. While the author never actually refers to these charms as *ody fitia*, he represents the women as acting out of exactly the same motives of jealous spite and desire for retribution. In fact, the words he puts in their mouth, 'if he won't be mine, he won't be anybody's' (*tsy ho ahy, tsy ho an'olona*), are the exact words he places in the mouths of users of vindictive *ody fitia*.[13] And as in the case of *ody fitia*, retribution takes the most visceral, tangible, and humiliating form.

In the nineteenth century, then, love medicine lay on the borders of witch-craft for the simple reason that it was most often employed when sexual desire was mixed with desire for revenge. Even when the ostensible pur-pose was winning a woman's affections, there was likely to be a very strong current of retributive violence in its effects. After all, there would be little reason to suspect anyone had actually used *ody fitia* in the first place unless someone, typically a young woman, began to suffer from suggestive symp-toms; her family's first reaction would presumably be to ask if there were any men whose advances she had recently turned down.

When I was living in Arivonimamo, on the other hand, if a woman de-veloped similar symptoms, the assumption would have been that someone was trying to drive her insane by means of a malevolent ghost.[14] The term *ody fitia* was normally confined to charms meant to inspire love, either as a means of seduction or as a way to inspire selfless devotion in one's cur-rent spouse or lover. In practice, it was undue devotion that people mainly tended to remark upon. If a man suddenly became infatuated, it might never occur to anyone to wonder if medicine were involved. But if he was seen to be slavishly indulgent of his wife or lover and, most of all, if she could be said to be enriching herself or otherwise exploiting him as a result, then rumors of *ody fitia* would inevitably begin to circulate. This was the reason people I talked to about the matter, men as well as women, would often point out that the motivations of women who used this kind of medicine often had less to do with love than with a desire for wealth and power.

In one village I knew well, there was a woman in her forties who had married into the community some eight or nine years before; both she and her husband had children from previous marriages. After several years, the man—who had, according to his neighbors, all this time grown increas-ingly moody and contentious—abruptly disinherited his own children by his former marriage and adopted hers. Whatever his wife tells him, they said, he does without question. This alone was evidence enough to compel several women to make me promise never, if I visited their home, to accept any food or drink she might offer me. After all, they pointed out, she still had several unmarried daughters, and she obviously knew how to use *ody fitia*.

An even more dramatic case had occurred a few years earlier. One of the wealthiest men in the village, a man of very modest origins who had raised himself to prominence by marrying a local heiress, had suddenly decided at the age of fifty to divorce his wife and marry a much younger woman he had met while off on business in the nearby town of Analavory. No sooner had the woman moved in with him than she began selling off his property—houses, fields, cattle, everything she could lay her hands on—as he dutifully signed the papers, refusing to discuss the matter with other members of his family. When after a few years there was nothing left to sell, she left him for an itinerant Tandroy cattle merchant, and eventually moved back to her old home in Analavory. At this point the man had nothing left to his name except for three cows. One by one, I was told, he sold them, each time using the money to fund a trip to Analavory to beg his wife to return to him. Each time she sent him away. The third time, he collapsed in exhaustion on the road back to Arivonimamo, had to be carried home to his village, and died there the next day. Almost everyone concluded she had not only used love medicine, but finally placed some kind of charm on him that would kill him as soon as he got home.

Other ody were referred to as 'kinds of *ody fitia*': the two most famous were *fanainga lavitra* ('fetching from afar') and *tsy mihoabonga* ('does not pass beyond the mountain'). The first was used to summon a person to the caster; once they fall under its effects, I was told, wherever they were or whatever they might be doing, they would fall into a trance, drop everything, and immediately travel to the caster by the quickest possible means available, not regaining consciousness until they arrived. *Tsy mihoabonga*, on the other hand, acts to confine its victim within a certain perimeter. If the victim tried to walk out of a village they were confined to, they would suddenly find themselves turning back again without being aware of doing so; if forcibly removed, they would grow seriously ill or even die. While the archetypical users of *fanainga lavitra* were woman trying to force lovers to return to them, and I heard several reports of rural women who were supposed to have used *tsy mihoabonga* to keep government functionaries posted to their villages from returning to their wives, these forms of medicine were often used in contexts which had nothing to do with 'love'.[15]

As these examples suggest, love medicine was typically the stuff of scandal. *Fanainga lavitra* was generally considered to be witchcraft pure and simple, no matter what the pretext for its use.[16] But if the moral standing of *ody fitia* had not much changed since Vig's time, the issues involved seemed to be entirely different. No one even suggested that *fanainga lavitra* was wrong because of the harm it could bring to its victims; in fact, it often did no immediate harm to them at all. What they stressed was that such medicine causes its victims to lose their autonomy, to act like slaves, to be completely at the will and bidding of another. And this is precisely what they stressed about more conventional forms of *ody fitia* as well. 'If a man always does whatever his wife tells him,' one woman told me, 'especially if she has him constantly out working, looking for new ways to get her money—that's how you can tell she probably knows how to use *ody fitia*.'

Bear in mind that most Malagasy medicine is not said to make its victims do anything. Legitimate medicine prevents others from acting; witchcraft attacks them. In fact, almost all forms of medicine which *are* said to have a direct effect on their victims' behavior are considered varieties of *ody fitia*.

And the one or two exceptions that do exist are looked on with much the same attitude of suspicion. A good case in point are ody used to protect crops from theft. Now, this is a purpose which would seem on the face of it about as intrinsically legitimate as one could get. Almost all farmers in Imerina use some variety of medicine to protect their crops, and most fields are decorated with *kiady*, flags of brightly colored strips of cloth and plastic or poles topped with bundled straw. These usually contain medicine said to guard against birds or animals, and perhaps also to prevent thieves from entering the field or alert the owner if they do. Some downplayed the importance of the medicine in *kiady* altogether, saying they were mainly just marks of ownership. Almost everyone stressed that any medicine they did contain was likely to be very mild in its effects. The really potent medicine, called *kalo*, tended to be buried in the ground rather than placed around the field on poles. Some *kalo* made thieves sick: if anyone ate food taken from the field protected by such a *kalo*, I was told, their feet or stomach would swell up to twice their normal size. Often they would die as a result. Almost everyone I talked to considered this simple witchcraft, not a legitimate way to protect one's crops. A more acceptable form of *kalo* trapped intruders: having entered the field, a would-be thief would find himself unable to leave it until the owner returned to release him. This, most considered inoffensive; but it was only one step from here to the most notorious variety of all, called *kalo mampiasa* or 'kalo which make one work'. A proprietor could leave a shovel or basket out on his property before heading home; if anyone entered the field intending to make off with it, or with the crops, he would suddenly be seized by the power of the medicine and find himself compelled to grab the tool and start working there, digging the owner's ditches or carrying his fertilizer for as long as it took him to return. These were clearly witchcraft, almost as reprehensible as poisoning one's victims outright, and most of the people I knew cast quite a jaundiced eye on anyone rumored to have anything to do with them.

I have suggested that these new concerns were the result of a general re-evaluation of modes of power and authority which followed the French conquest of Madagascar. Perhaps the easiest way to understand what happened is to follow the changing meaning of the term *fanompoana*, usually translated 'service', which is used throughout Madagascar to describe the obligations of subjects to their rulers and, secondarily, of slaves to their masters. In early Imerina, as in most Malagasy kingdoms, obligations to rulers centered on certain ceremonial tasks, particularly the building and rebuilding of royal houses and tombs. But in principle such obligations were unlimited; and under the Merina government that ruled most of Madagascar during the nineteenth century *fanompoana* was used to justify any number of newly created obligations, including a program of forced labor applied on a massive scale both in the provinces and in Imerina. After the French conquest colonial authorities continued the use of forced labor, which they too referred to as *fanompoana*.

In most of Madagascar, the French usage was not taken very seriously. Gillian Feeley-Harnik reports that the Sakalava people of western Madagascar never referred to colonial corvée labor as *fanompoana*, reserving the term instead for the ritual labor they continued to perform on royal tombs and dwellings. By continuing to carry out these rituals under French rule, she suggests, they were in effect making covert assertions about what they considered legitimate authority to be.[17] In Imerina, what happened was entirely different. There, the meaning of *fanompoana* had already been broadened before the French arrived to include most of the institutions— church, school, and government—that were soon to become the basis of colonial rule. Most Merina therefore seem to have accepted that what the French imposed on them was, indeed, a kind of *fanompoana*. Certainly, unlike Feeley-Harnik's Sakalava, they still refer to it as such today. The result was that the concept of *fanompoana* itself was thoroughly discredited. It came to be thought of not as service but as servitude, as something tantamount to slavery.

This change of meanings had profound consequences, in part because *fanompoana* had provided perhaps the only context in which it was considered appropriate for adults to give direct orders to each other. Within local communities and among kin, authority had long been seen most of all as a matter of imposing taboos or otherwise preventing others from acting, rather than telling people what to do.[18] Before the nineteenth century, the distinction between the two ways of exercising authority might have been little noticed; but after the French conquest, once the notion of *fanompoana* had become inextricably caught up in relations of servitude and foreign domination, it began to take on a broader political meaning. Traditional, ancestral authority—what I have called negative authority— became the only kind which people accepted as fully legitimate. It has come to be seen as the 'Malagasy' way of doing things and explicitly opposed to relations of command, which are seen as typical of foreigners and the French.

In other words, where other Malagasy have used relations of domination and control (and to be possessed by a spirit is to be under the control of another in about as total a form imaginable) to define a sort of autonomous, 'Malagasy' sphere for themselves in opposition to the colonizer, 'Malagasy' identity in Imerina has instead come to be based on the very rejection of such relations.

It is worth pointing out again that all this was not simply ideology, a utopian image of a Malagasy identity which could be counterposed to the French regime or, later, to the national government that replaced it. In fact, it was not really a self-consciously formulated ideology at all. It has always remained somewhat implicit, immanent in the moral standards by which people judge each other's actions, the traits they single out for criticism in others. I never heard anyone say 'we Malagasy do not give each other orders' (such a statement would have been obviously untrue); but the whole issue of giving orders had clearly become a tremendous problem, and this in turn has had all sorts of effects on domestic and political relations. These were the issues and anxieties that took shape in fears of *ody fitia*.

These issues and anxieties also had their roots in Imerina's historical experience. King Andrianampoinimerina (1789–1810) had already invoked the principle of *fanompoana* to draft his subjects into vast irrigation projects around the capital; but the reign of his son Radama (1810–1828) marks the real break with past traditions. After the British governor of Mauritius agreed to provide him with military trainers, missionary teachers and artisans, Radama used the principle of *fanompoana* as the basis for recruiting young men for a standing army, industrial projects, and mission schools. The army allowed Radama to expand Merina rule across most of Madagascar and, over the next several decades, to bring home a steady supply of captives to be sold as slaves. The influx of slaves, in turn, was to permanently transform the demography of Imerina. Property censuses carried out in the early 1840s indicate that slaves already made up about 40 per cent of the Merina population, and ownership was remarkably widespread.[19] Greater access to slave labor in turn allowed for increasing labor exactions on the free population. From the time of Radama, adult males not serving in the military were organized into brigades that were called up regularly for months of *fanompoana*. After Queen Ranavalona II converted to Protestant Christianity in 1869, the scope of *fanompoana* expanded even further to include compulsory education in mission schools, building of and attendance in local churches, and a host of new labor obligations. Most of these appear to have been widely resented, even while most Merina continued to accept the underlying principle of personal service to the sovereign.

The immediate effect on daily life was undoubtedly a vast growth in the scope of relations characterized by the direct giving and taking of orders. It is important to remember that the nineteenth-century Merina government was essentially a military government. Almost all important officials, even in the civil administration, held military rank, and civilian *fanompoana* brigades were organized in exactly the same way as military units. Even the schools—primary education became compulsory by the late 1870s—acted mainly as recruiting centers for the military. From the beginning, there is evidence that these principles of organization and conduct were considered profoundly alien from those which applied in everyday affairs, where authority was still imagined to be mainly a matter of preventing harmful actions. The Malagasy language did not even have a word for 'order' or 'command', and the term coined, *baiko*, had the additional meaning of 'foreign speech'.

But even within households, this was a time when more and more of the daily interaction was taking place between masters and slaves. In the early years, the slave population was made up overwhelmingly of women and children who were generally under the direct authority of their owners. But as the flow of slaves into Imerina tapered off in the 1850s and the proportion of slaves born to their condition increased, so too did the proportion of adult males. Apparently, owners found it extremely difficult to keep grown men under their systematic control. While the matter needs much further research, most male and a substantial proportion of female slaves appear to have won a large measure of autonomy, becoming a floating stratum of itinerant craftsmen, porters, laborers and petty traders who were only occasionally under the direction of their masters.[20] In addition, it appears that slaves were almost the only people willing to work as wage laborers. For instance, when in the 1880s abolitionists in England were scandalized to discover that Protestant missionaries were regularly being carried around by slaves and employing slaves as domestic servants, the missionaries insisted that despite their best efforts they had found it impossible to find anyone else willing to work for wages.[21]

In 1895 a French expeditionary force seized the Merina capital, Antananarivo. Within a year, Madagascar's new rulers had issued a series of edicts which abolished virtually all the institutions that had been the basis of the Merina state: the monarchy, aristocratic privileges and, finally and most dramatically, the institution of slavery itself. *Fanompoana* in fact was about the only major institution left in place. If anything, forced labor probably intensified in the first years of colonial rule, with the mass levying of men for such projects as the building of roads and bridges. Of course, under the colonial regime labor obligations applied equally to every inhabitant of Imerina, regardless of their former status; for masters and slaves to have to work side by side under foreign oversight must have made an enormous impression as a tangible expression of their new-found equality in common subjugation to the French.[22] In theory, *fanompoana* was maintained for only a few years. In reality, forced labor continued in one form or another until the late 1940s, maintained by an ever-changing series of laws and legal subterfuges. And since colonists found it extremely difficult to find anyone willing to sign labor contracts, additional laws were issued exempting those holding such contracts from corvée; this allowed employers to set pretty much whatever terms they cared to, and made wage labor appear from the Malagasy point of view a mere extension of forced labor, which in effect it was.[23]

During the first generation of colonial rule, the old rural elite largely abandoned the countryside, finding themselves places in the administration, commerce, or liberal professions and leaving their rice fields to be sharecropped by former slaves. Those who remained quickly fell into a fairly uniform poverty. Partible inheritance and constant migration to new lands may have prevented any extreme disparities of wealth from re-emerging, but the steady increase of population also ensured that most families did not have access to enough land to support themselves. This process only intensified with independence, by which time almost everyone in Imerina was forced to combine farming with crafts, petty commerce, wage labor, or some combination of the three.

Wage labor is by far the least popular alternative. Most descendants of free people will only fall back on agricultural day-labor when there is absolutely no alternative, and even then prefer to work for kin on a temporary basis. In the countryside and small towns where the vast majority of Merina live, long-term relations of wage labor between adults basically do not exist. Even in the city they are rare, outside of the very limited formal sector which consists mainly of the government itself and other colonial institutions. The only stratum of the population that does not share this aversion to wage labor is composed of the descendants of slaves, still a third of the population, and still considered a caste apart, who do not, generally speaking, intermarry with the descendants of former slave-owners. With little access to land or other resources, they follow much the same occupations they did at the end of the nineteenth century. They remain the only people who are normally willing to work for wages.

Two years after the emancipation of 1896, a colonial official wrote,

> Questioned on this occasion, a woman of the highest caste of nobility, rich, the owner of numerous slaves, responded with melancholy: 'What does it matter if our slaves have been freed? Haven't all Malagasy, beginning with the Queen, now become slaves of the French?'[24]

If this was a mere figure of speech, it has proved a remarkably enduring one. Even when talking with very well-educated people I would often hear comments like 'the French you know treated their slaves much better than the British', referring by this to policies of colonial rule. Discussions of chattel slavery would slip seamlessly into discussions of colonialism and back. In fact, almost all political relationships, including those identified with the Merina kingdom itself, appear to have been re-evaluated and largely reshaped in the popular imagination through assimilation with slavery. In modern Malagasy the meaning of the word *fanompoana* is closer to the English term 'servitude' than it is to 'service'; it implies work carried out under threat of coercion, and is most often used as a euphemism for slavery.[25] There were any number of such euphemisms. One of the more striking was 'soldier'. It took me some time to figure out that when someone recounting oral traditions referred to a lord's 'soldiers', they usually meant his slaves; in fact, the terms 'soldier' and 'slave' were often used interchangeably—a startling identification, since in the nineteenth century slaves would have been the last people ever allowed to carry guns. The connection seemed to be simply that both were people who obey orders. In oral traditions, historical relations of command always tended to be treated as so many refractions of slavery, and therefore as essentially unjust.

But if slavery had the importance it did in setting the measure of all other relations, this did not mean it was a subject anyone enjoyed discussing. It was more the sort of issue that no one wanted to talk about but everyone always seemed to end up talking about anyway, if only in hushed tones and euphemistic language, whenever they talked about the past. It was as if the continuing presence of a population of ex-slaves, living in close if often uncomfortable proximity with the descendants of their former masters, had made the whole issue so troubling that it had to be continually hidden, until in the end it began to be seen as the hidden reality behind everything.[26]

This attitude was almost certainly the legacy of the early years of colonial occupation. By the time the French appeared on the scene, the meaning of *fanompoana* had already been broadened to include obligations to pay taxes, perform military service, attend state schools and even churches—all the institutions that were soon to become the bulwarks of the colonial state. The organization of such institutions was already seen as essentially military, based on relations in which some were giving orders and others were expected to obey without question, and therefore as standing at a certain remove from daily life. After the French conquest, this remove became a chasm. Colonial phrase books, for instance, leave one with the impression that French officials and colonists hardly spoke to their subjects in anything but the imperative voice. (In literary Malagasy French is still known as *ny teny baiko*, 'the language of command.' One is reminded, too, of the proverb *aza manao Vazaha fito antrano*. A Malagasy version of 'too many cooks spoil the broth', it literally means 'don't act like seven French people all in the same house'—the idea being that if this were to happen everyone would just sit around giving everyone else orders and nothing would get done.) At the same time, in the small towns and rural villages where most of the population lived, people appear to have become increasingly averse to using imperative forms at all. When Elinor Ochs carried out a socio-linguistic study in a Merina village in the late 1960s, her informants insisted that giving direct orders to another person was not a 'Malagasy' way to behave, explicitly contrasting it with the manners of the city and the French.[27]

I should point out here that while I have been following conventional usage and calling these people Merina, I never heard anyone there spontaneously refer to themselves as such. They always spoke of themselves as 'Malagasy', just as they spoke of 'Malagasy' customs, 'Malagasy' beliefs, and 'Malagasy' forms of knowledge, all of which they defined in contrast to those they considered foreign, European, or French. After the French conquest, then, all these institutions (forced labor, wage labor, military, schools) came to be seen as so many tokens of foreign domination, analogous with slavery, and people's identity as Malagasy became in large part defined in opposition to them. One reason the constant reminders of slavery in daily life became so embarrassing, then, was that they made clear that Merina had once treated their fellow Malagasy in the same way as foreigners were now treating them. It had become an acute contradiction within their sense of national identity.

This political identity became embedded in daily life and standards of moral judgment. The reluctance openly to command others is part of a more general aversion to any relationship in which one party is seen as directing the actions of another. I think this aversion is the real explanation for the reluctance to engage in wage labor. Most rural people nowadays will occasionally hire themselves out as day laborers; but when they do, they work in teams that operate autonomously. Often I found myself watching workers hired to replant or harvest someone else's rice fields animatedly discussing how best to proceed while their employer watched silently from a few yards away, not presuming to tell them how to go about their task. Even fathers would avoid openly directing their adult children; in fact, of all the inhabitants of a rural community, the older men who were its primary figures of authority were also the least likely to be seen giving orders in public. Their quintessential role was seen to lie in preventing any action that might prove disruptive to solidarity: breaking up fights or 'admonishing' the young when their individualistic projects seem likely to lead to conflict.

Perhaps if one had shown up in a Merina village two hundred years ago, things would have not looked very different. But once the principle of *fanompoana* began to be identified with foreign domination, this sort of negative authority became the only kind people took to be wholly legitimate. To be Malagasy came to mean rejecting entanglement in relations of command as far as it was practical to do so.

Madagascar of course is no longer a French colony, but these attitudes have by no means disappeared. The rural population (and for that matter the bulk of the urban poor) still tend to see the government and governing class as existing at a certain fundamental remove from 'Malagasy' life. As one might expect, the educated, urban elite, who live their lives in a context of cash employment, have a much more accepting attitude towards relations of command.[28] Even in the country, though, relations of command have not been by any means eliminated. They continue to exist, if often in rather euphemistic forms, in any number of different aspects of daily life. Teachers and bureaucrats have affected a more consensual, 'Malagasy' style since independence, but the schools and offices are basically the same. Malagasy do hire one another, if rarely for very long; elders do direct other people's actions, if usually indirectly or under a consensual veneer. Like memories of slavery, relations of command in everyday life tend to be suppressed and hidden, and as such they become social issues much more important than they would otherwise have been.

From here it's easy to see how the pieces fall together. While something like an ethic of negative authority had long existed in Imerina, during the twentieth century it came to be explicitly framed as the true 'Malagasy' ethic and opposed to relations of command, which were increasingly conceived as intrinsically foreign, military, oppressive and unjust. However, such a position was full of obvious contradictions. First of all, everyone was perfectly well aware that Malagasy people used to treat each other this way: there were once kings and slaves, and both still had descendants whose typical occupations were not so very different from their ancestors'. More immediately, there is a reason why all languages have imperative forms; it is absurd to imagine a society in which no one ever told anyone else what to do.

Not only was the ideal of negative authority practically impossible; it also created a social world rife with hidden purposes, in which everyone— elders most of all, perhaps—was trying to influence others to do things without being able to fully acknowledge they were doing it. It was in this social environment that people in towns and villages across Imerina began to grow increasingly concerned with the prospect of women enslaving men by means of medicine; with images of people seized by *fanainga lavitra*, compelled to travel to their summoners; with thieves forced to spend the night carrying baskets of manure for their intended victims. Not all of these dangers were identified with women. But many were. Perhaps the most dramatic change, in fact, involved images of witches, which during the colonial period became increasingly interwoven with ideas about *ody fitia*.

I should explain here that the term *mpamosavy*, which I have rendered 'witch' or 'sorcerer', has always had two somewhat different meanings. On the one hand, it can refer to anyone—archetypically, to men—driven by envy, spite, and resentment to harm others by means of medicine. But there are also 'witches who go out at night', creatures of absolute depravity who prowled the surroundings of Merina villages after dusk. These were the ultimate image of moral evil. Even in the nineteenth century, they were also seen as predominantly women:

> No village is free from supposed witches, who are said to take their walks abroad at midnight to visit the tombs, on top of which they dance and revile the dead. They are said to be mainly elderly females of sinister aspect, joined by young women of bad character, with occasional male associates…. At the dead of night they knock at the doors of neighbors they wish to injure, and should there be anyone sick, they howl most dismally around the house.[29]

Witches were said to gather together to plan and carry out their more elaborate acts of sorcery, or terrorize those keeping vigil over the dead, accompanied by wild cats and owls. They went about naked, their clothing bundled on their heads and their fingers tipped with poisons. They had tremendous, uncanny strength, could span great distances almost instantly, dive into moats or out of windows and land unscathed.

As for how these women became witches, only one source—Vig again—suggests an explanation. 'According to Malagasy ideas, whoever lends himself to the adoration of a charm is drawn irresistibly to do whatever that charm's task may be.'[30] The power of ody, the reader will recall, was seen as coming from an invisible spirit, which gave it a consciousness and agency of its own. Witches, then, were people taken over by their own evil medicine, people who were driven by spite and resentment to harm others until finally the power of their ody drove them to band together with others of the same kind and work evil for its own sake. Indeed, most nineteenth-century descriptions of witches focus on the elaborate ceremonies bands of witches would undertake at night, including elaborate mock funerals, to make new victims waste away and die.

Many of these details still appear in descriptions of modern-day Merina witches; witches still dance on tombs, for instance, and they still have the same extraordinary physical powers. But the emphasis on malicious sorcery, mock funerals and the like has very much faded into the background. Instead, almost everyone insisted to me that, if women ended up prowling the outskirts of villages at night, it was not because of the abuse of malicious medicine but because of the abuse of *ody fitia*.

The way it was commonly expressed was this: if a woman uses too much love medicine or gets love medicine that is 'too powerful', she may in the end be overwhelmed by the power of her own medicine.[31] When night falls, the ody's spirit will take possession of its owner in much the same way an evil ghost possesses a victim of *ambalavelona*, or the soul of an ancient king who possesses a medium. Such witches are no longer in control of their own actions; by some accounts they are not even conscious of them. 'Carried' by the power of their ody, they strip off their clothes and abandon their houses to find and meet with other witches and work evil.[32] Women would usually insist that the typical witch was an old woman; but I suspect this mainly reflects the fact that older women, particularly those who head households or are otherwise independent, were the most likely to be suspected by their neighbors of 'going out at night'. Just about everyone I talked to who claimed to have themselves had run-ins with witches were men, and they always seemed to have a more sexualized image of a younger woman in mind.

Accounts of what happens to a man unfortunate enough to meet up with a witch at night were pretty much unanimous. If you see the witch before she sees you, then generally speaking you'll be able to get away. But if she sees you first, she will immediately make use of her ody and you will suddenly find yourself unable to move or even to cry out. Once captured, the helpless victim may be tormented by the witch—or more likely by a group of them—in various (usually vaguely specified) ways. But what witches are really famous for is riding men like horses. (This is always something women do to men; people would laugh when I so much as suggested other possibilities.) They mount their victims' backs and drive

them along until dawn, they make them eat dirt or otherwise abase themselves, and finally they abandon them, filthy and exhausted, on their door-
steps before dawn. Often, the victim awakes with only distant memories of
his ordeal; sometimes he is mute for days afterwards and cannot speak of
it; in extreme cases, his strength never returns to him and he dies.

In the last century witchcraft was a nightmare image of human malevo-
lence carried to its ultimate extremes. In the twentieth century, it has
become an extension of love medicine. And if stories about love medicine
told nowadays can be said to reflect a deep-seated suspicion of any sort
of relationship in which one person gains complete control of the actions
of another, the image of a woman 'carried' by her medicine riding a man
who is 'carried by' her, of a man possessed by a woman who is herself
possessed by a charm, is one of control stripped of any rationale or even of
any agent. An ody, after all, has no identity apart from its purpose, so that
a witch's ody is really a pure abstraction, the sheer desire to dominate
others and nothing else. Stories about women who try to win over men
through medicine but who end up riding men at night are fantasies about
the principle of control bursting all possible boundaries, stories which,
through an elaborate series of reversals and displacements, end up in a
rather similar place to those about nineteenth-century *ody fitia*: in a highly
sexualized image of degradation and cruelty.

Why, finally, should it be women in particular who are seen as embodying
the frightening power of command—a power which, after all, is otherwise
located mainly in images of slave-owning lords and French colonial
officials? This is a subtle question, and no doubt there are many reasons.
But one is obvious: Merina women tend to use the imperative form much
more than do men.

Ochs makes a great point of this in her analysis of speech patterns.
Avoiding giving others orders in public, she said, was part of a broader
feeling that one should never place others in a situation which might prove
publicly embarrassing. But it was men in particular, and most of all, older
men in positions of authority, who were expected to behave this way. Men
were assumed to be by nature more discrete, shy, and less competitive than
women, whose behavior even in public was more assertive and direct. This
was even more true within the household, where women are very much in
charge. Older women especially spend much of their time issuing orders
and coordinating tasks, casually dispatching siblings and children off on
errands. (Rarely if ever did I see a man giving a direct order to a woman;
but I very often saw women using the imperative form when speaking with
men.) Having read Ochs's work before I arrived in Madagascar, I was rather
surprised to discover how often the imperative form actually was used in
such contexts. And when I asked women why men were so much more
reserved in public and women so forthright, they would almost invariably

reply that women were responsible for running households and had to be assertive in order to do so.

But as Maurice Bloch has pointed out,[33] it is precisely through such mild postures that older men assert their authority: by acting this way, they are seen as embodying in their own comportment the solidarity and moral unity of the community as a whole. In public fora, it is women's very direct manners, their greater propensity, if not to issue commands, then at least to make direct demands on others, to propose schemes of action, which ensures they will not be seen as real figures of authority. There are few formal barriers to women becoming elders, but in fact they only rarely do. This is not only because of styles of action. It is also because it is precisely those women who are the most obvious candidates for an independent political role, especially the venerable women heads of large families or other older, independent women, who are most likely to be accused of 'knowing *ody fitia*' or even 'going out at night', sufficient tarnish on any-one's character to ensure they can never be taken seriously as public figures. For most women the only safe way to achieve a position of public influence is indirect, as the wife, mother or daughter of some significant man. The end result of course is that Merina women (like any group with little or no access to the formal mechanisms of power) tend to acquire a reputation as manipulators, which, in turn, ends up reinforcing the impression that they are more likely than men to have access to mysterious powers.

We are left with an image of three social levels, each with its own arche-typal figure of authority. On the level of the household, this was the woman giving orders, directly overseeing household tasks; on the communal level, most closely identified with 'Malagasy' tradition, the mild and self-effacing male elder, ready to step in to break up disputes and impose restrictions but otherwise a passive embodiment of solidarity; on the level of the over-arching state, a whole plethora of images—the colonial official barking orders, the military officer or gendarme, the ancient king with his retinue of 'soldiers'—of figures who operate within formal hierarchies of command. If nothing else, this makes it easier to understand the political color that talk of *ody fitia* always seemed to take. A woman who used love medicine in fact was often said to 'rule' over her husband (the same word used for kings or governments[34]) or even to 'enslave' him. Even in its most fantastic forms, where it detached itself from any human purposes and became a sheer force of domination that turned its owners into night-riding witches, it was still basically a political image, of a certain type of power distilled to its purest form and, in so far as it was also an image of utter evil, perhaps the single most dramatic statement of the ethos of negative authority. It was as if the moment a woman was in a position to exert any real authority or even influence on the communal level, she was likely to be accused of secretly drawing on arcane powers to exert a shadowy version of the very kind of foreign authority against which the communal sphere defined itself.

All this of course is something of an abstraction; political reality is much more complicated. For one thing, it is overwhelmingly women who actually tell these stories. This seems to make the narrators prime agents in their own political suppression, but since women by such means control much of the moral discourse about public affairs, it is also one of the main ways in which women do exert political influence. While there is hardly room here to go into the subtleties of practice, it might help to end with an illustration.

A friend of mine from Arivonimamo told me that when she was eight or nine, her father, then a wealthy and respected teacher, became obsessed with another woman. Before long he had moved in with her and began running through his savings to shower her with gifts, all the time sending his wife and numerous small children back empty-handed whenever they would come begging for support. What she particularly remembers about those trips, she said, was that at dinner, the woman would be openly scraping bits of wood into his food. The psychology was no doubt complex but, at the very least, by doing so she provided him with a ready-made alibi to excuse his behavior in the eyes of his family. Not that it was completely successful. He came back to his family a year or two later, but his daughter has hardly spoken to him since.

In the beginning of this essay, I suggested that the fantasies surrounding *ody fitia* have always been fantasies about power. Stories about medicine were perhaps the closest there was to an abstract idiom in which the nature of power itself could be defined. In both periods, images of power in the raw were almost always images of women: in the nineteenth century, of the woman invested with sudden and overwhelming strength, tearing herself from the arms of her family (from their entirely vain effort, one might say, to exert negative authority), or in the twentieth century, of night witches, with their uncanny speed and physical strength. These stories were not just a medium through which people could think about the nature of power; even more, they were a medium through which they could argue about its rights and wrongs. It was through endless arguments about hidden powers and hidden motives—about envy, sexual desire, pride, greed, resentment—that people worked out their common understandings of how it was legitimate for human beings to influence each other. In this light it is not surprising that the basic logic of what I have been calling negative authority was first made explicit in the ethic of protection, that is, in ways of talking about the morality of medicine, long before it emerged as a way of imagining a traditional Malagasy political morality. This also makes it easier to understand how intimate anxieties and domestic politics could have been transformed as a result. After all, these might have been ways of imagining power and authority, but they were not abstractions; they were the kind of representations, one might say, that helped to bring into being the things they represented. Political reality—and by this I mean both domestic or sexual politics and communal or national politics, in so far as these terms have any reality in practice—can never really be distinguished from its representations, if only because politics itself is largely a matter of manipulating and arguing about representations, of circulating stories and trying to control how those stories are interpreted. This was a game in which Merina women were certainly as much players as were men.

Notes

I would like to thank Jennifer Cole, Jean Comaroff, Gillian Feeley-Harnik, Michael Lambek, Pier Larson, Nhu Thi Le, Stuart Rockefeller, Marshall Sahlins, Johanna Schoss, and Raymond T. Smith for all sorts of useful comments and suggestions. My fieldwork in Madagascar was funded by a Fullbright/IEE. I should also note that the language and people of Madagascar are referred to as Malagasy, the inhabitants of Imerina are called Merina, and *ody fitia* is pronounced OOD fee-TEE.

1. A Foucauldian approach might emphasize how imported disciplines of education or hygiene transformed domestic relations, but this is not my project either. At least among the majority of people in Imerina, colonial disciplines did not really have so direct an impact on the kind of issues I am dealing with here.

2. The richest source on nineteenth-century ody is the catalogue assembled by the Norwegian Lutheran missionary, Lars Vig, between 1875 and 1902, entitled *Charmes: Spécimens de Magie Malgache* (Universitetsforlagets Trykningssentral, Oslo, 1969). But there is a fairly abundant literature, including material by Malagasy authors: R. P. Callet, *Tantara ny Andriana Eto Madagasikara* (Academie Malgache, Tananarive, 1908), pp. 82–103. Other European authors include: Lars Dahle, 'Sikidy and Vintana: Half-Hours with Malagasy Diviners', *Antananarivo Annual and Malagasy Magazine*, 11 (1886), pp. 218–34, 12 (1887), pp. 315–24, and 13 (1888), pp. 457–67; William Edmunds, 'Charms and Superstitions in Southeast Imerina', *Antananarivo Annual and Malagasy Magazine*, 22 (1897), pp. 61–7; Charles Renel, 'Les amulettes malgaches, Ody et Sampy', *Bulletin de la Academie Malgache*, (n.s.) 2 (1915), pp. 29–281. Some material extends to the middle of the present century: S. Bernard-Thierry, 'Perles magiques à Madagascar', *Journal des Africanistes*, 29 (1959), pp. 33–90; Jørgen Ruud, *Taboo: A Study of Malagasy Beliefs and Customs* (Humanities Press, New York, 1969). I have discussed the relation between spirit and object in much greater detail in 'Beads and Money: notes toward a theory of wealth and power', *American Ethnologist*, 23 (1996), pp. 1–36.

3. Richard Andriamanjato, *Le Tsiny et le Tody dans la pensée Malgache* [Blame and Retribution in Malagasy thought] (Presénce Africaine, Paris, 1957).

4. John Haile, 'Malagasy Village Life: Pen and Ink Sketches of the People of Western Imerina', *Antananarivo Annual and Malagasy Magazine*, 17 (1893), pp. 12–13.

5. My information is drawn mainly (though not exclusively) from women, whereas the nineteenth-century material was presumably drawn almost entirely from men, which may be the cause of some distortion. But I did talk to dozens of men as well, and never found their basic understanding of *ody fitia* to be significantly different. If anything, women were more likely to point out that men could occasionally employ such medicine, perhaps because for them the fact was more a matter of immediate practical concern.

6. Since all the accounts I draw on assume a female victim, when speaking in the abstract, it seems best to follow their usage. Still, the reader should note that Vig at least occasionally indicates that any of these charms could be used by women against men, and cites two charms said to have been used primarily by women. Vig, *Charmes*, pp. 94–7.

7. Vig, *Charmes*, pp. 30–1. Here as elsewhere, my translation from the French.

8. Vig, *Charmes*, p. 92.

9. Vig, *Charmes*, pp. 87–8.

10. Vig, *Charmes*, pp. 84–97.

11. If a woman was consistently 'proud', he notes, this was felt to be an affront to sociability. 'The man could tell her "why are you proud towards me? ... The custom of our ancestors applies to us all."' 'During the persecution of Christians under Ranavalona I,' he adds, 'one accusation made against the Christians was that their wives were chaste ....' Vig, *Charmes*, p. 20.

12. Callet, *Tantara ny Andriana*, pp. 106–7.

13. Callet, *Tantara ny Andriana*, pp. 106 and 108.

14. The condition, called *ambalavelona*, was often said to have been used by rejected suitors out of spite. It involved many of the symptoms Vig described—the great strength of the woman, the raving, the fits, the throwing off of clothes in public—but it was never thought of as inspiring love. It was merely a means of revenge.

15. Other medicines referred to as 'kinds of *ody fitia*' included *tsy tia mainty* ('to despise', or literally 'hate blackly'), which causes enmity to rise up between lovers or spouses, and *manara mody* ('follows one home'), the ody used by coastal women to kill their Merina lovers and which apparently killed the man with three cows. Most considered *manara mody* a form of witchcraft pure and simple, and some denied it was a kind of *ody fitia* at all. In every story of its use I heard, however, it was used in conjunction with other forms of *ody fitia*.

16. Even women whose lovers abandoned them on learning they were pregnant would not publicly admit to having used *fanainga lavitra* to bring them back. The only people I found willing (quietly) to admit they had employed it were a married couple who had used it to recover a teenage daughter who had run away from home.

17. Gillian Feeley-Harnik, *A Green Estate: Restoring Independence in Madagascar* (Smithsonian Institution Press, Washington, D.C., 1991), p. 349. Something along these lines appears to have happened throughout most of Madagascar during the colonial period; *tromba* cults, in which the spirits of ancient kings began to possess the living and demand ritual propitiation, brought royal service even to parts of the island which had never been ruled by kings at all. See Gérard Althabe, *Oppression et libération dans l'imaginaire: les communautés villageoises de la côte orientale de Madagascar* (Maspero, Paris, 1969). Here too, *fanompoana* rendered to ancient kings became a principle by which people could assert their cultural autonomy in the face of colonial rule.

18. I have written of the importance of taboo in 'Dancing with Corpses Reconsidered: An Interpretation of Famadihana in Arivonimamo (Madagascar)', *American Ethnologist*, 22 (1995), pp. 258–78, and in more detail about negative authority in 'The Disastrous Ordeal of 1987: Memory and Violence in Rural Madagascar' (Ph.D. diss., University of Chicago, 1996), ch. 3.

19. While the class of truly large-scale slave-owners was always relatively small, perhaps only the poorest fifth of Merina households had no access to slave labor whatever. Most of the figures that follow are derived from documents preserved in the IIICC and EE sections of the Malagasy National Archives.

20. Owners would usually accept a portion of their earnings and expect their attendance at certain critical moments, such as harvest, when labor was in particular demand. But it was often difficult to enforce even these requirements, and some masters appear to have been forced to pay wages to their own slaves. The situation was further complicated by the fact that by the end of the century partible inheritance had ensured that many slaves, perhaps most, had several different masters. For some contemporary accounts see Joseph Sewell, *Remarks on Slavery in Madagascar* (Elliot Stock, London, 1876); William Cousins, 'The Abolition of Slavery in Madagascar: with Some Remarks on Malagasy Slavery Generally', *Antananarivo Annual and Malagasy Magazine*, 21 (1896), pp. 446–50; and J.-B. Piolet, 'De l'Esclavage à Madagascar,' *Le Correspondant* (Paris), 10 February 1896, pp. 447–80.

21. See the debate in the *Anti-Slavery Reporter*, February–March 1883.

22. The transformation affected women as well as men; some observers note that many wealthy women had to learn to do manual labor for the first time in their lives after the liberation of their slaves. John Pearse, 'Women in Madagascar: Their Social Position, Employments and Influence', *Antananarivo Annual and Malagasy Magazine*, 23 (1899), pp. 263–64.

23. Jean Fremigacci, 'Mise en valeur coloniale et travail forcé: la construction du chemin de fer Tananarive-Antsirabe (1911–1923)', *Omaly sy Anio*, 1–2 (1975), pp. 75–137, and Jean Fremigacci, 'L'administration coloniale: les aspects oppressifs', *Omaly sy Anio*, 7–8 (1978), pp. 209–37; Jean-Pierre Raison, *Les Hautes Terres de Madagascar et leurs Confins Occidentaux: enracinement et mobilité des sociétés rurales* (Karthala, Paris, 1984), pp. 180–4.

24. Jean Carol, *Chez les Hova (au pays rouge)* (Pavanne, Paris, 1898), pp. 38–9.

25. I do not believe that in all the time I was in Imerina I ever heard the term used with anything but negative connotations. Apart from its political meaning, the only other phrase in which I heard it employed was the expression *fanompoana sampy* ('serving the idols'), adopted by the missionaries to translate the English 'heathenism'. The expression is only used as a term of denigration; no one, no matter how nominal their Christianity, would ever apply it to themselves.

26. This was much less true of the educated, urban elite than it was with rural people, white or black. Members of the former class would often speak quite casually about their 'ancestors' slaves' (*andevon-drazana*), clearly seeing their existence as a token of their former glory. Rural people, on the other hand, when they did discuss the matter openly, made it equally clear that they saw it as evidence of their ancestors' misdeeds. Quite a number who claimed noble descent confided in me that they believed their own present-day poverty was a judgment rendered on their ancestors for having kept other Malagasy as slaves.

27. Elinor [Ochs] Keenan, 'Norm-makers, Norm-breakers: Uses of Speech by Men and Women in a Malagasy Community', in *Explorations in the Ethnography of Speaking*, ed. Robert Bauman and John Sherzer (Cambridge University Press, Cambridge, 1974), pp. 125–43; quotations from pp. 131–4. See also Elinor [Ochs] Keenan, 'A Sliding Sense of Obligatoriness: The Polystructure of Malagasy Oratory', *Language in Society*, 2 (1975), pp. 225–43.

28. Interestingly, so do the descendants of their former slaves, who were also considered more loyal to the colonial regime, and more amenable than other Merina not only to wage labor but also to taking part in the hierarchically organized institutions identified with it; for instance, they served in greatly disproportionate numbers in the military and police, as well as converting in large numbers to Catholicism. Significantly,

too, I found them to be much more accepting of the use of *kalo* and even certain varieties of *ody fitia* than other Merina.

29. Haile, 'Pen and Ink Sketches', p. 11. Other sources on nineteenth-century witches include James Sibree, *Madagascar: the Great African Island* (Trübner & Co., London, 1880), p. 202; Bessie Graham, 'Notes', in 'Report of the Medical Mission for 1882', *Friends' Foreign Missionary Society Annual Report*, 62–64 (1883), pp. 62–3; Vig, *Charmes*, pp. 112–24.

30. 'So the brigands and thieves who present themselves to me to be catechized throw away their charms, being persuaded that they will lead them back to their careers as brigands without their being able to resist'. Vig, *Charmes*, pp. 123–4.

31. *Tsy mahazaka an'ilay herin'ilay fanafody.*

32. Unfortunately there is very little literature on witchcraft from the colonial period itself. The one exception is Mary Danielli, 'The Witches of Madagascar', *Folklore*, 58 (1947), pp. 261–76. Danielli's information, which comes from exactly half-way between my two periods, also offers a kind of unique synthesis between the two sets of ideas: there are *ody fitia* which simply cause love and devotion, Danielli's informants told her, and these women do not become witches; but some love medicine has punitive effects, driving its victims mad or making them violently ill, and it is women who acquire this type of medicine who end up becoming possessed and 'going out at night'. I never heard anything of the sort when I was there.

33. Maurice Bloch, 'Death, Women and Power', in *Death and the Regeneration of Life*, ed. M. Bloch and J. Parry (Cambridge University Press, Cambridge, 1982), pp. 211–30; Maurice Bloch, *From Blessing to Violence: history and ideology in the circumcision ritual of the Merina of Madagascar* (Cambridge University Press, Cambridge, 1986). Aside from Elinor Ochs's work, Pier Larson has contributed important insights into differences in male and female speech: see Larson, 'Multiple Narratives, Gendered Voices: Remembering the Past in Highland Central Madagascar', *The International Journal of African Historical Studies*, 28 (1995), pp. 295–325.

34. *Manjaka* ('to rule', nominalized as *fanjakana*, 'government') is in fact the reciprocal of *manompo* (to serve, nominalized as *fanompoana*). 'To enslave' is *manandevo*.

'Fork Up and Smile': Marketing, Colonial Knowledge and the Female Subject in Zimbabwe

TIMOTHY BURKE

In 1959, Nimrod Mkele, a South African advertising agent employed by the firm of J. Walter Thompson, commented to his colleagues: 'You will have noticed the highly significant role that women are playing ... they are bringing in new tastes into African homes. After all, it is they who determine what shall or shall not be bought. The role of a hubby is to fork up and smile.'[1] Mkele's comment reflected a broad consensus among his professional contemporaries. In identifying and imagining an allegedly untapped 'African market', these men argued that African women were identical socially to 'the' consumer and that the project of making Africans into mass-market consumers in the postcolonial world necessarily had to address itself to what advertisers saw as distinctively female practices and female roles in indigenous African culture.

From the beginnings of industrial capitalism to the contemporary era, a wide variety of discourses and institutions in Euro-American societies have depicted or imagined the consumer and practices of consumption as characteristically female. As a leading American advertising executive put it in 1970, 'we in the advertising business instinctively think of the customer as a woman. Because, for the most part, she is. Men make money, women spend it.... In order to sell a woman anything, you have to appeal to her tastes.... Step away from the world you're in and get into her shoes.'[2] In this article, I will argue that efforts by capitalist professionals to connect female subjects and consumer markets within modern southern Africa were predicated to a significant degree on colonial institutions and discourses about gender and race and, as a result, developed some of the characteristic contradictions and crises endemic to colonial culture. I am primarily concerned with the ideological and discursive figuration of the consumer as female by transnational advertisers, marketers and manufacturers from the 1920s to the present in Zimbabwe and South Africa, thus speaking to the gendering of consumption in the 'imaginary landscape' of transnational capitalism. But what exactly is 'gendering' in this sense? Does it describe the internal discourse of capitalist manufacturing, the way that it imagined the construction of mass markets in underdeveloped societies? Or is gendering best used to describe the ideological presumptions about audiences and consumer psychology built into the actual text of advertisements in southern Africa? Perhaps we should speak of the gendering of consumption itself, the actual distribution of commodity purchase, ownership and use between men and women in a particular society.

In some measure, all of these aspects of consumption can be described as gendered, and none of them can be easily disconnected from the others. The internally circulated perceptions of capitalist professionals have powerful effects both on the content of advertising and on the development of marketplaces; in turn, both the content of advertising and the configuration of marketing strategies help to construct social practice among consumers themselves. At the same time, these varying experiences pose separate analytic challenges. Multinational corporations have perceived Third World women from within transnational institutions which have been materially and ideologically connected to other institutions of colonial and neocolonial domination. On the other hand, the way that women in urban southern Africa have made use of Sunlight Soap is only *directly* comparable to the experience of women elsewhere in the colonial and postcolonial world through unsatisfying and unspoken axioms about the essential unity of the 'Third World woman' as a subject. Lines of connection exist, but they should be traced back through transnationally salient pathways: common advertising campaigns, marketing techniques, and colonial laws regulating women. Seizing upon singular gendered features in these local consuming practices and casually regarding them comparatively would be a surrender to what Mike Featherstone has described as the leading 'temptation' of current approaches to global culture, an emptying out of deep histories for a momentary voyeurism.[3]

In describing the influence of colonial thought on postwar marketing in the developing world, it is important to begin with a look at the historical development of transnational marketing in the capitalist periphery. In the first two decades of the twentieth century, professionalized advertising and market research were only just securing a niche within *metropolitan* capitalism. At the same time, most investment in Europe's colonies was oriented towards extraction. Proletarianizing processes were typically uneven in many locations throughout the colonized world. As a consequence, colonial subjects consumed manufactured goods sporadically as wage earners in a cash economy. There were considerable prewar markets for manufactured goods among colonized peoples, but much of this exchange was fundamentally governed by older mercantile patterns of global trade, or was supplied by classically nineteenth-century industrial concerns rather than by the new modern monopoly firms which were at the heart of metropolitan capitalism by the 1920s. In colonial Zimbabwe, much of the merchandise sold by so-called 'truck' merchants, retailers who sold goods to African customers, involved cheap textiles produced either in the old industrial heartland of England or in peripheral factories in Japan, India or Argentina.

As a consequence, advertising in the colonial world generally tended to be spottily developed prior to and immediately following World War II. In her studies of the history of global advertising, Noreene Janus has accurately described international advertising up to the 1960s as 'anything but well controlled and functional'.[4] The historic shifts in the world system that developed during and after World War II, including the dominance of American businesses over European concerns, expanded and reoriented transnational marketing and advertising in southern Africa. The 1950s saw significant new investments by multinational corporations, resulting in the growth of local manufacturing, mostly in light consumer industries producing such goods as tinned foods, soaps and other toiletries, clothing, alcoholic beverages, patent medicines and cigarettes. Their manufacture necessarily required a mass market, which white settlers or administrators alone could not possibly provide. In contrast, indigenous Africans throughout the region were already important consumers of industrially produced commodities, both imported and local, and had been so since the 1920s. In addition to clothing, Africans consumed agricultural implements, medicines, foodstuffs, soaps, bicycles and gramophones.

The characteristically modern capitalist enterprises that moved to the economic forefront in the region after World War II were driven by both practical considerations and the momentum of institutional practice and discourse to seek the consolidation of complex and diffuse prewar channels of distribution and exchange that shaped Africans' consumer habits. The postwar objective was to establish what manufacturers considered to be 'normal' markets among Africans. The firms that spearheaded this drive—such as Unilever, the giant British multinational firm particularly known for its production of toiletries and foodstuffs—looked most centrally to their marketing and advertising divisions as the institutional tools which could facilitate this consolidation and expansion.

Similar projects, though as yet relatively little studied by historians and political economists, seem to have taken place across the developing world during the postwar era, though conditioned by local and regional histories.[5] Judging from the case of southern Africa, the labor of the advertisers who were called upon to imagine and organize mass markets in the capitalist periphery after World War II was influenced not only by large-scale features of the world system but also by pre-existing local institutional and ideological arrangements of colonial hegemony. This occurred not only because of the inertial weight of the past but also because of concrete connections between transnational advertising and the colonial state. Marketing firms in southern Africa acquired many of their copywriters and researchers during their postwar expansion into the 'African market' from state offices dedicated to 'native administration' or from the anthropology departments of local universities.

Making a mass market from the raw material of ex-colonial subjects was a deeply contradictory project, understood by Western professionals as the conversion of alien peoples with alien needs into individuals possessed of a putatively new and familiarly Western style of desiring things. This was in many ways a restatement of the 'civilizing mission' that was central to colonialism.[6] As one of the postwar inheritors of this mission, international advertisers in southern Africa investigated how the 'natives' experienced wants and could be induced to form a new relationship with manufactured goods. Many firms in southern Africa turned to anthropologically-trained individuals when they were first establishing divisions to tackle the 'African market'. These professionals warned their employers: 'It is only when we realise the cultural implications of marketing to Africans that we appreciate how fundamentally different our task of selling to these people is … in marketing to the African we are faced with a completely new situation.'[7] Over the past half-century, market researchers and advertisers have gradually developed procedures for dealing with what one marketing study commissioned in 1921 by the US government termed the 'puzzling unlikeness' of consumer demand among non-Western peoples.[8]

The conditions established by colonial and postcolonial institutions of rule led marketers to understand their target as an alien identity (female) within an alien identity (African). Women were regarded as crucial to producing markets and reproducing consumer practices for many reasons. The goal was to decipher indigenous cultures and re-orient the rules that governed desire, and both colonial and postcolonial institutions had already laid the foundations for positioning women as central to this project. Women were supposedly being 'liberated' from indigenous patriarchy, and were thus seen as culturally pliable. The goods being manufactured for the peoples of the colonial world were mostly intended for consumption within the household, regarded as a feminized sphere. The reproduction of new habits and practices was regarded as a female province, accomplished within the context of family life.

The engagements between empire and gender that channeled marketers towards female subjects came in part from attitudes towards cultural reproduction in nineteenth-century imperial discourse.[9] One common imperial view of cultural reproduction located it within the increasingly circumscribed realm of the private, the household, the feminine. There were, to be sure, other senses of the developing notion of culture that worked in active contradiction to this strain of thinking: for example, the Tylorian understanding of culture as the 'complex whole' which thematically linked all the practices of a defined 'people' to some coherent principle or conceptual proposition; culture in Matthew Arnold's sense, as an elevated and distinctly masculine world of elite taste and distinction; culture as the civilized, masculine opposite to elemental, feminine nature.[10] But even given the multiple meanings of the idea of culture, the gendered partition of the public and political from the private and cultural was often pronounced in colonial discourse.

The degree to which early ethnographic thinking and, by extension, the entire imperial project were tied up in the making of domains of gender which were also coded by race has been of increasing interest to scholars in the last decade. As Ann Laura Stoler has observed, 'the very categories of "colonizer" and "colonized" were secured through formal sexual control that defined the domestic arrangements of Europeans and the cultural investments by which they identified themselves … gender-specific sexual sanctions and prohibitions not only demarcated positions of power but prescribed the personal and public boundaries of race.'[11] The implications of such an analysis of colonialism are far-reaching.[12] The challenges of establishing a colonial order were considered by European rulers to hinge upon the reconfiguration of gender roles, while colonial subjects' knowledge of imperial power and of their own identities often worked against and within these hegemonic arrangements of masculinity and femininity.[13] Many of the most persistent crises and controversies circling around imperial authority were defined simultaneously as questions of culture and of gender: attempts to ban or restrict *sati* in India,[14] control sexual license and exchange in Hawai'i, prohibit clitoridectomy in East Africa, ban beer-brewing in southern Africa, or transform such practices as bridewealth and child marriage throughout the colonial world.

Colonial domesticity in particular was one of the key sites where these tensions played themselves out.[15] In colonial Zimbabwe, promoting new forms of domesticity among African women became a major preoccupation almost immediately following the establishment of colonial rule in the 1890s. In southern Africa as a whole, missionaries at the end of the nineteenth century had increasingly come to believe that the reproduction of Christian communities was contingent upon wresting away female converts from indigenous family structures. Missionary emphasis on the maintenance of nuclear households within an economy dependent upon male migrant labor carried within it the presumption that the Christian and 'civilized' habits of succeeding generations could only be guaranteed through the conversion of women in their roles as mothers and wives.

As a consequence, state officials and missionaries alike shared a powerful inclination to rail against 'the dead weight of the female influence' in African culture and to identify women as the primary force retarding the 'civilizing mission'.[16] There was a powerful conceit that remaking culture through the private and feminine sphere would ultimately insure the transformation of the whole of what was imagined as problematically 'African'. For example, a government official entrusted with establishing educational programs for female pupils called for 'dynamic activities which shall enrich the life of Native womanhood … cleansing the home and through it the race'.[17] Another concluded, 'the study of Home Economics develops women and girls on natural lines ... if it is well taught it should raise the Native to a higher state of civilization and mental development.'[18]

Mission schooling for African girls and women in Zimbabwe during the colonial era typically included lessons on homecraft, cooking and infant care. Personal, household and social hygiene (an especially intense pre-occupation in settler colonies like Zimbabwe, South Africa and Kenya) was also very important. A limited amount of medical training and gardening was also included, partly because both skills were much in demand among the prospective clients and dependents of mission-trained women. Missions in Zimbabwe and elsewhere in Africa also variably stressed the adoption of European manners.[19] The number of colonial Zimbabwean institutions dedicated to domesticity multiplied over time. By the 1950s, there were a number of mission-trained African women serving as roving 'home demonstrators', a model 'Homecraft Village' for use in domestic training programs was built by community groups and the Rhodesian state, there was a growing network of African Women's Clubs, and the state was funding extensive propaganda campaigns around domesticity in media aimed at African audiences, including mobile demonstration vans equipped to show films.[20] The training of African 'home demonstrators' in colonial Zimbabwe closely resembled programs in Western, Equatorial and Eastern Africa, though there were important variations in the scale of the programs, the degree to which they served the particular needs of a settler population, and the institution sponsoring the projects. Other variations came from the highly contingent development of particular discursive and institutional forms in different African localities. Nancy Rose Hunt, for example, has described how missionaries in one area of the Belgian Congo came to understand African boys as 'elves', a frame of reference not repeated elsewhere in colonial Africa but which had a significant local impact.[21]

Postcolonial interest in 'development' was intimately and dialogically based upon these kinds of colonial logics and programs, particularly as the project of development was reoriented during the 1970s and practitioners successively identified 'problems' which explained its failure to fulfill heady postwar prognoses. As Gustavo Esteva points out, each of these problems has 'followed for a time an independent career, concentrating both public and institutional attention'.[22] 'Women' have constituted one predominant class of 'problem'. Like their colonial predecessors, development experts have frequently described women both as obstacles, conservative guardians who stand resolutely in opposition to modernity, and as objectives, passive and helpless victims who must be rescued by foreigners from local forms of domination and backwardness.[23] It is still not uncommon to find both visions simultaneously shaping policy and discourse among international aid workers and planners.[24] In some cases, the linkages between development work and colonial perspectives on women have been very direct. In southern Africa, many international aid organizations funded programs for women which were overt continuations of colonial domesticity, such as the teaching of handicrafts or household skills. Much of the attention paid to domesticity in colonial Zimbabwe during the 1960s and 1970s, through the Federation of African Women's Clubs in particular, was an outgrowth of the Rhodesian government's cynical 'community development' apparatus, which freely sought and received aid from various foreign institutions.[25]

The manner in which European empires generated and confronted crises over cultural practices in their colonies, the specific programmatic construction of colonial domesticity, and the postcolonial refinement of these notions within 'development' all helped to gender postwar marketing in southern Africa (as well as elsewhere in the capitalist periphery) in a very particular fashion. Most of the consumer goods manufactured for sale to colonial peoples, whether produced in southern Africa or elsewhere in the Third World, were household items, largely inexpensive non-durables: cleansers, toiletries, foods, clothing, medicines. Manufacturers might well have argued that if it was a cultural bias of some sort to connect the household with female purchasing, it was none of their doing, nor was it their province to undo. Such a bias could hardly be said, especially in the 1950s and 1960s, to be particular to the developing world.
    Nevertheless, these connections relied underneath the surface on colonial domesticity and its postcolonial analogues within development practice. Some of these linkages were simply a by-product of marketing institutions. Just as international marketing generally made use of anthropological and administrative personnel and resources from colonial institutions, so its tools for reaching women in the Third World were often seized directly from colonial programs for domesticity. Many postwar southern African marketers appropriated most of their characteristic infrastructure—cinema vans, leafleting, low-cost single-channel radio sets, home demonstration of products —directly from state propaganda programs directed with particular intensity at African women, and they continued to develop this infrastructure in close cooperation with local and international institutions dedicated to 'community development'. As this typical account of a 'home demonstration' session from 1970s Zimbabwe makes clear, the characteristic sites of female activity created by colonial domesticity were heavily infiltrated by capitalist marketing:

> Mrs. Rusere of Colgate-Palmolive has given a number of most enjoyable demonstrations of the use of coldwater washing powder, showing how it can even be used for the washing of woolies.... Each member then took it in turns to wash a cup and saucer under the eagle eyes of the watching club members who had learned from Mrs. Rusere's demonstration.... Each member took home with her a plastic bag containing toothbrush and Colgate toothpaste, a packet of Cold Power washing powder and toilet soap.[26]

Because marketers identified the making of mass markets in the Third World as a project which entailed the reconstruction of cultural standards, practices and sensibilities, they were bound to focus on women. Creating mass consumption was, in the words of one South African executive, a matter of trying to change 'the African way of life, the African culture, to make it conform to European standards'.[27] Marketers like Nimrod Mkele were deeply conditioned by the weight of colonial knowledge to regard women as the 'bringers of new tastes into the home'. Advertisers and executives whom I interviewed in 1990 and 1991 in Zimbabwe and South Africa testified to the strength and persistence of these perceptions of the 'African market'.[28]

These perceptions were intimately dependent upon the infrastructure of domesticity and reflected the proposition that many African women had been made into loyal and dedicated wives and mothers who had assumed responsibility for 'modern,' single-family households. Professional assessments of the potential of the 'African market' and the design of methodologies for reaching it relied on such presumptions. One Lever Brothers (Rhodesia) executive declared, 'the woman now features as the major decision maker for the purchase of day-to-day consumer goods.'[29] Another analysis argued, 'the changing status of women is particularly noticeable … today the housewife … does the shopping.'[30] Mkele put it even more distinctively: 'Women are … the vanguard of progressive ideas in today's emergent African Society in so far as the home is concerned. This factor is so important from a marketing and advertising point of view that it cannot be overlooked. To paraphrase a well-known idiom: Never under-estimate the size of a woman's thumb—there may be a man under it!'[31] Many marketing techniques were held to function effectively only because women were now capable of relatively free movement and were not bound by cultural 'tradition'. Fashion shows, for example, were a common strategy for marketers, reflecting the increasing commodification of women themselves. The advent of such shows was celebrated by advertisers as a sign of the modernity of African femininity: 'In old African society, there were no such things as Beauty Contests.... Now it is an accepted form of entertainment. African girls will even parade in bikinis!'[32] Marketers presumed that their ability to advertise to African women was a sign of the defeat of pre-colonial family structures, which had rested on the power of the senior members of a lineage. Consequently, a declaration of interest in women as the linchpin of a new mass market was often accompanied by a parallel denunciation of the power of 'traditional taboos' and of the 'elderly' over consuming habits.

If southern African women were targeted as responsible for the reproduction of new consumer habits in ways that recalled the colonial logic of gender relations, their envisioned relationship to the production of new mass markets was also enmeshed in some of the contradictions that had marked that logic, as well as some new countervailing forces peculiar to the needs and priorities of transnational capitalism.

The conventional wisdom that mass markets had to expand through segmentation of the consuming population provided a powerful disincentive to regard 'the' African consumer as essentially female. For the most part, the doctrine of market segmentation has remained merely theoretical in Third World marketing. Despite some fairly elaborate schemes for distinguishing 'lifestyle' groups and social classes in particular national marketplaces,[33] transnational capitalists have ended up treating various formerly colonized peoples as 'Others' who desire goods according to a consistent set of cultural rules which vary only by gender. While marketers may have seen African women as the key to changing consumer habits, they also wanted to stress that women and men should develop particular, gendered needs of their own. For certain classes of goods associated with men, advertisements and marketing strategies appealed directly to male audiences, presuming that men would purchase these goods themselves. In the 1960s and 1970s in Zimbabwe, for example, advertisements in the African media for alcoholic beverages, certain types of toiletries and patent medicines, and educational courses were invariably directed at male audiences, using what white advertisers believed were characteristically masculine images and phrasings in urban African culture. In particular, advertisers repeatedly invoked the term 'power', believing that African men understood this term to be a direct reference to sexual potency.[34] Many of the advertisements most identified with women, such as the perennial campaigns for Feluna Pills (iron supplements), addressed women as women, not as the quintessential consumer.

Other views among marketers about how mass markets could be created within peripheral economies also relied on the legacy of colonial thought, but in rather different ways. Many marketers envisioned the successful identification and nurturing of a 'middle class' as the key to the stimulation of consumer demand in African (as well as other Third World) societies. Such a view has been bedeviled by contradictions of its own. In postcolonial Africa, small local elites frequently have been the only economically important consumers of imported goods, but the ideological presumption that elite taste will automatically reproduce itself in other social classes has proved both culturally false and structurally impossible in most of southern Africa to date, regardless of whether we take the gap between white and black or between black elites and other Africans as the key example. Nevertheless, this line of argument has represented important discursive competition for marketers' contentions about the role of women in taste transfer. One advertiser acidly remarked in 1970s Rhodesia that his colleagues were forever searching for an 'Excalibur' that would magically open the 'African market'; it was either women or the middle class, but rarely both.

The issue of social status opens up some additional lines of connection between marketing wisdom and gendered colonial knowledge. The example of postwar southern Africa is instructive. Women were seen as the doorway through which Western-style consumer habits could pass into the lives of non-Western peoples, through which the alien could become familiar, but, at the same time, indigenous women were also the most alien of the aliens. Information is the capital of marketing and advertising, but information about the reality of women's lives often turned out to be hard to come by.

Marketers needed to believe that the project started under colonial domesticity was mostly complete, that many African women were becoming members of single-family households with stable housing and a private sphere of social life. At the same time, they knew full well that this was not the case in southern Africa; actually, it was not even intended to be the case. The realities of migrant labor coupled with decades of segregationist land removal policies meant that government officials, settler associations and other powerful interests, including many capitalists, regarded the rural countryside as the true and proper abode of women and a peasant lifestyle as their proper mode of life.

The entire discursive structure of what marketers knew about African women rested on one set of assumptions about African households. Budget surveys and connected market research from the 1950s to the 1970s in both Zimbabwe and South Africa organized their data in terms of a single-family household and concentrated on urban populations which were both accessible to researchers and financially capable of purchasing manufactured goods. Yet the structural place marked out for African women when these surveys were conducted was the countryside, and the governments of the region, in alliance with many senior male African patriarchs, were continually striving to prevent urban settlement and to restrict female mobility. Marketers knew very little about rural lifestyles, and they generally had few plans to learn more. Even in urban or peri-urban settings, African men were far more visible and audible to marketers. Moreover, households in both areas were profoundly marked by male migrancy and thus by fluid configurations of family life and familial authority. The single-family household, even in fairly stable urban townships with semi-permanent inhabitants, had its greatest currency in the social imagination of bureaucrats and marketers, rather than in the lived reality of township life.

This paradox not only recalled deeply ingrained and widespread tensions that had marked colonial society as a whole but testified, at least in the southern African context, to stresses within the prior evolution of commodity culture among African peoples. Before efforts to construct mass markets in the 1950s, the 'kaffir truck' merchants who sold manufactured goods to Africans found that women were often their primary customers in rural areas. This pattern provoked a continuous triangular tension in the countryside among traders, female shoppers, and traditional African male elites. Depending upon the shifting balance of power between traders and rural cultivators, male elites spoke of 'truck' stores either as a dangerous opportunity for women to exercise economic power and social independence or as a form of exploitation which uniquely victimized 'their' women.

This sense was deepened and complicated by the anxiety and anger that many settlers expressed about the expansion of Africans' consumption. The growing African urban middle class in particular attracted the ire of whites, beginning in the 1920s and 1930s, for its use of fancy clothing, cosmetics and other manufactured goods which whites considered to be a sign of privilege and racial superiority. The confluence of these attitudes with the concerns of African men about female mobility and economic power and the role of African women in commodification put into circulation a powerful set of cultural stereotypes that envisioned the most active and socially visible black female consumers as corrupt and culturally degenerate, as temptresses and prostitutes. Such stereotypes had power among most whites and some African men. For example, a representative diatribe by a white colonial official reprimanded 'over-dressed, heavily rouged and lipsticked cigarette-smoking females',[35] while African journalist Lawrence Vambe spoke bitterly of 'emancipated ladies' who were 'well-washed, sweetly scented and finely dressed', cruelly stealing men away from 'simple work-worn wives and sweethearts'.[36]

One of the consequences of such stereotypes was that programs designed to reproduce domesticity made great emphasis on 'thriftiness', stressing that African women must learn to consume humbly, within their means and appropriate to their racial place. Women were held responsible for reconstructing and reproducing consumer behavior for the whole of the African population, but within a logic which called for restraining rather than expanding their role as consumers. Female consumption in this light was portrayed as a potential drag on male aspirations, another of the many ways that a woman could be selfish and self-absorbed, a 'bad wife'.

Consumption by African women was thus already a highly contentious subject that underlined important schisms within colonial society when marketers began to set out their strategy in the 'African market' in 1950s southern Africa. The units of data and various received wisdoms about cultural reproduction through which market research understood African women were profoundly at odds with the social realities of racial capitalism. Rather than being the most accessible segment of African communities, women were in fact often the most remote from the information-gathering and planning apparatus of capitalist marketing. Moreover, male interlocutors within African communities, including black marketing professionals recruited in increasing numbers, regarded the expansion of consumption through women ambiguously, even angrily. Though Mkele saluted African women as the harbingers of the mass market, he also betrayed a certain typical resentment about agreeing to 'fork up and smile' and being 'under a woman's thumb'. The African man, he said, 'tends to be conservative', but 'this conservatism is of course encouraged by women'.[37]

In one sense, this formulation accurately reflected the social history of gender during the colonial era. Colonial domesticity and the construction of 'customary law' by the Rhodesian state increasingly redefined the household and its relationship to production in ways that were highly disadvantageous to African women. Many rural women responded by articulating and defending their own readings of 'tradition' which sought to preserve some of their power over cultivation and exchange and which resisted the intrusion of younger women working to promote domesticity on behalf of missionaries or the state by defining 'African culture' in opposition to 'modern ways'. Equally, in urban communities, women defended their own capacity for accumulation through prostitution or entrepreneurship against an alliance of African men and township administrators. One of their key strategies was to assert their right to control household expenditures; another was publicly to mock and satirize masculine dependency and wastefulness. Colonial domesticity provided unintended resources for women to articulate their own agenda, through the emphasis on thrift and the female management of the household.[38] Some of the most striking examples of female satire can be found in persistent rumors circulated by township women that commercially-produced beer caused impotence in men.[39]

Marketers were generally concerned not to represent female control over consumer behavior as existing outside the context of the patriarchal order. In southern Africa, marketers often stressed that women were purchasing for others. In some cases, advertisements and marketing materials showed women purchasing goods while subordinate to the command of husbands and fathers. Moreover, marketers invariably represented African men as the decision-makers when it came to 'major' purchases of durable goods. Finally, colonial domesticity was the premise upon which marketers approached African women as modernized shoppers who controlled the budget and habits of a single-family household, but it also reflected the deep anxieties of colonial elites about the prospect of their subjects actually becoming 'civilized'. Domesticity attempted to outline and enforce boundaries around consuming practices, to restrain African women to what whites felt were racially appropriate habits of consumption. This had inevitable echoes within the social vision of white capitalist professionals in southern Africa. For example, in one instance, a commercial journal trying to assess the market for cosmetics among African women offered a resoundingly negative perspective: 'The horrible sight of a dark-skinned woman whose face is plastered with cosmetics which obviously were manufactured exclusively for use by a light-skinned person is a common sight in Rhodesia.... African woman frequently lacks taste.... She entirely ignores the final effect in her anxiety to do what the white woman does.'[40] In a similar vein, a Rhodesian manufacturing executive reproduced domesticity's vision of the consuming wife as a 'bad wife': 'It is a known fact that the women in African society ... exert enormous influence, good and bad, on their men. The man is obliged to provide his wife with anything she desires however reluctant he may be to purchase it.'[41]

Much in this last set of arguments should be seen as particular to southern Africa. The structure of racial capitalism, the effects of migrancy, the social vision of a settler society, the local content of domesticity programs, and the evolution of controversies over female consumption did not have precise analogues elsewhere. Yet it is reasonable to suppose that equally powerful contradictions arose in other contexts, with similar effects on capitalist marketing discourse. For example, the significant expansion of female wage labor in much of postwar south and southeast Asia has certainly had different but equally important effects on the general inheritance of colonial knowledge about gender roles. Marketing discourse over the last five decades about new habits of mass consumption and women in the Third World has been affected everywhere by peculiarly local forms of wider colonial propositions about gender, cultural reproduction and domesticity. Moreover, some of the forces which have worked against identifying women as the essence of the consumer, such as the desire to segment markets, have been common across the span of transnational capitalism.

What does the preceding analysis suggest? In one sense, it might simply represent a version of several lines of existing scholarly analysis. For example, within marketing and business discourse, some studies have long warned male executives not to be misled by their own cultural stereotypes regarding gender roles, particularly the statistical and organizational presumptions that shape international or comparative marketing practice.[42] In another vein, this article could be viewed as a rather indirect contribution to the long tradition of debate about the definition and meaning of the household as a social unit within feminist and anthropological scholarship.[43]

I would like to suggest another possible use for the analysis initiated in this paper. We are coming to realize that the matter of gender lay at the heart of subtle and yet vitally important crises of imperial authority. In equally subtle and crucial ways, gendered perspectives within transnational capitalism about cultural reproduction, alterity and development may mark the gradual evolution of another domain of crisis, with important historical and contemporary implications. The predominant interpretation promoted in modernization theory of capitalist development in non-Western societies as inevitably homogenizing now seems questionable. Instead, what is increasingly clear is that capitalist professionals have often simultaneously sought to produce and erase social difference, to fix and erode boundaries between identities and cultures. Women have been seen as the ideal subjects of marketing campaigns throughout the postwar Third World, yet they have also been known as the least accessible, the most alien, the furthest away from what transnational capitalism understood as the form of 'modernity' which it monopolized. The consuming 'modernity' which has emerged in different sites throughout the postcolonial world, with all of its gendered aspects, seems richly local and meaningful for all that it is also uneven, contested and impoverishing.

Notes

1. Nimrod Mkele, 'Advertising to the Bantu', *Second Advertising Convention in South Africa* (Society of Advertisers, Durban, 1959), p. 129.

2. Gordon Effer, 'Act Like a Man, Think Like a Woman', *International Advertiser*, 11 (1970), pp. 32–3.

3. Mike Featherstone (ed.) *Global Culture: Nationalism, Globalization and Modernity* (Sage Publications, London, 1990), p. 2.

4. Noreene Z. Janus, 'Advertising and the Mass Media in the Era of the Global Corporation', in *Communication and Social Structure: Critical Studies in Mass Media Research*, ed. Emile G. McAnany, Jorge Schnitman and Noreene Janus (Praeger Publishers, New York, 1981), p. 291.

5. For some examples, see Steven Langdon, 'Multinational Corporation, Taste Transfer and Underdevelopment: A Case Study From Kenya', *Review of African Political Economy*, 2 (1975); Jeffrey James, *Consumer Choice in the Third World* (St. Martin's Press, New York, 1983); Noreene Janus, 'The Making of the Global Consumer: Transnational Advertising and the Mass Media in Latin America' (Ph.D. diss., Stanford University, 1980); Richard Wilk, 'Consumer Goods as Dialogue About Development', *Culture and History*, 7 (1992), pp. 79–100; Daniel Miller, *Material Culture and Mass Consumption* (Basil Blackwell, Oxford, 1987); T. G. McGee, 'Mass Markets—Little Markets: Some Preliminary Thoughts on the Growth of Consumption and its Relationship to Urbanization: A Case Study of Malaysia', in *Markets and Marketing*, ed. Stuart Plattner (University Press of America, Lanham, Maryland, 1985); Benjamin S. Orlove and Henry J. Rutz (eds) *The Social Economy of Consumption* (University Press of America, Lanham, Maryland, 1989).

6. See Timothy Burke, *Lifebuoy Men, Lux Women: Consumption, Commodification and Cleanliness in Modern Zimbabwe* (Duke University Press, Durham, 1996), for further comments on the 'civilizing mission' and advertising. I am grateful to Leonardo Paggi for forcefully pointing out how important social difference has been to global marketing.

7. J. E. Maroun, 'Second Address: "Bantu Market" Session', *Third Advertising Convention in South Africa: The Challenge of a Decade* (Statistic Holdings Inc., Johannesburg, September 1960), p. 124.

8. See J. W. Sanger, *Advertising Methods in Japan, China and the Philippines*, US Department of Commerce Bureau of Foreign and Domestic Commerce Special Agents Series #209 (Government Printing Office, Washington, D.C., 1921), p. 26.

9. Chris Jenks (ed.) *Cultural Reproduction* (Routledge, London, 1993). For nineteenth-century examples, see Christopher Herbert, *Culture and Anomie: Ethnographic Imagination in the Nineteenth Century* (University of Chicago Press, Chicago, 1991); Raymond Williams, *Culture and Society 1780–1950* (Chatto & Windus, London, 1958); and George Stocking, *Victorian Anthropology* (Free Press, New York, 1987).

10. For these perspectives on culture, see Herbert, *The Invention of Culture*; Stocking, *Victorian Anthropology*; and Williams, *Culture and Society 1780–1950*. On the discursive opposition between nature and culture, see Sherry B. Ortner, 'Is Female to Male as Nature Is to Culture?', in *Woman, Culture and Society*, ed. Michelle Zimbalist Rosaldo and Louise Lamphere (Stanford University Press, Stanford, 1974); Carol P. MacCormack, 'Nature, Culture and Gender: A Critique', and Marilyn Strathern, 'No Nature, No Culture: The Hagen Case', both in *Nature, Culture and Gender*, ed. Carol P. MacCormack and Marilyn Strathern (Cambridge University Press, Cambridge, 1980),

and Donna J. Haraway, *Simians, Cyborgs and Women: The Reinvention of Nature* (Routledge, New York, 1991).

11. Ann Laura Stoler, '"Carnal Knowledge and Imperial Power": Gender, Race and Morality in Colonial Asia', in *Gender at the Crossroads of Knowledge: Feminist Anthropology in the Postmodern Era*, ed. Michaela di Leonardo (University of California Press, Los Angeles, 1991), p. 52.

12. In addition to the work of Ann Stoler, also see Margaret Strobel, *European Women and the Second British Empire* (Indiana University Press, Bloomington, 1991); Nupur Chaudhuri and Margaret Strobel (eds) *Western Women and Imperialism: Complicity and Resistance* (Indiana University Press, Bloomington, 1992); Helen Callaway, *Gender, Culture and Empire: European Women in Colonial Nigeria* (University of Illinois Press, Urbana, 1987); Kenneth Ballhatchet, *Race, Sex and Class Under the Raj: Imperial Attitudes and Policies and Their Critics, 1793–1905* (St. Martin's Press, New York, 1980); Anna Davin, 'Imperialism and Motherhood', *History Workshop*, 5 (1978), pp. 9–57.

13. Veena Das, 'Gender Studies, Cross-Cultural Comparison and the Colonial Organization of Knowledge', *Berkshire Review*, 21 (1986).

14. This practice of immolating widows after their spouses' death exerted an immense fascination for British administrators. For two interesting discussions of sati's place in imperial policy and imperial knowledge, see Das, 'Gender Studies', and Lata Mani, 'Contentious Traditions: The Debate on Sati in Colonial India', in *Recasting Women: Essays in Indian Colonial History*, ed. Kumkum Sangari and Sudesh Vaid (Rutgers University Press, New Brunswick, 1990).

15. Jean Comaroff and John Comaroff, 'Home-Made Hegemony: Modernity, Domesticity and Colonialism in South Africa', in *African Encounters With Domesticity*, ed. Karen Tranberg Hansen (Rutgers University Press, New Brunswick, 1993).

16. Zimbabwe National Archives (ZNA) S138/150, Native Commissioner (NC) Sinoia to Superintendent of Natives, February 1924. For analyses of these kinds of sentiments among missionaries and officials in Africa, see Elizabeth Schmidt, *Peasants, Traders and Wives: Shona Women in the History of Zimbabwe, 1870–1939* (Heinemann, Portsmouth, New Hampshire, 1992), esp. ch. 5; Hansen (ed.) *African Encounters With Domesticity*; Nancy Rose Hunt, 'Domesticity and Colonialism in Belgian Africa: Usumbura's Foyer Social, 1946–1960', *Signs*, 15 (1990), pp. 447–74; Jacklyn Cock, *Maids and Madams: A Study in the Politics of Exploitation* (Ravan Press, Johannesburg, 1980); Audrey Wipper, 'The Maendeleo Ya Wanawake Movement in the Colonial Period: The Canadian Connection, Mau Mau, Embroidery and Agriculture', *Rural Africana*, 29 (1975–76).

17. Southern Rhodesia Department of Native Education, *Report of the Director of Native Education* (Salisbury, 1929), p. 57.

18. M. Waters, 'Home Economics and Practical Hygiene', Department of Native Education Occasional Paper No. 1 (Salisbury, May 1929), p. 2.

19. See Nancy Rose Hunt, 'Colonial Fairy Tales and the Knife and Fork Doctrine in the Heart of Africa', in *African Encounters With Domesticity*, ed. Hansen, and Norbert Elias, *The History of Manners* (Pantheon Books, New York, 1978; orig. German pub. 1939).

20. See Schmidt, *Peasants, Traders and Wives*; Sita Ranchod-Nilsson, '"Educating Eve": The Women's Club Movement and Political Consciousness Among Rural African Women in Southern Rhodesia, 1950–1980', in *African Encounters with Domesticity*, ed. Hansen; and Burke, *Lifebuoy Men, Lux Women*.

21. See Hunt, 'Colonial Fairy Tales'; Karen Tranberg Hansen, *Distant Companions: Servants and Employers in Zambia, 1900–1985* (Cornell University Press, Ithaca, 1989); Hansen (ed.) *African Encounters With Domesticity*; and Callaway, *Gender, Culture and Empire*.

22. Gustavo Esteva, 'Development', in *The Development Dictionary*, ed. Wolfgang Sachs, p. 14.

23. For a unique perspective on the pull of these contradictions, see Norman Rush's novel, *Mating*, which focuses on an imaginary development expert's project for women in Botswana.

24. See Haleh Afshar (ed.) *Women, Development and Survival in the Third World* (Longman, London, 1991); Jane Parpart, 'Who is the "Other": A Postmodern Feminist Critique of Women and Development Theory and Practice', *Development and Change*, 24 (1993), pp. 439–65; Kay B. Warren and Susan C. Borque, 'Women, Technology and International Development Ideologies', in *Gender at the Crossroads of Knowledge*, ed. di Leonardo.

25. Southern Africa may also seem unrepresentative, for decolonization came slowly and painfully to the region. Yet many of the economic and political transformations which were so characteristic of postcolonial societies elsewhere in the world were clearly a part of the otherwise formally colonial societies of southern Africa. This included 'development', albeit in a segregationist costume.

26. 'Hygiene', *Homecraft Magazine* (Salisbury), May 1970, p. 6.

27. 'Questions from "Bantu Market" Session', *Third Advertising Convention in South Africa*, p. 133.

28. Cornell Butcher, Francis Makosa, Wellington Chikombero, Harare, 26 November 1990; Clive Corder, Johannesburg, 30 May 1991; Roger Dillon, Harare, 3 April 1991; Douglas Kadenhe, Harare, 23 May 1991; Maurice Mathewman, Harare, 13 May 1991; Jack Wazara, Harare, 15 May 1991. Interview tapes are held privately by the author.

29. Charles Nyereyegona, 'Marketing to the Urban African', *Marketing Rhodesia* (Salisbury), 1 (May 1973).

30. Rhodesian Ministry of Information, *A People's Progress* (Salisbury, 1969).

31. Mkele, 'Advertising', p. 129.

32. ZNA S 2113/1-2, Rhodesian Ministry of Information, 1962.

33. See for example Nick Green and Reg Lascaris, *Communication in the Third World: Seizing Advertising Opportunities in the 1990s* (Tafelberg Publishers/Human and Rosseau Ltd., Cape Town, 1990); P. J. du Plessis (ed.) *Consumer Behaviour: A South African Perspective* (Southern Book Publishers, Pretoria, 1990).

34. See Burke, *Lifebuoy Men, Lux Women*, ch. 5, for further discussion of these campaigns.

35. ZNA ZBJ 1/2/3, testimony of Location Superintendent, Gwelo.

36. Lawrence Vambe, *An Ill-Fated People: Zimbabwe Before and After Rhodes* (University of Pittsburgh Press, Pittsburgh, 1972), p. 200.

37. Mkele, 'Advertising', p. 129.

38. See Schmidt, *Peasants, Traders and Wives*, and Diana Jeater, *Marriage, Perversion and Power: The Construction of Moral Discourse in Southern Rhodesia 1894–1930* (Clarendon Press, Oxford, 1993).

39. See Burke, *Lifebuoy Men, Lux Women*, and essays in Jonathan Crush and Charles Ambler (eds) *Liquor and Labor in Southern Africa* (Ohio University Press, Athens, 1992).

Timothy Burke

40. 'On the Frontiers of Trade: Cosmetics for the African Woman', *Commerce of Rhodesia*, July 1955.

41. Joe Van den Bergh, 'Marketing in the Tribal Trust Lands', *Marketing Rhodesia*, 2 (1974), p. 61.

42. For the most recent example, see Rena Bartos, *Marketing to Women Around the World* (Harvard Business School Press, Boston, 1989).

43. For a recent example which also directly addresses consumption and offers a quick overview of the literature, see Barbara Diane Miller, 'Gender and Low-Income Household Expenditures in Jamaica', in *The Social Economy of Consumption*, ed. Rutz and Orlove.

Glossary

ambalavelona (Malagasy) sorcery which caused the victim to be possessed by an evil ghost and driven insane

atani [sing. *mutani*] (Meru) older women who performed excisions on adolescent girls

baiko (Malagasy) order or command; also, foreign speech

efundula (Ovambo) female initiation rite

fanafody (Malagasy) medicine, or magic

fanompoana (Malagasy) forced labour, initially of subjects to rulers and subsequently of slaves to masters

fiarovana (Malagasy) medicine used for protection from harm

kafir/kaffir (Afrikaans) whites' term for native Africans

kalo (Malagasy) medicine buried in the ground to protect crops

kiady (Malagasy) flags placed on fields to protect crops

kiama gia ntonye (Meru) 'council of entering', composed of older women, which organized female initiation

Maendeleo ya Wanawake (Kenya) state-sponsored women's groups which taught home economics

mpamosavy (Malagasy) witches or sorcerers

Muthirigu (Ovambo) dance-song performed by women to protest colonial policies

ngaitana (Meru) 'I will circumcise myself'

Njuri Ncheke (Meru) local council of male elders

ody (Malagasy) 'charms'

ody fitia (Malagasy) love medicine

'Shongola' (Ovambo) 'the whip', African nickname for 'Cocky' Hahn

sjambok (Ovambo) rhinocerous-hide whip

truck (South Africa) trade with native Africans

Index

Printed and bound by CPI Group (UK) Ltd, Croydon, CR0 4YY

09/06/2025

14686137-0004